Al-ʿArabiyya

Journal of the American Association of Teachers of Arabic

مجلة رابطة أساتذة اللغة العربية

Volume 44 and 45 | 2011–2012

Al-ʿArabiyya: Journal of the Association of American Teachers of Arabic

Editor: Reem Bassiouney, Georgetown University
Assistant Editor: Emily Severy, Georgetown University
Book Review Editor: Reem Bassiouney, Georgetown University

Editorial Office (essays and book reviews)
Reem Bassiouney
Al-ʿArabiyya Journal
Department of Arabic and Islamic Studies
Georgetown University
1437 37th St NW, Poulton 206
Washington, DC 20007
al-arabiyya@hotmail.com
202-687-3925

Business Office
American Association of Teachers of Arabic
3416 Primm Lane
Birmingham, AL 35216

Publisher (purchase and copyright)
Georgetown University Press
3240 Prospect Street NW
Washington, DC 20007
http://press.georgetown.edu

Al-ʿArabiyya (ISBN 978-1-58901-948-5; ISSN #: 0889-8731) is published annually by the American Association of Teachers of Arabic.

AATA Membership
A subscription to *Al-ʿArabiyya*, which is published annually, is included in a membership to the American Association of Teachers of Arabic (AATA). The annual cost of membership is US $50 for individuals, US $15 for students, and US $200 for institutions. AATA welcomes members who live and work throughout the world; AATA does not have a residency or citizenship requirement for members. For more information about AATA membership, to join AATA online, or to download an AATA membership application, please visit the AATA website at: http://aataweb.org/signup.

Institution and Library Subscriptions
A single issue of *Al-ʿArabiyya*, which is published annually, or a one-year subscription may be purchased by institutions and libraries for US $60. Place orders at 800-537-5487 or online at http://press.georgetown.edu.

Back Issues
To order back issues, please visit the AATA website at: http://aataweb.org/purchase_publications. Back issues can be ordered for US $35 each for institutions/agencies and US $20 each for individuals. Most volumes are available in the original edition. If an issue is not available, we can offer a photocopy for US $5 each.

Advertising
AATA is pleased to accept a limited number of advertisements, which appear after all editorial content in *Al-ʿArabiyya*. For information about advertising your institution, organization, publications, or other products or services that relate directly to the needs and interests of AATA members and subscribers, please contact the Executive Director at admin@aataweb.org.

If your subscription copy of *Al-ʿArabiyya* has not yet reached you, please contact AATA at: American Association of Teachers of Arabic, 3416 Primm Lane, Birmingham, AL 35216 USA. Phone 205-822-6800, fax 205-823-2760, info@aataweb.org.

Contents

Editor's Note

I am delighted and honored to take over the task of editor of *Al-'Arabiyya*. Georgetown University Press has kindly agreed to give this journal a home, and a very appropriate one at that. I am grateful to Richard Brown, the director of the press, and to Hope LeGro, director of Georgetown Languages, for their trust and willingness to take on a promising project. The press staff has been very accommodating in adding this new title to their offerings.

I hope that you will enjoy the current and future issues of *Al-'Arabiyya*. As we begin publication with a new publisher, our journal retains its wide scope and offers strong contributions by established and new scholars in our field. As part of this renewal of the journal, issues will be published annually in the fall of each year. We welcome everyone to look for our calls for papers and submit suitable essays. As always, each essay will be peer reviewed so that we continue to include the highest-quality scholarship about Arabic teaching.

I would also like to thank people who have supported this new endeavor. I would particularly like to thank Chester Gillis, dean of the Faculty of Languages and Linguistics at Georgetown University, for the institutional and financial support that he provided, and for his encouragement. I also want to thank Elliott Colla, chair of the Arabic and Islamic Studies Department, for useful suggestions at the beginning of this project and for his support on many levels. Elizabeth Bergman, the executive director at AATA, was, as usual, very supportive throughout the process of bringing the journal back into regular circulation. Special thanks go to Emily Severy, assistant editor, who was indispensable in preparing this issue for publication.

In addition to thanking the editorial board, I also want to thank the following scholars for reviewing papers for this issue:

Mahmoud Al-Batal, *University of Texas at Austin*
Mohammad Attia, *The British University in Dubai*
Kirk Belnap, *Brigham Young University*
Elizabeth Bergman, *Miami University of Ohio*
John Eisele, *College of William and Mary*
Hussein Elkhafaifi, *University of Washington*
Amira El-Zein, *Georgetown University*
Annie Higgins, *College of Charleston*
Terrence Potter, *Georgetown University*

Reem Bassiouney, *Editor*

College-Level Teachers of Arabic in the United States

A SURVEY OF THEIR PROFESSIONAL AND INSTITUTIONAL PROFILES AND ATTITUDES

■

Mahmoud Abdalla, Monterey Institute of International Studies
Mahmoud Al-Batal, The University of Texas, Austin

Abstract

The present study reports the results of a survey of 209 college teachers of Arabic in the United States, representing close to 50 percent of the Arabic teachers' population. The survey was conducted in 2009 and aimed to provide comprehensive analysis of the teachers' profiles, perspectives, and needs in the following areas: demographics, institutional and programmatic settings, curricula, study abroad, and professional attitudes, needs, and opportunities.

We believe that the results of this survey will enable all those concerned about the Arabic teaching profession to better understand the dynamics of the Arabic field, gauge the transformations that have occurred within the past decade, and predict its future direction. The survey results will also help them understand the needs of teachers and determine how these needs could be met.

Introduction

Over the past ten years, the teaching of Arabic in the United States has experienced phenomenal growth, to the extent that Arabic has been transformed from an exotic less commonly taught language into a mainstream one. The unprecedented number of new Arabic programs established in colleges and universities across the United States and

Table 1. MLA-reported college Arabic enrollments in the United States 1998–2009

Year	Arabic enrollments	Increase (%)
1998	5,505	—
2002	10,584	92
2006	23,974	126.5
2009	35,083	46.3

the increasing student enrollments in Arabic classes since 2001 have propelled Arabic to the eighth position among languages taught in the United States, ahead of Latin, Russian, and ancient Greek, as reported by the Modern Language Association of America (MLA) (Furman, Goldberg, and Lusin 2010; Welles 2004). Table 1 provides the figures and percentages of increase reported by the MLA for enrollment in Arabic at institutions of higher education in the United States since 1998.

This remarkable surge of interest in Arabic has posed a number of significant challenges to the Arabic teaching profession that have mounted to a national crisis of unprecedented dimensions (Al-Batal 2006). Perhaps the most daunting of these challenges is how to cope with these record levels of demand for Arabic at a time when the field is facing a substantial lack of professionally trained Arabic instructors and low numbers of graduate students specializing in Arabic (Betteridge 2003). In an effort to meet the demand, universities, colleges, and government agencies have had to hire language instructors who have not been trained as language teachers. Belnap (2006) points out that thousands of American students want to acquire professional-level fluency in Arabic, but relatively few succeed because the United States lacks sufficient numbers of well-trained language professionals who can help these students move efficiently and effectively forward in the pursuit of their linguistic and cultural proficiency goals. While there are some excellent teachers of Arabic and a few institutions that are succeeding in recruiting and training professional teachers, the teaching situation remains a challenge to the Arabic field at large. Ryding states that in order to achieve language-teaching success, "the most essential and influential components are the teachers: teachers and professors with high expectations of their students, with clear goals and methods, who use Arabic themselves almost all time in the classroom, and who pave the way for students to engage in spoken Arabic" (2006, 18).

Information about the status of teachers in the Arabic field remains scarce. While a number of surveys have been conducted on students taking Arabic (Belnap 1987, 2006; Husseinali 2006; Kuntz 1996; Smadi and Al-Abed Al-Haq 1998), there are very few surveys aimed at college-level Arabic teachers. An important study in this area is Belnap's 1995 survey of the institutional setting of Arabic language teaching. This survey focuses on aspects of teaching and provides valuable information on teachers and some of their profiles within a larger context of programmatic aspects. In addition, the National Middle East Language Resource Center (NMELRC) in 2004 conducted a comprehensive survey on teachers of Arabic within an overall survey of teachers of Middle Eastern languages. These surveys informed the design and construction of our own survey, and we compare our results with theirs wherever applicable.

In the present study we report the results of a survey of college teachers of Arabic in the United States with the aim of providing comprehensive demographic, institutional, and programmatic profiles of these teachers and their professional attitudes and needs. Understanding teachers' beliefs, attitudes, and perceived needs is a key component in developing effective foreign language teaching. We believe that the results of this survey will enable teachers, language program supervisors, and administrators to better understand the dynamics of the field and gauge both the extent and the future direction of the transformations that have taken place within the field. They will also allow us to understand the needs of the teachers and see how these needs can be met.

Survey and Methodology

The survey used for this study consisted of sixty-nine items that addressed the following areas[1]:

1. Demographics (gender, age, native language and dialect, years of employment, rank, etc.)
2. Institutional and programmatic settings
3. Attitudes and perspectives on curricular issues
4. Perspectives on study abroad
5. Professional attitudes, needs, and opportunities

We based most items in the survey on the Likert scale and asked participants to make a choice among four possible answers: strongly agree, agree, disagree, and strongly disagree. No neutral response choices appeared in order to encourage participants to make a choice. Some open-ended items on the survey required the participants to provide their own answers.

Prior to administering the full version of the survey, we administered a pilot version to a small number of teachers at the University of Texas to ensure the clarity of the items and the smooth operation of the survey. We made adjustments based on feedback received during the pilot, and administered the final version of the survey between May 13 and June 14, 2009. The survey generated responses from 209 teachers of Arabic. While we do not have any published statistics on the number of instructors teaching Arabic in the United States, our own research of Arabic teachers listed on websites of colleges and universities offering Arabic in the United States yielded close to 400 names.[2] This suggests that our sample reflects the views of about 50 percent of Arabic teachers at the college level in the United States, which, we believe, constitutes a representative sample.

Teacher Demographics

The survey reveals a gender distribution of 56.5% male teachers and 43.5% female. Almost half of the teachers surveyed (49%) reported they were in the 30- to 45-year-old range, 43.5% were over 45 years old, and only 7.2% were under the age of 30. The age maturity reflected by the survey indicates the fact that close to half of the teachers surveyed hold doctoral degrees.

Native speakers of Arabic make up the majority of teachers surveyed (73%) while nonnative speakers account for the remainder (27%). The percentage of teachers who are nonnative speakers represents a positive development for the Arabic field in a number of ways. It demonstrates that the field has matured and has begun to produce learners who have reached higher levels of proficiency and who are ready to teach the language. It also shows that Arabic is breaking away from the pattern of the dominance of native teachers, a phenomenon that is particularly noticed in the less commonly taught languages.

In addition, our survey reveals that there is growing awareness in the field of the important role of nonnative teachers. In response to the question *"Do you think that nonnative speakers can be successful teachers of Arabic?"* the majority of teachers (92.7%) responded in the affirmative (48.3% strongly agree and 44.4% agree) whereas 5.8% disagreed, and 1.4% strongly disagreed. This is a welcome development because it reflects

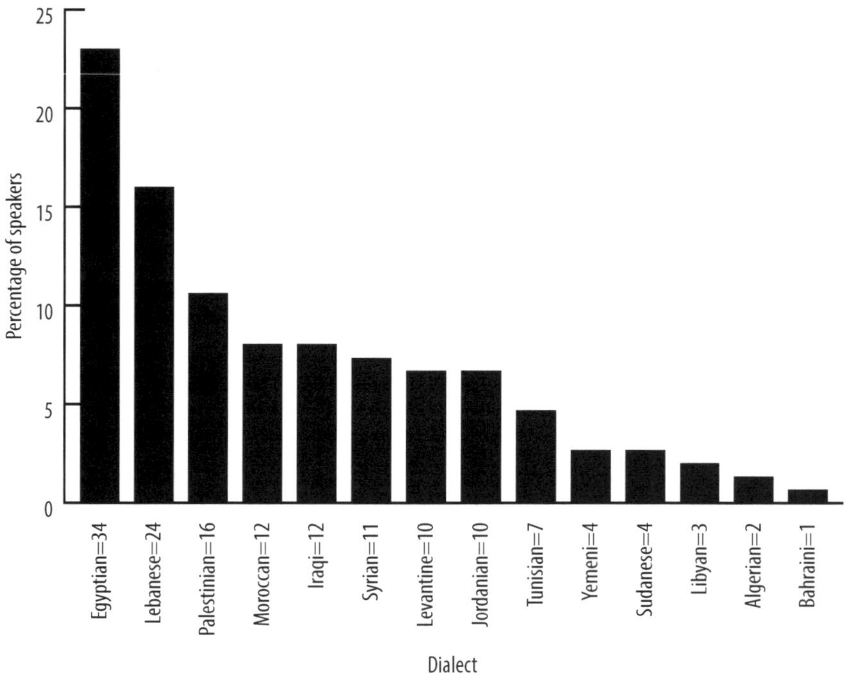

Figure 1. Native Arabic dialect

field-wide cognizance of the important role nonnative teachers play as cultural mediators in the teaching of Arabic.

Among native-Arabic-speaking teachers there is a wide array of dialects represented, with speakers of Egyptian Arabic comprising the majority, followed by Lebanese, then Palestinian, as reflected in figure 1. This distribution of native dialects can help us understand the emphasis placed on teaching the Egyptian and Levantine/Shami dialects in many Arabic programs in the United States. The dialectal diversity reflected in the survey represents a wealth of linguistic resources that need to be further utilized in teaching Arabic so that learners of Arabic can benefit from exposure to more regional dialects of Arabic.

As for nonnative teachers, the vast majority (80%) are native speakers of English while the remaining 20% comprises speakers of Russian, Serbo-Croatian, Urdu, Gujarati, German, Spanish, Greek, and Chinese. In addition to their linguistic skills, these nonnative speakers have had considerable cultural experiences in Arabic-speaking countries. Of these teachers, 48% reported living in Arabic-speaking countries for a period ranging between two and five years, and 19.5% reported spending between twenty and thirty years. Only five of the nonnative teachers reported zero years of living in an Arabic-speaking country.

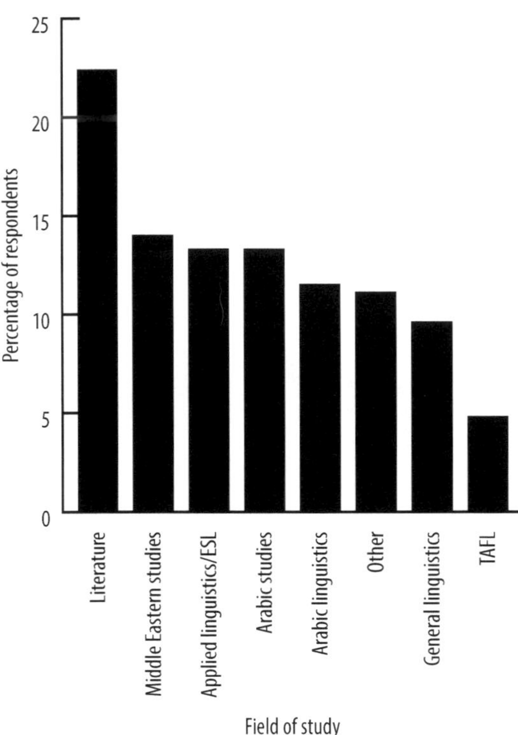

Figure 2. Fields of specialization

In addition to the vast cultural background, Arabic teachers demonstrate high levels of education. Our survey shows that the majority (47%) of Arabic teachers in the United States hold PhD degrees in various disciplines, 2% hold EdD degrees, 40% hold master's degrees (MA/MS), and 5.5% hold a bachelor's degree (BA/BS). Figure 2 details the different fields of specialization and shows that most teachers of Arabic in the United States specialize in literature, whereas only about 18% hold degrees in applied linguistics or teaching Arabic as a foreign language (TAFL). The "other" category includes fields such as computer science, law, educational management, religion, communication, and business. These figures confirm the widely held assumption that the vast majority of those who teach Arabic in the United States have not been trained as language professionals and underscore the need for in-service training for the majority of Arabic teachers. These training needs are discussed in more detail in the section on professional needs.

Teacher training is particularly relevant when viewed in light of the number of new teachers who have joined the profession. Figure 3 demonstrates that 30.3% of the teachers entered the field within the past five years and 31.7% within the past five to ten years. This shows that close to two-thirds of the teachers of Arabic in the United States today have been recruited within the past ten years as part of the national effort to accommodate the dramatic increase since 2001 in the number of students studying Arabic. Also related to length of service is the significant mobility among Arabic teachers due to this development. Many Arabic teachers leave their programs and move to other programs in search of better working conditions. Responses to our survey reveal that the

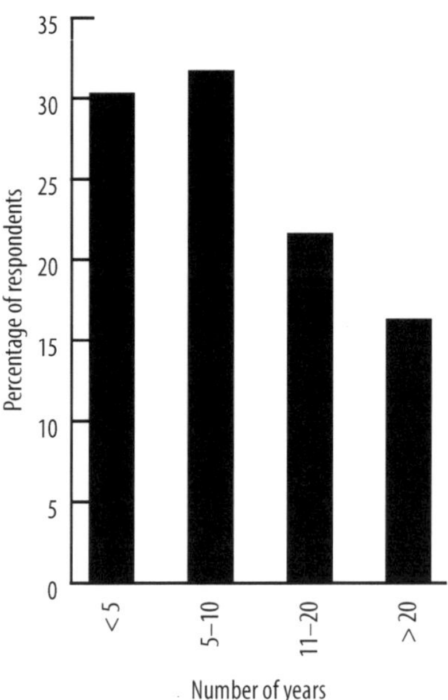

Figure 3. How many years teaching AFL?

vast majority of Arabic teachers (68.4%) have been teaching at their current institutions for five years or less, 17% for six to ten years, 5.7% between ten and fifteen years, and only 8.6% for more than fifteen years. This remarkable mobility seems to be continuing as more colleges and universities open a variety of new Arabic positions at the professor, senior lecturer, and lecturer levels.

In terms of job status, 76.4% of the teachers surveyed reported that they hold full-time appointments versus 23.6% who reported part-time status. Of those who hold full-time appointments, only 29.6% occupy tenured or tenure-track positions, while the rest occupy nontenured positions, as shown in figure 4. The numbers in our survey reflect a different pattern than the one reported in Belnap's 1995 survey, in which the number of professorial tenured and tenure-track positions in the sample surveyed was slightly higher than the number of lecturer positions. These figures reflect a trend to shift language teaching positions away from tenure into nontenure lines, which seems to have started in the Arabic field in the 1990s. Our data confirm this shift and show that the majority of new Arabic teaching positions created in the past ten years as part of the Arabic surge have been nontenure positions. Tenure-track lines in Arabic seem to be reserved for nonlanguage disciplines. This decision has serious implications because it

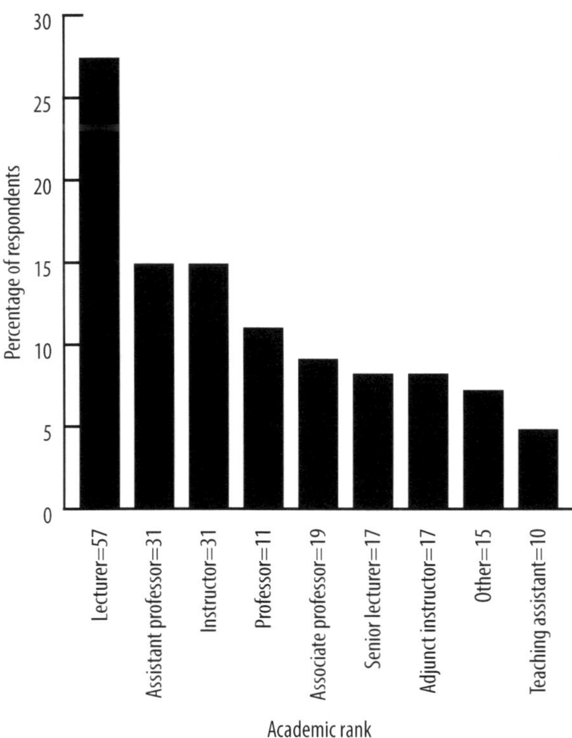

Figure 4. Academic rank of Arabic teachers

contributes to creating a two-tiered system: one for those who teach language and one for those who do not.

As for the reasons that lead teachers to choose teaching Arabic as a profession, our data show that the reasons are ranked as follows in terms of importance: (1) love for Arabic, (2) love of teaching, (3) desire to share knowledge about Arab culture with American students, and (4) financial reasons. These responses reflect the teachers' high levels of commitment to their field and their students and show that teaching Arabic is part of a larger project of facilitating cultural understanding between Americans and Arabs.

Institutional and Programmatic Settings

In this section we analyze the teachers' responses to the survey questions that deal with the institutional and programmatic settings within which they function.

Institutional Type and Program Location

Our survey shows that the majority (54.5%) of college teachers of Arabic in the United States teach at public institutions; the remaining 44.5% work at private institutions. Within these institutions, Arabic teachers are housed in a wide array of academic departments, including Language and Literature departments (41.6%), Middle (Near) Eastern Studies departments (17.7%), and Middle (Near) Eastern Civilizations and Cultures departments (6.7%). Only two of the teachers surveyed reported that they are housed in an Arabic Studies department. The rest of the teachers surveyed identified other departments such as Asian Studies, Linguistics, African Studies, Classics, and Religious Studies as their academic homes.

Class Size, Class Composition, and Teaching Load

In an effort to explore the variations that exist among the Arabic programs, we included several questions related to the number of contact hours offered, class size, class composition, and teaching loads in the survey. The participants' responses show that the average number of contact hours offered at the various levels of instruction in US colleges and universities is as follows[3]:

First Year:	4.8 hours /week
Second Year:	4.5 hours /week
Third Year:	3.8 hours /week
Fourth Year:	3.0 hours /week

In terms of teaching load (excluding office hours), figure 5 exhibits a wide spread that is due perhaps to the various ranks where tenured and tenure-track professors and senior lecturers have lighter teaching loads and lecturers usually have heavier workloads. The numbers in figure 5 demonstrate that except for a small minority of teachers who teach twenty hours per week—an excessive load—the majority of teachers (38%) have a teaching load between six and eleven hours per week, and 34% have loads between twelve and sixteen hours per week.

Figure 6 reveals that close to half of the teachers surveyed do not have teaching assistants (TAs) who can provide instructional support. For those who reported having full or partial TA help, the most important activity performed by the TAs is tutoring students outside class (63%), followed by grading (50.5%) and helping with group work inside class (41.9%).

In terms of the average Arabic class size, our data illustrate in figure 7 that the vast majority of Arabic teachers teach classes that have enrollments ranging between fifteen and twenty students. This is a reasonable average and shows that despite the increase in the number of Arabic students overall, the classroom average is still manageable. Enrollments in Arabic, as in other languages, tend to show higher numbers in the first year but go down significantly in later years due to attrition.

We also asked teachers for information about their students' backgrounds. Figures 8 and 9 provide valuable information on the percentage of heritage students found in Arabic classes. They show that the majority of teachers teach classes that have 1%–10% of Arab and Islamic non-Arabic heritage students, whereas a smaller percentage of teachers teach classes with an average of 10%–20% of heritage students. These figures also show

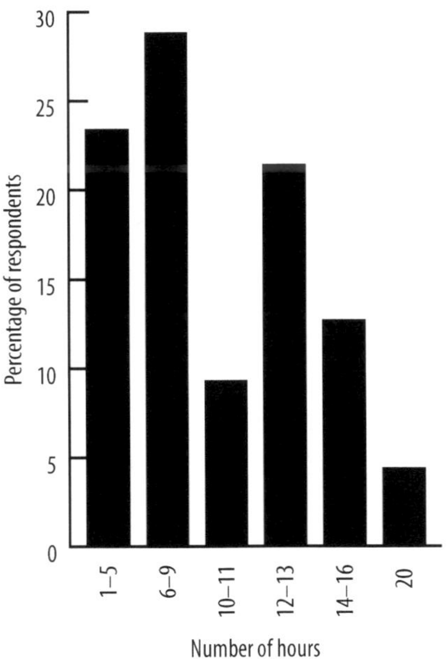

Figure 5. Number of contact hours taught per week (not including office hours)

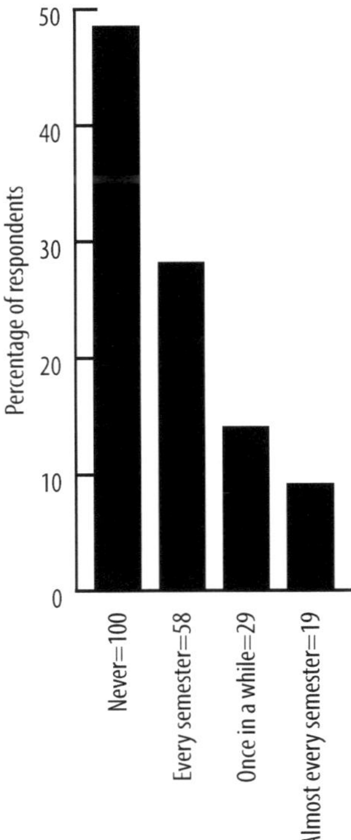

Figure 6. Do you have teaching assistants?

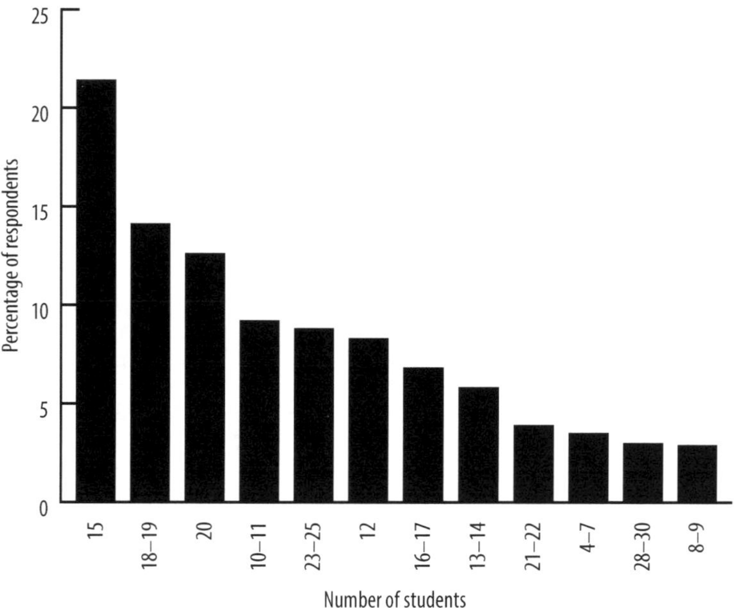

Figure 7. Average class size you teach

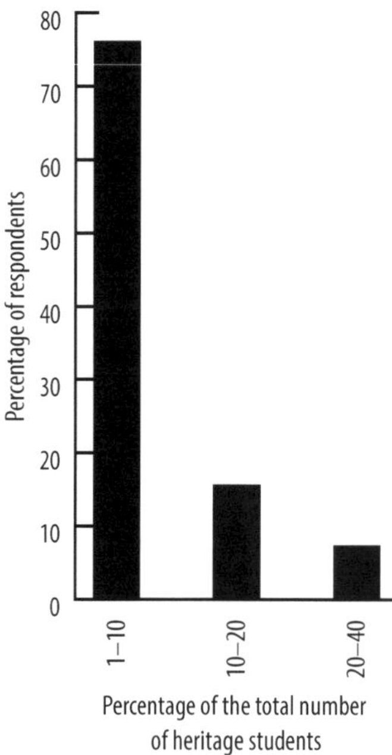

Figure 8. Percentage of teachers with Arab heritage students in their classes

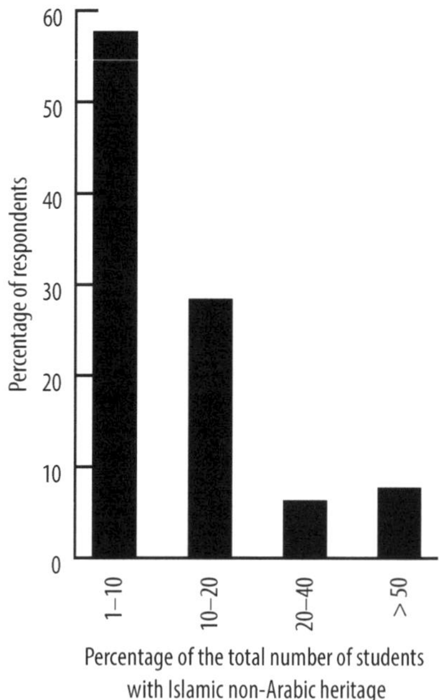

Figure 9. Percentage of teachers with Islamic non-Arabic heritage students in their classes

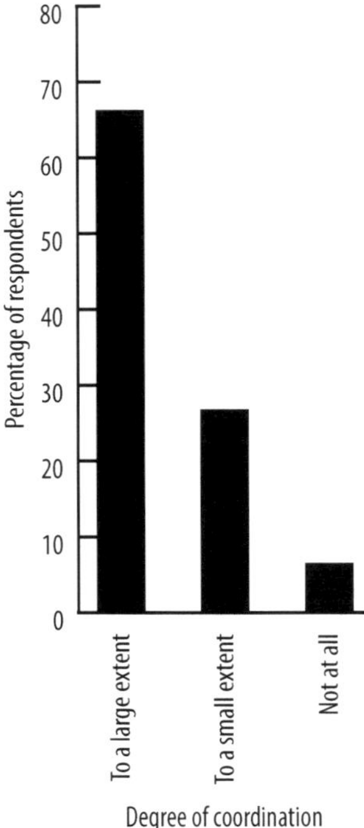

Figure 10. To what extent is there coordination among multiple sections of the same Arabic courses?

that the percentage of Muslim non-Arab heritage students is higher than that of the Arab heritage students.

Philosophy and Coordination

One of the positive findings of our survey is that the majority of Arabic teachers in the United States believe that the program in which they teach has a well-defined and well-articulated philosophy for teaching Arabic. Of the respondents, 43.5% indicated that they feel this to a large extent, 40.7% agree to some extent, 13.4% agree to a small extent, and only 2.4% didn't believe it at all. This is a significant result that shows that the Arabic field has developed in terms of setting instructional goals and practices. It also shows that the significant investments made by the universities and the US government in training, assessment, and development of materials have begun to yield results.

This well-defined program philosophy is clearly reflected also in teachers' responses to the question related to the level of coordination that exists among different sections of the same Arabic course within their programs. Figure 10 demonstrates that the majority of the teachers feel that there is a great deal of coordination among the various sections of the same year. As further evidence, the teachers in our survey responded to other questions stating that a similar high level of coordination exists at the syllabus level:

The majority of teachers reported that they use the same syllabus for all sections every semester (63.5%) or almost every semester (18.8%), whereas 17% indicated that they seldom or never use the same syllabus for multiple sections.

However, while coordination among teachers of different sections of the same level seems to be strong when it comes to syllabi, it is not as strong when it comes to testing. Only 39.5% of the teachers surveyed indicated that they use the same exam for all sections every semester, whereas 19% indicated that they use the same exam almost every semester. A sizable group of teachers indicated that they use the same exam once in a while (21.5%) or never use the same exam (20%). This discrepancy raises further questions about the extent of coordination in the area of methodology and classroom practice.

Attitudes and Perspectives on Curricular Issues

General Attitudes toward Arabic and the Language Skills

One of the prevailing perceptions of Arabic among students and some instructors is that it is a difficult language. As part of our survey we wanted to explore the extent to which this perception is present among teachers of Arabic in the United States. Our survey shows that the teachers are evenly divided in terms of their perception of the difficulty of Arabic. Of all respondents 50.3% agree strongly (9.3%) or agree (41%) that Arabic is a difficult language, whereas the other half disagree strongly (12.7%) or disagree (37.1%) with this statement. For teachers, such perceptions are important because they influence the way teachers approach teaching and their expectations from students. A teacher who believes Arabic is difficult may have lower expectations and may not challenge the students enough because he or she does not want to reinforce the perception of the difficulty of the language, whereas a teacher who does not believe Arabic is difficult may be able to challenge his or her students further because he or she will expect stronger abilities from them.

To quantify what aspects of Arabic are most difficult for American learners, we asked the teachers to rank the level of difficulty of the following components on a scale from 1 (extremely difficult) to 6 (not difficult). This is how these language components were ranked:

Pronunciation	(average rating of difficulty = 2.85)
Dealing with the different registers	(= 2.9)
Grammar	(= 3.11)
Vocabulary	(= 3.28)
Understanding the culture	(= 4.16)

What is striking about this order is that the two aspects that teachers consider most difficult are not among the aspects that are strongly emphasized in most existing Arabic curricula. Teachers usually deal with pronunciation in the first weeks or months when the Arabic alphabet is introduced but do not treat it in a systematic way in subsequent

Table 2. Ranking of Arabic language skills by importance, %

	1 Most important	2	3	4	5 Least important
Speaking	74.3 (N=150)	19.8 (N=40)	5.0 (N=10)	1.0 (N=2)	0
Listening	60.8 (N=124)	29.4 (N=60)	7.4 (N=15)	2.0 (N=4)	0.5 (N=1)
Reading	49.0 (N=100)	36.3 (N=74)	11.3 (N=23)	2.5 (N=5)	1.0 (N=2)
Culture	44.7 (N=89)	31.2 (N=62)	13.6 (N=27)	5.5 (N=11)	5.0 (N=10)
Writing	26.2 (N=53)	38.1 (N=77)	22.3 (N=45)	8.4 (N=17)	5.0 (N=10)

years of instruction. Similarly, because most programs do not provide much exposure to colloquial Arabic, students do not get enough opportunities to learn how to deal with the different registers of Arabic. These figures suggest a need for more curricular attention to these aspects of teaching in the form of materials and approaches to address these two important challenges.

As for the attitudes of teachers toward the language skills and their importance for learners, table 2 reflects that teachers perceive speaking and listening to be the most important of the skills, followed by reading, culture, and writing. These results are consistent with the results reported in Belnap's (1995) and Husseinali's (2006) surveys of students taking Arabic in the United States. The fact that speaking continues to be perceived as the most important skill poses some questions about our approaches to the various registers of Arabic and the speaking tasks connected with these registers.

Textbooks and Teaching Materials

In terms of textbooks used in teaching Arabic, our survey shows that a variety of textbook series are being used and that *Al-Kitaab fii ta 'allum al-'Arabiyya* by Brustad, Al-Batal, and Al-Tonsi seems to be used by the majority of the teachers surveyed, as shown in figure 11. Among the responses given within the "other" category is *Dardasha* by Mughazy, *Formal Spoken Arabic* by Ryding, *Standard Arabic* by Schulz et al., self-prepared materials, grammar notes, and children's stories.

Our data also show that the vast majority of teachers favor the use of textbooks in their classes. In response to the statement *"I prefer to develop my own materials rather than use a designated textbook,"* 55.3% of the respondents disagree with the statement and 9.7% strongly disagree, bringing the total of those who disagree to 65%, whereas 27.2% agree with the statement and 7.8% strongly agree.

Proficiency and Proficiency-Based Teaching and Assessment

Responses to the questions regarding the proficiency guidelines of the American Council on the Teaching of Foreign Languages (ACTFL) and their relevance to Arabic teachers provide another positive indication of the maturity of the Arabic teaching profession. The majority of the teachers reported that they are very familiar (62.2%) or somewhat familiar (30.1%) with the guidelines. In addition, most teachers reported

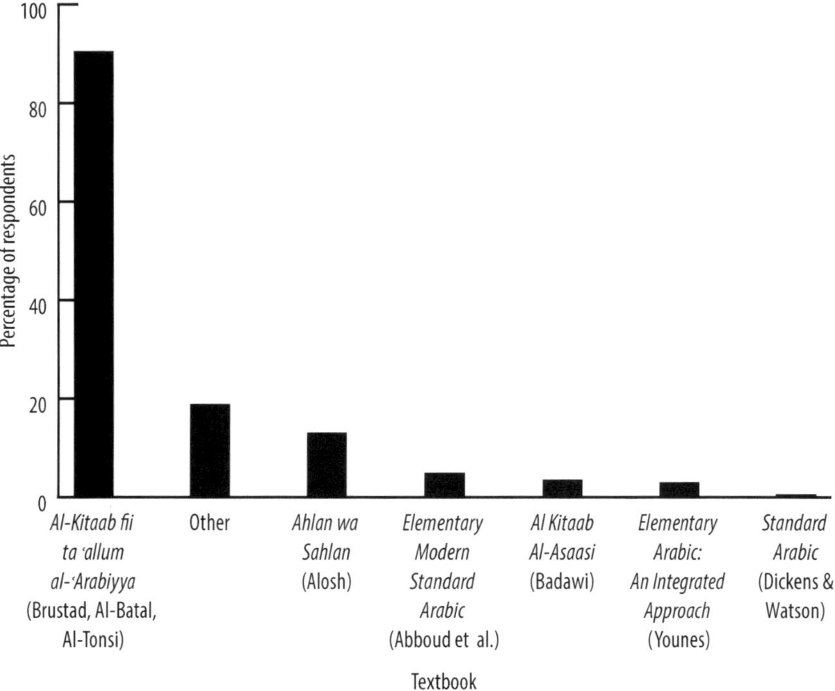

Figure 11. What textbook(s) do you use in teaching?

that their Arabic curricula incorporate the ACTFL guidelines to varying degrees. Of the teachers surveyed, 35.9% indicated that the guidelines are incorporated to a large extent, 35.9% indicated that they are to some extent, and 12.1% indicated that they are to a small extent. Only 7.8% indicated that the guidelines aren't incorporated, and a small group (8.3%) didn't know whether the guidelines are incorporated. These responses provide strong evidence of the impact the ACTFL guidelines have had on the Arabic field since they were introduced in the 1980s.

Additionally, a little over half of the teachers reported that their programs utilize proficiency testing to a large extent (23.4%) or a moderate extent (28.8%), whereas the others reported that they use it to a small extent (22.4%) or not at all (25.4%). As expected, the most widely used proficiency test is the ACTFL oral proficiency interview (OPI), which is used by 79.5% of those who reported that they use proficiency testing in their programs. A much smaller number of the teachers (15.7%) indicated they use ACTFL's writing proficiency test (WPT), 7.9% use the Center for Applied Lingusitics (CAL) for reading and listening, and 5.5% use the University of Michigan's Arabic proficiency test developed by Raji Rammuny. While these figures show that proficiency testing—especially in the area of speaking—is widely used in Arabic programs, they also reveal the need for new standardized proficiency tests for reading and listening to be used alongside the OPI.

Of the 209 teachers surveyed, 106 reported that they had participated in OPI training and 17 indicated they had taken the CAL simulated OPI training. Twenty-four of the respondents indicated that they were certified ACTFL testers and twenty-one reported they were in the process of being certified. This excellent development will enhance assessment in our field. However, the fact that the remaining 41% of the respondents have not had training in any kind of proficiency testing points to another gap in the field.

In-Class and Out-of-Class Activities

Our survey shows that daily written homework assignments constitute a major part of out-of-class activities. The majority of teachers (68.8%) reported that they assign their students daily homework that takes between one and two hours, 21.6% reported assignments that require two to three hours to complete, and 8.7% reported giving homework that requires one hour or less.

As for the type of activities that constitute homework assignments within the first two years of instruction, teachers listed the following activities, shown below in order of frequency:

1. Listening to a CD/DVD to learn vocabulary
2. Writing vocabulary sentences
3. Doing grammar drills/preparing for oral presentations in class
4. Reading grammatical explanations
5. Essay writing

Only 12 teachers of 209 indicated that they assign listening comprehension activities as part of the homework. This small percentage conflicts with the much larger percentage of teachers who rank listening as the second most important skill.

We asked the teachers about the extent to which they utilize group work in their classes for various activities, and their responses are presented in table 3. The responses show that a large majority of teachers utilize group work at all levels of instruction, reflecting a substantial pedagogical shift away from a teacher-centered classroom.

Table 3. How often do you use group work for different class levels?, %

	More than 50% of the time	25%–50% of the time	Less than 25% of the time	Never
Beginning level	42.1 (N=85)	39.1 (N=79)	17.8 (N=36)	1.0 (N=2)
Intermediate	42.5 (N=79)	47.3 (N=88)	9.1 (N=17)	1.1 (N=2)
Advanced	45.2 (N=75)	36.1 (N=60)	15.1 (N=25)	3.6 (N=6)

In supporting use of group work, teachers emphasized the value of peer learning, cooperative learning, motivation, activation, interactive learning, giving students control of their own learning, and communication. However, some teachers indicated that they prefer to do group work only at the intermediate and advanced levels because beginning students need the teachers more. One teacher explained that he or she opposes group work because "it takes precious class time."

We also wanted to see how much time teachers devote to grammar explanation in class. The teachers' responses show that 39.1% explain grammar to a large extent, 58.5% explain grammar to a small extent, only when dealing with complex grammatical structures, and 2.4% do not explain grammar at all.

These responses reflect that the field is undergoing the transition from a teacher-centered classroom to a more learner-centered environment in which the teacher's role is to facilitate learning as opposed to initiating it.

The Role of Colloquial Arabic in the Curriculum

Our survey included a number of questions aimed at understanding the role that colloquial Arabic plays in the curriculum. Our data reveal that most survey respondents (45%) teach in programs that provide instruction in Modern Standard Arabic (MSA) without offering any dialect classes, whereas 34.5% indicated that their programs offer dialect classes and 20.4% said that these courses are offered sometimes.

Within programs that offer separate colloquial classes, 39.8% of the teachers reported that their programs require a prerequisite of two years of MSA before a student can take a course in colloquial, 35.3% reported a one-year prerequisite, and 20.3% said their programs do not have any prerequiste for colloquial classes.

Given the emerging trend within many Arabic programs in the United States toward integration of colloquial Arabic in instruction, we wanted to gauge the teachers' reaction to this principle. Figure 12 reveals that there is wide acceptance of the principle among teachers; the majority of them (over 65%) strongly agree or agree that training in a dialect should start at the early stages of instruction. These figures reflect a noticeable change in the Arabic field, which has, for a long period of time, mainly focused on the teaching of MSA at the lower levels of instruction despite the fact that colloquial is the variety used to perform all functions related to the ACTL Novice and Intermediate levels.

Despite this acceptance, however, the responses in figure 13 show that the incorporation of colloquial in the first two years of instruction is still limited within the existing Arabic curricula. According to our survey, the majority of programs incorporate colloquial Arabic to a small extent or not at all. So, here we see a contradiction between the beliefs of the teachers reflected in figure 12 and the actual teaching practice reflected in figure 13. This disconnect suggests that existing curricula may undergo change in the future as teachers engage the question of the place of colloquial in the curriculum.

In programs where dialects are introduced, Egyptian Arabic continues to have a sizable lead with 110 out of 166 respondents indicating that their programs offer it, followed by Levantine Arabic, with 63 respondents saying their programs have classes in Levantine.

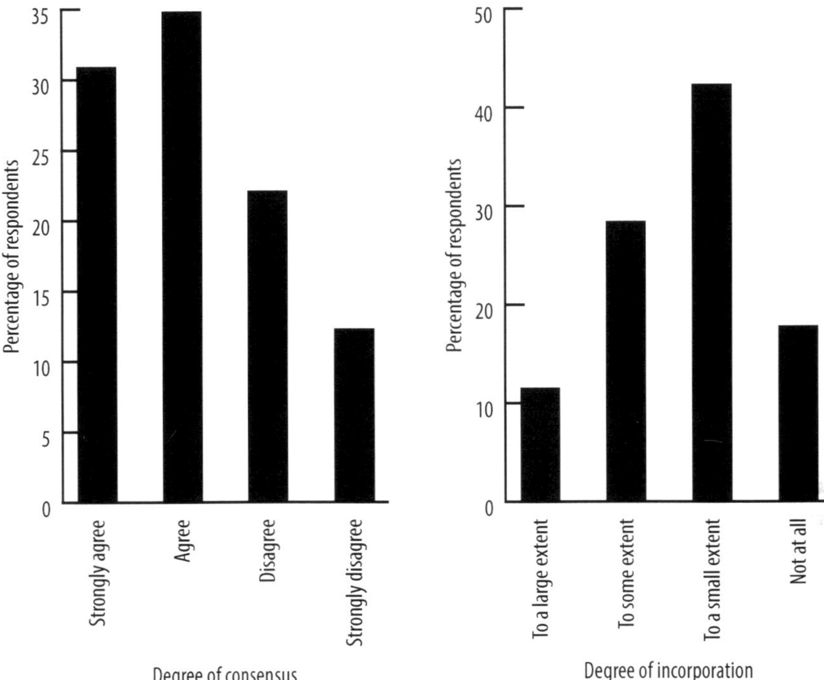

Figure 12. The Arabic curriculum should provide training in a dialect of Arabic from early stages of instruction

Figure 13. To what extent is colloquial incorporated into Arabic classes during the first 2 years of instruction in your program?

An interesting observation that has emerged from our data is an overall positive attitude of teachers regarding their willingness and ability to teach the basics of an Arabic dialect different from their own. One argument against integrating colloquial elements at the early stages of instruction in Arabic programs bases itself in statements such as "I am a speaker of dialect X and cannot or do not feel comfortable teaching dialect Y." Figure 14 demonstrates that most teachers are willing to teach and feel comfortable teaching the basics of a dialect that is not their native one. Among the teachers who indicated they are comfortable, one commented that "the more I read and practice teaching it, the more comfortable I feel about it," and another said, "with little effort, an Arabic native speaker could easily master any Arabic dialect. Therefore, I would feel comfortable teaching the basics of any dialect." However, the issue remains a sensitive one ideologically, as is reflected in the words of another teacher who indicated his unwillingness to work with another dialect: "Although I feel more than capable to teach Levantine or Egyptian, I do not desire to have any dialect imposed on me."

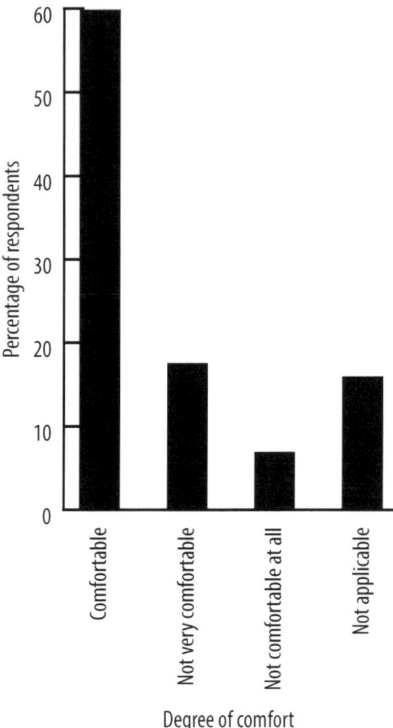

Figure 14. If a dialect other than the one you are familiar with is introduced in the 1st or 2nd year, to what extent do you feel comfortable teaching it?

Perspectives on Study Abroad

Research on study abroad (e.g., Martinsen et al. 2010; Medina-Lopez-Portillo 2004) provides ample evidence of the linguistic and cultural benefits of the experience, and these benefits have clearly not been lost on teachers and learners in our field. Arabic study-abroad programs began to expand in the late 1990s and have experienced rapid growth in the past ten years as part of the overall Arabic surge in the United States. Recent surveys of study-abroad destinations for American students (Bhandari and Chow 2008) show that study in the Arab world is concentrated in a handful of countries, with more than half of the students choosing to study in Egypt, as shown in figure 15.

To understand the perceptions and expectations of teachers regarding study abroad and the links that exist between their US-based programs and Arabic programs overseas, we asked a number of questions about the study-abroad experience. First, we asked the teachers to indicate the percentage of students in their programs who participate in Arabic study-abroad programs. Thirty-one teachers reported percentages that range between 50%

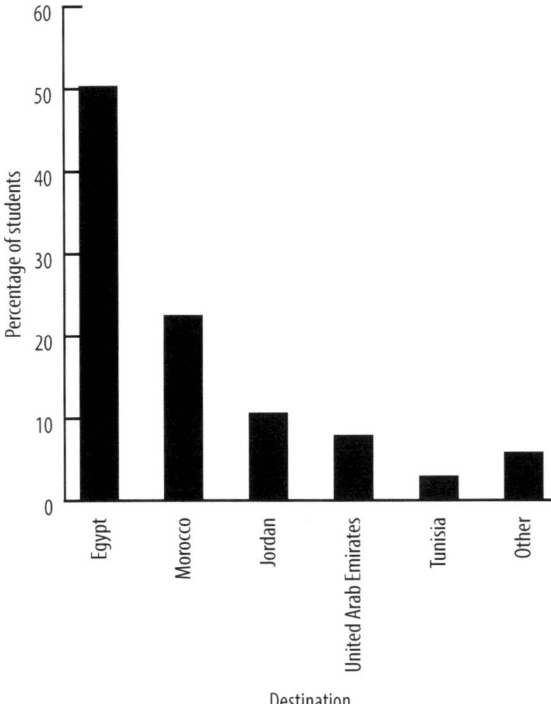

Figure 15. Arab-world destinations of US study-abroad students, 2006–7

and 70% of the number of students, sixty-two teachers reported percentages between 15% and 25%, and seventy-four teachers reported percentages between 5% and 10%. The majority of teachers believe that the study-abroad experience is crucial for the achievement of superior-level proficiency in Arabic. In response to the statement that "superior-level proficiency in Arabic can be attained without the need to spend time in the Arab world," 35.9% of the teachers strongly disagreed and 46.6% disagreed, bringing the total dissent to 82.5%.

These numbers suggest that study abroad is becoming more integrated into Arabic programs in the United States. Yet these numbers have significant implications for curriculum design in Arabic: If such large numbers of students are participating in programs overseas, what kind of linguistic and cultural training is needed to prepare them to fully utilize this experience abroad? Should programs do more to expose students to colloquial Arabic before their overseas experience, and should more cultural content be incorporated in the curriculum? Our survey did not address these questions or others dealing with articulation between the stateside and overseas programs or effective immersion of students within the overseas environment.

Our study asked whether programs of teachers surveyed have an official study-abroad program and where it is located. Ninety-eight teachers indicated the presence of

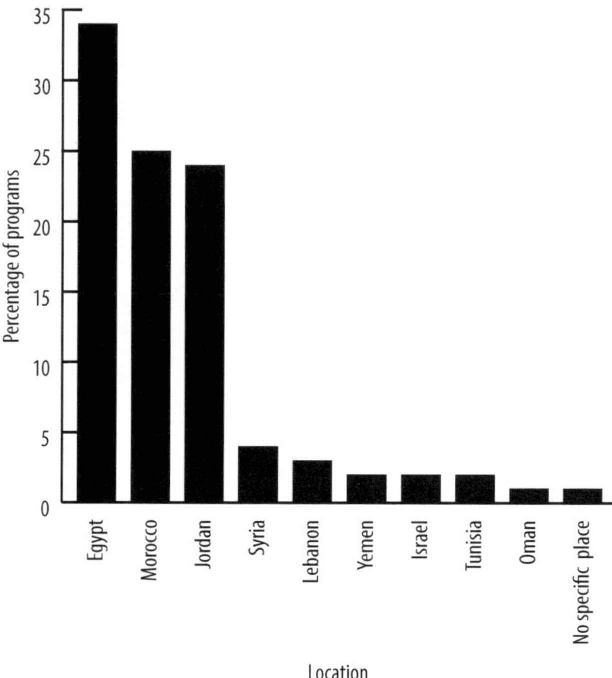

Figure 16. Location of official Arabic study-abroad programs

one, and their responses show that Egypt is the destination of choice for Arabic study-abroad programs, followed by Morocco and Jordan. The location and distribution of official Arabic study-abroad sites are shown in figure 16. In terms of specific institutions, the American University in Cairo (AUC) seems to be the preferred site for 28% of the teachers who have study-abroad program participants, followed by al-Akhawayn University in Morocco (12%), Alexandria University in Egypt (11%), and the University of Jordan (6%). Among the other institutions mentioned but with lower percentages are Qasid Institute, the Hashemite University, and University of Yarmouk in Jordan; Alif Institute and University of Moulay Isma'il in Morocco; and Hilwan University and International Language Institute in Egypt.

Our data regarding study abroad reflect the recent growing interest of US-based Arabic programs in private language centers that are keen to provide quality academic service. In the teachers' list of eighteen overseas programs, there are seven private centers, which represent 39% of all institutions listed. While enrollment at the traditional study-abroad sites such as AUC is still high, the emergence of new study-abroad programs and the interest in private language centers can be attributed to a number of factors, including program capacity, logistical and financial constraints, and the interest in providing further exposure to various Arab communities and cultures.

For Arabic programs that do not have official study-abroad programs, teachers stated that they encourage their students to travel abroad, and they pointed out that Egypt,

Morocco, Jordan, and Syria are the most popular destinations. Again, AUC, al-Akhawayn University in Morocco, University of Jordan, Damascus University, and Alexandria University in Egypt top the list in addition to other private language centers and universities such as the American University of Beirut, AMIDEAST, Institute Francais du Proche-Orient in Damascus, and the Arab American Language Institute in Meknes, Morocco.

Professional Attitudes, Needs, and Opportunities

We believe that developing an understanding of teachers' beliefs, attitudes, and perceived needs is crucial in helping departments, program supervisors, and higher administration identify the resources needed to help teachers advance professionally. For this reason we included in the survey questions aimed at gauging the teachers' overall level of satisfaction and assessing their professional needs and how these needs might be fulfilled.

Our survey shows that the majority of the Arabic teachers in the United States express satisfaction with their job, as is reflected in figure 17. When asked about the extent to which each teacher feels valued by his or her department, the vast majority

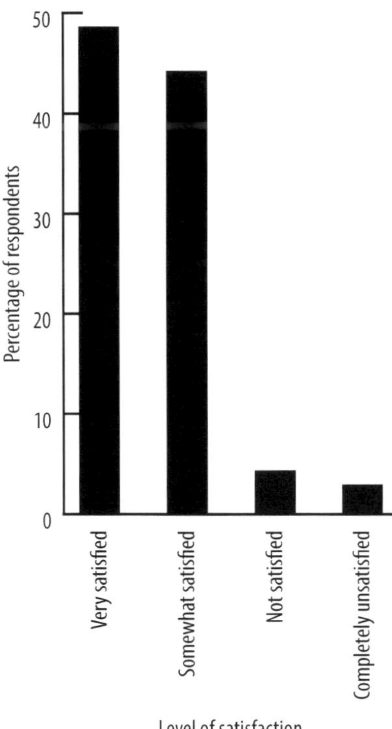

Figure 17. How satisfied are you with your current job as an Arabic teacher?

Table 4. Most pressing needs facing the Arabic-language teaching profession, %

	1 Very important	2	3	4	5	6	7 Not important	Rating average	Response count
Materials development	63.9 (N=131)	21.0 (N=43)	9.3 (N=19)	4.4 (N=9)	1.0 (N= 2)	0.5 (N=1)	0.0 (N=0)	1.59	205
Teacher training	63.0 (N=126)	21.5 (N=43)	11.0 (N=22)	2.5 (N=5)	1.0 (N=2)	1.0 (N=2)	0.0 (N=0)	1.60	200
Improved textbooks	55.4 (N=112)	22.3 (N=45)	11.9 (N=24)	6.9 (N=14)	3.0 (N=6)	0.5 (N=1)	0.0 (N=0)	1.81	202
Improved means of evaluating student performance	35.8 (N=72)	27.4 (N=55)	25.4 (N=51)	7.5 (N=15)	3.5 (N=7)	0.5 (N=1)	0.0 (N=0)	2.17	201
Increased access to authentic materials	38.2 (N=78)	28.9 (N=59)	16.2 (N=33)	7.8 (N=16)	3.4 (N=7)	5.4 (N=11)	0.0 (N=0)	2.25	204
Testing tools	32.2 (N=64)	26.1 (N=52)	25.1 (N=50)	8.5 (N=17)	6.5 (N=13)	1.5 (N=3)	0.0 (N=0)	2.36	199
Other	84.6 (N=22)	7.7 (N=2)	3.8 (N=1)	3.8 (N=1)	0.0 (N=0)	0.0 (N=0)	0.0 (N=0)	1.27	26

responded in the affirmative, with 66.8% indicating that they feel very valued, 27.9% somewhat valued, and only 5.3% not valued. In addition, the majority of the teachers (47.1 strongly agree and 37% agree) indicated that they feel they have a voice in setting their curriculum and program policies, although 11.5% disagree with this assessment and 4.3% strongly disagree. Moreover, our data show that 77.3% of the teachers surveyed feel satisfied with their job security within their current positions (with 39.1% indicating they are very satisfied, 38.2% somewhat satisfied), whereas 15% feel unsatisfied and 7.7% completely unsatisfied. These are very positive numbers that indicate that the growth in enrollment in Arabic in the United States has stimulated institutional and governmental investments in Arabic that have, by and large, resulted in more job security and job satisfaction for the majority of teachers.

In the area of teacher needs, our survey shows that financial support for professional development represents a high priority for teachers, as indicated in the responses of 129 out of 205 respondents (69%). Other areas of need cited in-service training, high-tech media services, and an increase in the number of TAs and graduate interns to provide support for learners in review and follow-up sessions outside regular class time. Teachers also stressed the importance of mentoring and guidance from senior colleagues and supervisors.

On a scale of 1 to 7, where 1 is very important and 7 is least important, participants were asked to rate their most pressing needs as teachers of Arabic. Material development, teacher training, and the availability of effective assessment tools are the top three areas of need identified, as reflected in table 4.

In the area of instructional materials needed, table 5 points to materials for listening, culture, and reading as the most urgently required. These needs are further confirmed in participants' comments: One teacher stated his desire to see "a larger amount of authentic materials available for teaching reading and listening," and another remarked, "listening and cultural materials need to be up-to-date and therefore must continually be developed." The need to integrate dialect into the Arabic-language curriculum was expressed by a participant who called for new methods of teaching to integrate "spoken varieties in the teaching of Modern Standard Arabic."

With regard to teacher training, teachers' responses in figure 18 show that most feel that the opportunities currently available in the field are not sufficient to meet their needs. Half of the participants feel that such training opportunities meet their needs to a small extent or not at all. While teachers' specific comments vary according to their individual program needs, they all agree on the importance of providing quality teacher education and the necessity for cooperation and teamwork. Among the opinions expressed in this area: "I need my department to have a serious search for a trained teacher of Arabic"; "I can add that being a native speaker of the language does not entail the person is qualified to teach the language in a sound pedagogical way. A way that is congruent with second or foreign language acquisition"; and "the colleague in charge [in my program] does not speak Arabic and the other instructor is a native speaker but has no background in education or teaching."

Table 5. Rate the types of materials that need to be further developed for teaching Arabic from very urgent to not urgent, %

	1 Very urgent	2	3	4	5	6 Not urgent	Rating average
Grammar materials	26.6 (N=54)	26.6 (N=54)	23.2 (N=47)	8.4 (N=17)	8.9 (N=18)	6.4 (N=13)	2.66
Cultural materials	43.1 (N=87)	25.2 (N=51)	15.8 (N=32)	9.9 (N=20)	3.5 (N=7)	2.5 (N=5)	2.13
Reading materials	32.8 (N=67)	40.2 (N=82)	15.2 (N=31)	6.4 (N=13)	4.9 (N=10)	0.5 (N=1)	2.12
Listening materials	57.4 (N=117)	31.4 (N=64)	6.4 (N=13)	2.9 (N=6)	1.0 (N=2)	1.0 (N=2)	1.62
Computer programs for learning	38.7 (N=77)	28.1 (N=56)	18.6 (N=37)	6.0 (N=12)	5.0 (N=10)	3.5 (N=7)	2.21

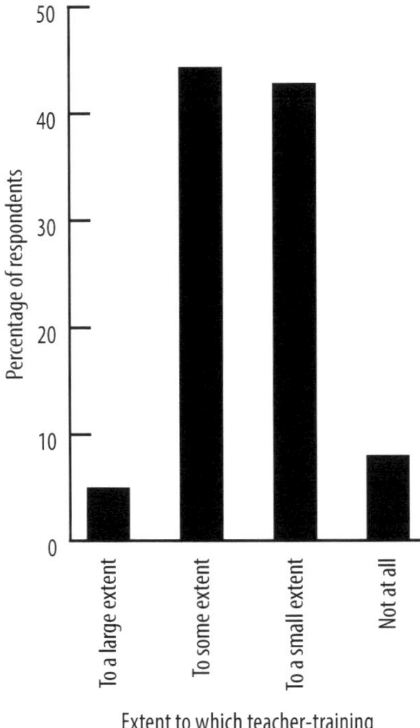

Figure 18. To what extent does the Arabic field provide teacher-training opportunities for teachers?

Conclusion

The results of our survey indicate that the dramatic growth in Arabic student enrollments in the United States over the past ten years has brought about a number of positive developments for Arabic teachers and programs. Thanks to this growth, the Arabic teaching profession today includes a diverse group of teachers representing different parts of the Arab world in addition to a growing number of nonnative teachers. This diversity represents a cultural and linguistic resource that has the potential to enrich individual programs and the field at large. In addition, Arabic teachers, by and large, seem to enjoy high levels of job satisfaction and security and feel valued by their institutions. More importantly, most of them feel that they have a voice in setting their curricula and program policies. Given the pivotal role of the teacher within any language program, these high levels of satisfaction speak well for the status of the Arabic-teaching profession in the United States.

At the programmatic level, our survey shows that advances toward setting standards have been made in a number of areas, including developing program philosophy and setting instructional goals, coordinating among various sections within the same levels, moving toward a learner-centered classroom environment, increasing focus on proficiency-based curricula and OPI assessment and training, and expansion of study-abroad opportunities for students.

Despite these positive developments, however, teacher responses to our survey have exposed a number of challenges that need to be addressed in order to set the Arabic-teaching profession on solid ground. These challenges include the following.

(1) Further professional development opportunities: Thanks to enhanced federal support for Arabic, significant professional development opportunities have been created for teachers in Arabic, facilitated by programs developed and implemented by NMELRC, STARTALK, and ACTFL. Yet, our survey points to strongly felt needs among the teachers for expanded opportunities for professional development, especially in the area of teacher training. The fact that most current teachers of Arabic have not been trained in language pedagogy as part of their graduate education makes in-service training one of the top priorities for the Arabic field. We see in these survey results the expression of an urgent need to further expand training opportunities and provide face-to-face workshops, online materials, and mentoring teams (see Al-Batal and Belnap 2006, 393–94) for teachers of Arabic in the United States and abroad as part of a national effort to address their professional needs.

(2) Enhanced articulation with Arabic overseas program: While our survey reflects the remarkable growth in study-abroad opportunities for students of Arabic, it also shows the need for more coordination and articulation between stateside programs and programs in the Arab world. Survey participants are keen to see such close collaboration in areas such as curriculum design, teaching methodology, development of instructional materials, testing and assessment, and program evaluation.

(3) Rethinking teaching the spoken varieties of Arabic: Our survey reveals some interesting observations regarding the incorporation of colloquial Arabic in the curriculum. On the one hand, it demonstrates that the majority of teachers are in support of incorporating the study of colloquial in the first two years of instruction. It also reveals that most teachers feel comfortable teaching the basics of a dialect other than their own. On the other hand, the survey shows that the existing Arabic curricula do not reflect the teachers' views, in that colloquial Arabic often follows and is separated from MSA. This disconnect between the teachers' beliefs and programmatic practices implies a perceived need for specific curricular approaches and models for integrating colloquial within the curriculum as an indispensable component of the process to develop the speaking skill in Arabic.

(4) Focus on teaching pronunciation and listening: Responses from the teachers to our survey reveal that there is a need to place more focus within Arabic curricula on the teaching of pronunciation and listening comprehension. Pronunciation has been identified as one of the areas that present particular difficulty for American learners of Arabic, and listening as one of the skills that do not receive much attention in out-of-class activities. Both areas need further research to determine the type of training needed at the various levels of instruction and the instructional materials needed to enhance students' performance.

Acknowledgments

We express our sincerest thanks to Dina Housny of the American University in Cairo, and Britt Milliman and Anita Hussein of the University of Texas, Austin, for their help with the design and research connected with this survey. We also thank all of the 209 teachers of Arabic who participated in the survey and made this study possible. *Alf shukr* to all of you.

Notes

1. A complete copy of the survey and the responses to all its questions can be found at the following websites: www.coerll.utexas.edu/coerll/projects/arabic and www.nmelrc.org/arabicteacherprofiles.

2. Our research on the number of teachers was confined to colleges and universities and did not target US-government Arabic programs such as the one offered at the Defense Language Institute (DLI) or the Foreign Service Institute (FSI).

3. Some teachers reported twenty, twenty-five, and forty contact hours per week. We filtered out these numbers in order to reflect regular, nonintensive program settings.

References

Al-Batal, Mahmoud. "Facing the Crisis: Teaching and Learning Arabic in the United States in the Post-September 11 Era." *ADFL Bulletin* 36, no. 2–3 (2006): 39–46.

Al-Batal, Mahmoud, and Kirk Belnap. "The Teaching and Learning of Arabic in the United States: Realities, Needs, and Future Directions." In Wahba, Taha, and England, *Handbook*, 2006, 389–99.

Belnap, Kirk. "Who Is Taking Arabic and What on Earth For? A Survey of Students in Arabic Language Programs." *Al-'Arabiyya* 20 (1987): 29–42.

———. "The Institutional Setting of Arabic Language Teaching: A Survey of Program Coordinators and Teachers of Arabic in U.S. Institutions of Higher Learning." In *The Teaching of Arabic as a Foreign Language: Issues and Directions*, edited by Mahmoud Al-Batal, 35–77. Provo, UT: American Association of Teachers of Arabic (AATA), 1995.

———. "A Profile of Students of Arabic in U.S. Universities." In Wahba, Taha, and England, *Handbook*, 2006, 169–78.

Betteridge, Anne. "A Case Study in Higher Education International and Foreign Area Needs: Changes in the Middle East Studies Association Membership from 1990 to 2002." Paper presented at the Global Challenges and US Higher Education Conference, Duke University, Durham, NC, 2003. www.jhfc.duke.edu/ducis/globalchallenges/pdf/betteridge1.pdf.

Bhandari, Rajika, and Patricia Chow. *Report on International Educational Exchange*. New York: Institute of International Education, 2008.

Furman, Nelly, David Goldberg, and Natalia Lusin. "Enrollments in Languages Other Than English in United States Institutions of Higher Education, Fall 2009." Web Publication: The Modern Language Association of America, 2010. www.mla.org/pdf/2009_enrollment_survey.pdf.

Husseinali, Ghassan. "Who Is Studying Arabic and Why? A Survey of Arabic Students' Orientation at a Major University." *Foreign Language Annals* 39, no. 3 (2006): 395–412.

Kuntz, Patricia S. "Students of Arabic: Beliefs about Foreign Language Learning." *Al-ʿArabiyya* 29 (1996): 153–76.

Martinsen, Rob, Wendy Baker, Dan Dewey, Jennifer Bown, and Cary Johnson. "Exploring Diverse Settings for Language Acquisition and Use: Comparing Study Abroad, Service Learning Abroad, and Foreign Language Housing." *Applied Language Learning* 20, no. 1–2 (2010): 45–66.

Medina-Lopez-Portillo, Adriana. "Intercultural Learning Assessment: The Link between Program Duration and the Development of Intercultural Sensitivity." *Frontiers: Interdisciplinary Journal of Study Abroad* X (2004): 179–99.

Ryding, Karin. "Teaching Arabic in the United States." In Wahba, Taha, and England, *Handbook*, 2006, 13–20.

Smadi, O., and F. Al-Abed Al-Haq. "American University Students' Beliefs about Arabic Language Learning." *AbHaath Al-Yarmouk* 16, no. 1 (1998): 53–74.

Wahba, Kassem, Zeinab Taha, and Elizabeth England, eds. *Handbook for Arabic Language Teaching Professionals in the 21st Century*. New Jersey: Lawrence Erlbaum Associates, 2006.

Welles, Elizabeth. "Foreign Language Enrollments in United States Institutions of Higher Education." *ADFL Bulletin* 35, no. 2 (2004): 7–26.

Diglossia, Code Switching, Style Variation, and Congruence

NOTIONS FOR ANALYZING MIXED ARABIC

■

Gunvor Mejdell, University of Oslo, Norway

Abstract

The study addresses the complexity of describing and accounting for the highly variable forms of spoken "mixed Arabic" by presenting a survey on various approaches, concepts, and models that have recently been applied to such data in the sociolinguistic literature on Arabic. Merits and limitations of code-switching (CS) models receive consideration, as do the notions of the asymmetry of codes and constraints on switching and mixing; an alternative approach linked to style variation with patterns and principles; and the notion of lexical conditioning. The author suggests that the common ground of Arabic, the shared structures and features of the varieties, should receive more attention from analysts, and that close study of individual speakers' perceptions of their linguistic choices might be a next step.

Introduction

This study discusses sociolinguistic notions, principles, and models used to account for the very complex phenomenon variously labeled intermediate forms of Arabic, code-switched or mixed Arabic, *lugha wusṭā* or *lughat al-muthaqqafīn*: the analysis of language use that combines features and items from the two basic varieties: standard Arabic, *al-fuṣḥā*, and the everyday spoken vernacular, *al-ʿāmmiyya*. I assess (at least some of) the descriptive capacities of these notions, principles, and models. What can we claim is common ground, that is, insights achieved through various approaches, what are conceived as the major problems, and where should we go from here?

Reem Bassiouney and I have both been struggling with this issue over the years and both had books published on the topic by Brill in the same year (2006): Bassiouney, *Functions of Code Switching in Egypt: Evidence from Monologues*, and Mejdell, *Mixed Styles in Spoken Arabic in Egypt: Somewhere between Order and Chaos*. Our studies are based on the same kind of data: Bassiouney on extracts from political speeches, religious sermons, and a university lecture; Mejdell on only one genre, academic panel presentations. The data was approached from somewhat different perspectives, however. Both studies deal with structural analysis, but Bassiouney's main focus is motivations for and functions of switching between modern standard (MSA) and Egyptian colloquial Arabic (EA), whereas Mejdell focuses in some detail on interspeaker patterns of distribution and tries to identify some factors behind the patterns.

Diglossia and Intermediate Forms—Persistent Misconceptions

The issue of mixed, or intermediate, forms of modern Arabic has concerned Arabists ever since the publication of Charles Ferguson's seminal article "Diglossia" in 1959. One can almost say that it has become a rite of passage or an obligatory exercise for any new Arabist working in sociolinguistics to relate and position him- or herself in this tradition: starting from the diglossic dichotomy of High (H) versus Low (L), through defining three to five intermediate levels, and then on to recognizing a diglossic continuum between the poles of H and L. It is in fact enlightening to go back to the early contributions by Ferguson himself, Haim Blanc, and Heikki Palva in the 1960s, and Werner Diem and Elsaid Badawi in the early 1970s. The recirculation and summaries of these contributions, however, often overlook or obscure some of their keen observations and insights—so it is perhaps not such a bad exercise after all for students to track down the forebears.

For some reason, the widespread practice of using intermediate forms and the subsequent discussion of these forms and their functions have been largely neglected in mainstream sociolinguistic literature, which, with few exceptions, continues to represent H and L varieties in Arabic diglossia as discrete entities in categorical functional distribution (e.g., Romaine 1995; Hudson 1994; Myers-Scotton 1993). Schiffman (1997) represents one of the exceptions, mentioning that "though linguistic cultures think of diglossia as either-or, it is often a gradient cline, with one variant shading into another" (211).

Arabic is no doubt the prototypical case for Ferguson's initial model of diglossia, but the other defining cases (Swiss German, Haitian Creole, and Greek) have also reported intermediate forms and overlapping of domains and functions. In short, with regard to sociolinguistic typology, scholars should acknowledge the existence of mixed forms as a significant feature in the description of diglossia (better described as the diglossic continuum). Then misconceptions concerning Arabic and other linguistic communities may be avoided. For instance, Czech linguists describe a situation in their language community very similar to that of Arabic but conclude that since in the Czech case there are fuzzy linguistic boundaries, mixing of H and L features, there can be no diglossia.

The Code-Switching Approach to Mixed Styles

The concept of CS is rooted in studies of bilingual language contact. CS research looks for patterns in and constraints on the way the two codes in contact combine, whether CS is seen as linear, alternational, shifting from one code to the other in sequence, or as insertional, with elements of one code inserted or embedded in the structure of another code. CS models have also been applied to the combined use of two varieties of what is considered the same language on the assumption that "the social meanings linked with the varieties and the mechanisms underlying individual choices are sufficiently akin . . . to cover concurrent choices from both kinds of pairs [bilingual and monolingual] with a single term" (Coulmas 2005, 110).

One example is the well-known study on the Norwegian case of Hemnesberget (Blom and Gumperz 1972) with its situational and metaphorical switching between standard Norwegian and local dialect. Norwegian sociolinguists, however, have harshly criticized this study for its methodology and interpretation, for its unrealistic description, and notably for its representation of the variation as discrete (Mæhlum 1996).

Following the hard-to-kill strictly dichotomous view of diglossia to which I refer above, some leading sociolinguists assume that diglossia prevents CS because "there is an almost one-to-one relationship between language choice and social context" so that "only one code is usually employed at any one time" (Romaine 1995, 121). Similarly, Myers-Scotton: "The expectation is that unmarked CS should not occur at all in narrow diglossic communities (the Arabic-speaking nations of the Middle East, at least)" (1993, 128).

The first to apply syntactic CS models to Arabic diglossic switching is Mushira Eid (1982, 1988). Eid looks at switch points ("focal points") in view of the linear model and at constraints proposed by Sankoff and Poplack, and finds that they must be somewhat modified to fit her Arabic data. She made, however, some interesting observations to which I shall return.

In her dissertation and book on diglossic CS, Bassiouney (2006) applies the matrix language frame model (MLF) developed by Myers-Scotton from the early 1990s and on. Basic to the model is the notion that the languages, or codes, involved in CS have unequal status and play different roles in the mix: The dominant, or "matrix," language (ML) alone sets the morphosyntactic frame for the clause (word order and inflection), and provides the system morphemes and normally most of the content morphemes as well. The other code, the embedded language (EL), may provide constituents and single content morphemes, which are inserted into the ML base. This model (only grossly outlined here) has been most influential and has inspired many studies. It has also met with critique and counterevidence and is constantly developed, to the extent that it has lost its initial simplicity and thus, for many scholars, its attractiveness. Bassiouney (2006,

2009) demonstrates several problems with applying the model to her data. The main problem, she reports, is that "ECA and MSA are different codes but with a lot of shared content and system morphemes, and it is almost impossible at times to say whether a certain morpheme belongs to ECA or to MSA. Thus, it is not easy to come up with one ML, since it is sometimes difficult to decide which code is being used in the first place.

I argue that the existence of two codes that are partially overlapping and partially distinct, as in Arabic, may cause problems for both the ML and the 4-M model" (2009, 55). Another study on CS monologue in an MLF framework, by Boussofara-Omar, reports the same kind of problem, namely "the cooccurrence of system morphemes from both varieties within a single CP (projection of the complementizer)" (2006, 77).[1]

Congruent Lexicalization—A Way Out?

Similar problems—with stated CS principles and constraints that do not apply to sets of related languages, such as Dutch-English, or standard languages with distant dialects—made Peter Muysken (2000 and earlier versions) suggest a third kind of CS (in his terms, "code-mixing"). In addition to alternational mixing (mostly intersentential CS) and obvious cases of insertional mixing, he proposes a third category, congruent lexicalization. "Congruent lexicalization," he says, typically should be expected "when the languages in contact share basic sentence structure, such as the alignment of the major constituents—fully or in part" (Muysken 2000, 122). With regard to the vocabulary, it "may come from two or more different languages, but may also be shared" (ibid., 127).

Two conditions are typically conducive to congruent lexicalization: "an overabundance of homophonous words . . . that serve as bridges or triggers for the code-mix," and "general structural equivalence" (ibid.). In such cases, even multiconstituent code mixing may be so frequent that it does not make sense to think of it as shifting for some kind of function or pragmatic meaning. As examples of this smooth mixing back and forth, I cite the following:

- Bij mijn broer *y a un ascenseur* en alles. (At my brother('s) *there's an elevator* and everything.) (Dutch + *French*, Treffers-Daller 1994:222, in Muysken 2000, 126)
- Ja maar bij *ouwe mensen* komt dat *gauwer tot stilstand als* bij jonge mense wa. (Yes but with *older people* that comes *to a halt more quickly than* with younger people eh.) (*Standard* vs. dialect in Ottersum, data from Giesbers in Muysken 2000, 130)

Congruent lexicalization presents itself as a most relevant and attractive category for Arabic diglossic mixing, with its high degree of structural and syntactic congruence between codes, although not complete overlapping. Concerning word order, whereas the spoken language may prefer an SVO word order, and MSA a VSO order, both SVO and VSO are possible in both (Dahlgren 1998). Fronting as a discourse strategy may be more frequent in the vernacular, but it is not uncommon in MSA, even the written form. For most clause embedding, the subjunctions are lexically different, but the structure is mostly equivalent. There is a mismatch in the order of attributive demonstrative and head noun in MSA and EA, and asyndetic verb sequences (subordination) in EA must align with the MSA construction by adding a complementizer. The "structural gap hard to cross" as Palva (1969) characterizes it, namely the systemic opposition of modal distinction in the dialects and in MSA, is in practice overcome in mixed styles by the use of EA indicative marker *bi-* with MSA verbs, a strategy that works because *bi-* apparently has very low salience as a marker of EA, and thereby of style (Mejdell 2006, 383–85). Bassiouney (2006, 124) claims that MSA lexical verb forms with the *bi-* prefix are still perceived as MSA.

The following example illustrates this structural parallellism in mixed Arabic: "b-aʿtaqid ʾinnu bi-hādha n-naṣṣ bi-yadxul fī munāzarat al-mawāqif wil-ʾiqnaʿāt ʾilli bi-tukawwin-ha magmūʿat ʾan-nuṣūṣ ʾallati tatanāwal hāza l-mawḍūʿ." ("I believe that with this text he [the author] enters the controversial field of attitudes and convictions which all texts treating this issue are part of" (Mejdell 2006, 398).

Congruent lexicalization was explicitly intended as a bridge-building category between bilingual code mixing and monolingual style variation, allowing mixing of all kinds of constituents and single words, including grammatical features, that contradict constraints in the CS literature. Muysken also argues that the distinction traditionally made between code mixing—the alternation of two invariant systems in a single discourse—and variation or style shifting—the realization of different options within one single system—"has become less watertight, in the light of developments both in our view of grammatical systems and in our perception of the phenomenon of code-mixing. The phenomenon of style shifting can be seen as one subtype of code-mixing, namely congruent lexicalization" (Muysken 2000, 123).

Mixed Arabic as Stylistic Variation?

So let us cross the bridge from CS to a style-variation framework for our diglossic mixed data. The functions, the pragmatics, of diglossic mixing do not change. In both frameworks, language form (H vs. L or mixed) is linked to sociocultural context, especially to the formal-informal dimension typical for register or style variation.[2] The notion of style being the link between linguistic form and context rests on the assumption that a language community develops conventions for the language forms appropriate to various contexts, which are defined by setting, participant relations, and a number of other functions that may be specified. For diglossic variation these functions are mostly related to speakers' perception of the degree of formality, including the dimension of informational or interactional purpose, but they are also influenced by the individual speaker's degree of competence in the H variety, and whether the speech is planned or unplanned. Style may be responsive, when the speaker accommodates to the perceived formality (or otherwise) of a speech situation, or initiative, whereby the speaker by linguistic means defines or modifies the perception of the situation, for instance in order to alter the social distance to the audience or between interlocutors. In "'standard with dialects'-situations, linguistic features typically found at the high end of the *social* scale are similarly high on the *stylistic* scale and vice versa" (Gadet 2005, 1357), whereas in diglossia, there is an extra set of H variants for more elevated style, in addition to features at work for social stratification within L (such as phonology, lexicon, the use of English, H elements perhaps indexical of access to literacy, but also come with traditional, religious expressions used by lower social strata).

Significantly, style variation is "largely a matter of tendencies, rather than strict co-occurrence constraints" and is "explicitly or implicitly, an inherently comparative concept" (Levinson 1988, 162–63). Thus, the analytical focus to this approach is typically tuned toward relative frequency of linguistic style variables, across levels and across genres.

In my study of mixed styles, I compare interspeaker usage levels of some high-frequency grammatical diglossic variables, that is variables that have clearly distinctive EA and MSA variants: complementizers, demonstratives, negative markers, relative markers, and pronoun suffigation.[3] All occurrences were registered in their immediate linguistic environment, uncovering certain patterns of distribution, such as constraints on mixing and some collocational constraints.

My initial expectation was that variation patterns would reflect a certain conventionalization of linguistic strategies, or means for specific uses, such as the genre of academic panel presentations from which my data is recorded. However, the quantitative survey shows that the speakers have highly different ratios/usage levels for the variables, both among themselves and among the variables (Mejdell 2006, 375–76). Second, ordering the variants in a sequential survey (ibid., 399–404), I found that the distribution of variants also varied to a great extent: Some speakers used MSA variants nearly exclusively in some sequences, followed by a sequence with nearly exclusively EA variants, reflecting a CS strategy, whereas others had variants from both codes more evenly sprinkled throughout their presentation, reflecting code mixing. I had to conclude that there is no evidence of a stabilized style for this genre.

However, from comparing the frequency counts for the variables, I discovered that the speakers all had nearly the same hierarchy of preferences for MSA or EA features. The highest usage level of MSA variants was for the attributive demonstrative (DEM), followed by the negative markers (NEG), then the relative marker and/or the complementizer (REL/COMP), whereas the lowest usage level of MSA variants—and consequently the highest usage level of EA variants, was for pronoun suffixation:

MSA < DEM > NEG > REL/COMP > PRON < EA

We can read the same relative ordering of the variables from Bassiouney's study (e.g., 2006, 232 and 152), and from Schulz's data.[4]

Common Ground: Asymmetry and Constraints on Mixing

Researchers have long observed asymmetrical psycholinguistic status between languages involved in mixing for many different language pairs.[5] Petersen (1988) formulates this principle as the Dominant Language Hypothesis: In word-internal mixing, dominant-language (DL) grammatical items may combine with DL and with non-DL lexical items/stems, whereas non-DL grammatical items may only combine with non-DL lexical items. We note the parallel constraints formulated in the MLF model: ML system morphemes may combine with ML and EL content morphemes, whereas EL system morphemes may only combine with EL content morphemes (in an EL island). All the data on diglossic word-internal mixing in Arabic appears to confirm the principle.[6]

But the DLH also seems to operate as a constraint for switching between the relative (grammatical) marker and the verb (lexical) form, between complementizer and following verb or noun, between negative marker and verb, between demonstrative and noun, between pronoun suffix and head noun or verb. The DLH claims validity for word-internal mixing across languages, and the collocational constraints above seem to work for Arabic diglossic CS and mixing. Mushira Eid (1982, 1988) observes the same asymmetry: CS between variants before and after her focal points was not balanced between the codes, and in fact it patterned in accordance with DLH. Bassiouney (2006, 152 and 233) makes similar observations, reporting that the mixed forms involving her variables all consist of

- a negative marker in ECA and a verb in MSA,
- a demonstrative in ECA and a noun in MSA,
- an ECA aspectual(GM+/modal) marker and an MSA verb

I argue elsewhere for a terminological distinction between the notions of dominant language and matrix language (Mejdell 1999). The Dominant Language Hypothesis considers the dominant language to be the primary language of a person, usually acquired as the natural mother tongue, the deepest entrenched variety, in which one has the most automaticized competence and control. Secondary varieties or languages will not interfere with one's dominant language the way the dominant language interferes with secondary ones. However, close and prolonged contact with other varieties may affect the primary, dominant language to some extent, so it is not necessarily static. (For near-balanced bilinguals, the issue of language dominance may be more complex.)

The matrix language, on the other hand, is the main activated language form of an actual utterance: The matrix language of my article here is English, but the matrix language is under interference from my dominant language, my native variety of Norwegian, and would be much more so in a spoken presentation. Thus, matrix and dominant languages/varieties are not equal in status. The dominant language is stable (though not static); the matrix language changes with the communicative goal, it is the target language. For native Arabic speakers of diglossic mixed style, the dominant language will be the vernacular, but the matrix language may change with the communicative target. This distinction may account for an utterance such as: "*fa-yufakkir fi ʿalaqt-u bi-zamilt-u wa kayfa ʾanna ʾizāhit hāza l-ab ʾaw mawt-u.*" (and he thinks about his relationship to his colleague (f) and how the disappearance of his father or his death.) (Mejdell 2006, 431)

This speaker seems to have MSA as target, as the intended matrix for his utterance, choosing MSA lexical items and grammatical words, but the EA DL interferes (in the less-salient grammatical endings), resulting in mixed forms that are acceptable to the DLH. However, according to the MLF model, these forms would point to EA as the ML, or they should not, strictly speaking, occur at all.

Phonology and Lexicon : Lexical Conditioning, or "the Lexical Hypothesis"

In monolingual style variation, phonology and lexicon are normally important style markers. With regard to intermediate forms of the Arabic language, scholars generally recognize that the H variety provides a high amount of the lexical material and that with the lexical items come some phonological features not basic to the vernacular. Determining the lexical status of a word can be a complex issue, however: First, much vocabulary is shared between the MSA and the vernacular, and second, a cultural loan from the MSA may receive phonological adaptation, reflecting a gradual process of integration into the common spoken language. Whether there is phonological or lexical variation at play between variants of cognate words is a classic discussion in Arabic sociolinguistics, going back to Haim Blanc (1964)—"phonemic modification or lexical loan." Clive Holes, discussing such forms in his Bahrayni data, for example, variation between *jumʿa* and *yimʿa* (Friday), argues that speakers "choose between closed sets of alternative representations for the same underlying form (or function) . . . alternative lexical representations which speakers have internalized through exposure to MSA" (1987, 153). In line with Holes's Lexical Hypothesis, Palva (1969) observes that the variable pronunciation in his Palestinian texts appears to be "largely connected with the lexicon [and] to a considerable degree tied to the dialectal or literary lexical items" (1969, 26 and 28). Similarly, Miller (2005, 933) notes the co-occurrence of words with different realizations of /q/- /ʾ/variants in plain spoken Cairene.

Related to this is the notion of lexical specification, where words with MSA and EA phonological representations of the same stem, or root, have different lexical meanings. Badawi (1973) gives, for instance, EA *atar* (bad omen) vs. MSA *athar* (trace, antiquity), which come from the same stem and root, with EA vs. MSA variation between /t/and /th/; further, contrast MSA *muthallath* (triple; triangular) and EA *mitallit* (triple; three times twisted rope > strange [person]). In an example Bassiouney cites (2006, 248), "*ʿashān kānit qawiyya ʾawi*" (because it was very strong), the adjective *qawiyya* and the adverb *ʾawi* have the same root (*qwy*) but the lexical items come with different realizations of the first phoneme. The same phenomenon is noted by Holton (2002) for New Standard Greek as convergence taking place with the end of (Greek) diglossia: "In phonology: the separate systems of K and D have merged, so that, in the case of certain consonant clusters, for example, the phonology is word-specific or morpheme-specific, not systemic" (176).

Thus, diglossic phonological variables—for example, /q/and /ʾ/; /th/, /s/and /t/; /aw/and /ō/—should be studied in their lexical environment, so to speak, and variants do not necessarily reflect style variation, but in many cases are lexically conditioned.

Common Ground in Another Sense: An Alternative Perspective

> "I only distinguish between standard and dialectal language in so far as one word rather than another accurately expresses what I want to say"
>
> (Yusuf Idris, cited in Kurpershoek 1981, 124).

Although these words from the famous Egyptian writer refer to his use of vernacular items in his writing, it seems more and more reasonable to me in working with this kind of spoken data, whether from a switching, mixing, or variation approach, that producers of mixed style above all want to find the appropriate expression for the communicative purpose at hand. Trying to understand mental processes—and not being a psycholinguist, I am tentative and pretheoretical on this—it appears to me that speakers primarily access words, notions, and lexical items, and that these words and notions are accompanied by their usual linguistic environment, that they come in chunks, so to speak, which also may affect the wider environment of the utterance. [7]

Educated speakers have a (variably) large MSA lexicon added to their vernacular lexical repertoire and may quite freely choose the appropriate items from this common pool, either as single items or in chunks. They may modify the linguistic form with stylistic markers restricted by some principles that reflect the asymmetric psycholinguistic status of the varieties (DLH). Apparently, speakers are more consciously aware of some features than others; they may avoid the more-salient features of the vernacular when style raising, and actively use salient features of the H variety as markers of formality. Less-salient parts of speech, grammatical features that are phonetically close (*-at* and *–it*; *al-* and *il-*; pronoun suffixes; *ʾanna, ʾinna, ʾinnu*) or features less easy to monitor (supersegmental features such as syllable structure, vowel shortening, lengthening) may follow the lexical item, or automatically interfere as a reflex of primary language habits (including *bi-* as essential for the modal system). See the utterance cited above, in this light.

I do not believe that intermediate forms of the language, CS and mixed styles of Arabic, will ever turn into an autonomous variety in the normal sense, implying a certain structural cohesion. The native notion of *lughat al-muthaqqafīn*, or *lugha wusṭā*, is similarly if impressionistically defined as mixing and interaction between the high norm and the vernacular, a mode of speaking, at best a heterogeneous variety. We may, however, expect that individuals develop idiosyncratic individual norms and preferences among choices and that some conventionalization for specific genres emerges as speakers interact and influence each other.

I also believe that the congruent structures are basic to speakers' construction of their talk and provide a common ground for selecting items from the repertoire. We should pay more attention to this common ground, instead of hunting for the matrix language and insisting on classifying a text as having either EA or MSA as ML. The analytical concept of congruent lexicalization helps analysts out of the MLF trap but does not have further explicative value, as far as I can say. What it does is to link bilingual code mixing to the style-variation approach in a unified framework. For our kind of diglossic mixed data it may foreground shared forms and gradient features and tone down somewhat the flagging of EA and MSA markers. I finally wish to emphasize that CS and style variation are not mutually exclusive approaches, but complementary.

As a next step I propose that we do more in-depth case studies on individual styles, using qualitative methods and techniques such as interviewing and interpreting observed practice with speakers, in specific genres, not only on the diglossic variables, but on other stylistically relevant features as well, not least lexical choice.

Notes

1. As Bassiouney admits, the composite ML is not an appropriate category for these cases, either, because Myers-Scotton apparently reserves it for cases of language turnover.

2. I prefer the term "style" as more general, with broader connotations, including "personal style." "Register" is often associated with a more restricted sense of conventionalized use for specific settings and situations. The terms are often used interchangeably, though, and for some, "register" is considered the more general term, whereas "style" connotes some aesthetic values.

3. In David Schulz (1981) one finds a pure count of these and other variables occurring in various extracts from Egyptian radio.

4. Significantly, if pronominal demonstratives are also counted, negative markers and demonstratives have more equal distribution.

5. For a discussion of some such cases, see Mejdell (2006), 62–66.

6. For Arabic diglossic mixing R. W. Schmidt (1974) finds, in elicited data, that stems (lexical items) from both MSA and EA can combine with EA grammatical endings, whereas only MSA lexical items can be combined with MSA grammatical endings. I discuss this point at length in Mejdell (2006) and also in Mejdell (2012).

7. I believe Ad Backus has used this notion but am not able to trace this source at the time of writing.

References

Badawī, Al-Saʿīd Muḥammad. *Mustawayāt al-lugha al-ʿarabiyya al-muʿāṣira fī miṣr*. Cairo: Dār al-maʿārif, 1973.

Bassiouney, Reem. *Functions of Code Switching in Egypt: Evidence from Monologues*. Leiden: Brill, 2006.

———. *Arabic Sociolinguistics*. Edinburgh: Edinburgh University Press, 2009.

Blanc, Haim. *Communal Dialects in Baghdad*. Cambridge, MA: Harvard University Press, 1964.

Blom, Jan-Petter, and John Gumperz. "Social Meaning in Linguistic Structures: Code Switching in Northern Norway." In *Directions in Sociolinguistics: The Ethnography of Communication*, edited by John Gumperz and Del Hymes, 407–34. New York: Holt, Rinehart, and Winston, 1972.

Boussofara-Omar, Naima. "Neither Third Language nor Middle Varieties but Diglossic Switching." *ZAL* 45 (2006): 55–80.

Coulmas, Florian. *Sociolinguistics. The Study of Speakers' Choices*. Cambridge: Cambridge University Press, 2005.

Dahlgren, Sven-Olof. *Word Order in Arabic*. Göteborg: Acta Universitatis Gothoburgensis, 1998.

Diem, Werner. *Hochsprache und Dialekt im Arabischen*. Wiesbaden: Franz Steiner, 1974.

Eid, Mushira. "The Non-Randomness of Diglossic Variation in Arabic." *Glossa* 16, no. 1 (1982): 54–84.

———. "Principles of Code Switching between Standard and Egyptian Arabic." *Al-ʿArabiyya* 21 (1988): 51–79.

Gadet, Françoise. "Research on Sociolinguistic Style." In *Sociolinguistics/Soziolinguistik*, edited by Ulrich Ammon et al., 1353–61. Berlin: Walter de Gruyter, 2005.

Holes, Clive. *Language Variation and Change in a Modernising Arab State: The Case of Bahrain.* London: Keagan Paul International, 1987.

Holton, David. "Modern Greek: Towards a Standard Language or a New Diglossia?" In *Language Change: The Interplay of Internal, External, and Extra-linguistic Factors,* edited by Mary C. Jones and Edith Esch, 169–79. Berlin: Mouton de Gruyter, 2002.

Hudson, Alan. "Diglossia as a Special Case of Register Variation." In Biber and Finnegan, *Sociolinguistic Perspectives on Register*, 1994, 294–314.

Kurpershoek, P. Marcel. *The Short Stories of Yusuf Idris: A Modern Egyptian Author*. Leiden: Brill, 1981.

Levinson, Stephen. "Conceptual Problems in the Study of Regional and Cultural Style." In *The Sociolinguistics of Urban Vernaculars: Case Studies and Their Evaluation,* edited by Norbert Dittmar and Peter Schlobinski, 161–90. Berlin: De Gruyter, 1988.

Mejdell, Gunvor. *Mixed Styles in Spoken Arabic in Egypt: Somewhere between Order and Chaos.* Leiden: Brill, 2006.

———. "The Elusiveness of *Luġa Wusṭā*—or, Attempting to Catch Its 'True Nature.'" In *Arabic Language and Linguistics,* edited by Reem Bassiouney and E. Graham Katz, 157–67. Washington, D.C.: Georgetown University Press, 2012.

———. "Switching, Mixing—Code Interaction in Spoken Arabic." In *Language Encounters across Time and Space*, edited by Bernt Brendemoen, Elizabeth Lanza, and Else Ryen. Oslo: Novus, 1999.

Miller, Catherine. "Between Accommodation and Resistance: Upper Egyptian Migrants in Cairo." *Linguistics* 43, no. 5 (2005): 903–56.

Muysken, Peter. *Bilingual Speech: A Typology of Code-Mixing*. Cambridge: Cambridge University Press, 2000.

Myers-Scotton, Carol. *Social Motivations for Codeswitching: Evidence from Africa*. Oxford: Clarendon, 1993.

Mæhlum, Brit. "Codeswitching in Hemnesberget: Myth or Reality?" *Journal of Pragmatics* 25 (1996): 749–61.

Palva, Heikki. "Notes on Classicization in Modern Colloquial Arabic." *Acta Orientalia* XL (1969): 3.

Petersen, Jennifer. "Word-Internal Code-Switching Constraints in a Bilingual Child's Grammar." *Linguistics* 26 (1988): 479–93.

Romaine, Suzanne. *Bilingualism*, 2nd ed. Oxford: Blackwell Publishers Ltd., 1995.

Schiffman, Harold F. "Diglossia as a Sociolinguistic Situation." In *The Handbook of Sociolinguistics,* edited by Florian Coulmas, 205–16. London: Basil Blackwell, 1997.

Schmidt, Richard Wilbur. *Sociostylistic Variation in Spoken Egyptian Arabic: A Re-examination of the Concept of Diglossia*. Unpublished Ph.D. diss., Brown University, 1974.

Schulz, David Eugene. "Diglossia and Variation in Formal Spoken Arabic in Egypt." PhD diss., University of Wisconsin-Madison, 1981.

Sluicing in Libyan Arabic

■

Ali Algryani, Academy of Graduate Studies, Tripoli, Libya

Abstract

This study examines two issues related to sluicing in Libyan Arabic from a PF deletion perspective. First, it attempts to determine whether what appears as sluicing is sluicing or pseudosluicing. Second, it discusses the apparent violation of the preposition stranding generalization posited by Merchant (2001). The study shows that sluicing exists in the language and that it can be derived from regular wh-questions by wh-movement followed by TP deletion. Furthermore, the study argues that the apparent preposition stranding (p-stranding) effects under sluicing derive from a copular source and that therefore there are two sources of TP ellipsis: sluicing and pseudosluicing. Sluicing derives from regular wh-questions, and it conforms to the p-stranding generalization; pseudosluicing is an elliptical wh-cleft resulting from deletion of a clefted TP whose pivot is an extracted wh-phrase. The fact that the preposition in cleft wh-questions resides in the relative clause, which eventually deletes at PF in pseudosluicing, yields the illusion that sluicing involves p-stranding.

Introduction

This study investigates the ellipsis phenomenon of sluicing in Libyan Arabic (LA) and attempts to determine whether what appears as sluicing is sluicing or pseudosluicing.[1] It also aims to discuss the crosslinguistic and language-specific properties that sluicing displays. The study is organized as follows. The first section is an introduction to sluicing and its status in syntactic theory, and the second deals with sluicing and sluicing typology with reference to some crosslinguistic properties of sluicing. The third section examines LA sluicing and attempts to determine whether it is sluicing or pseudosluicing by applying some sluicing-defining diagnostics. The fourth section deals with the interaction between p-stranding and sluicing. Finally, the fifth section presents the conclusions.

Defining Sluicing

The term sluicing, originally coined by Ross (1969), refers to a form of sentential ellipsis in which a remnant wh-phrase functions as a wh-question despite the fact that such a question is reduced phonologically to a mere wh-phrase, as in (1). Sluicing constructions are similar to non-elliptical wh-questions in both distribution and interpretation. The sluiced wh-phrase is interpreted as a fully pronounced wh-question as it conveys a full interrogative force, as in (1) and (2).

(1) John bought something, but I don't know what.

(2) John bought something, but I don't know what *[John bought]*.

Sluicing in Syntactic Theory

Generally, there are two approaches to the syntactic structure of sluicing: the nonstructural and structural approach. The nonstructural approach assumes no syntactic structure in the ellipsis site: the sluiced wh-phrase is treated as a bare "wh-fragment", generated as an XP (DP, PP, AP) functioning as a complement to the main verb (Riemsdijk 1978; Culicover and Jackendoff 2005).

The structural approach argues for a structure in the elided material. However, there is some disagreement as to whether or not the unpronounced material contains lexically null elements. The two dominating structural approaches are LF copying and PF deletion. The former assumes a null category filled by copying the semantic component of the antecedent clause at LF (Chung, Ladusaw, and McCloskey 1995; Lobeck 1991, 1995). The latter argues for a syntactic structure within the null TP that gets deleted after a wh-movement operation (Ross 1969; Chomsky and Lasnik 1993; Lasnik 2001, 2007; Merchant 2001; Aelbrecht 2010). This study adopts the PF deletion approach to sluicing as a working hypothesis.

Following the deletion theory in positing a syntactic structure in the ellipsis site of sluicing, the question is how we can determine the nature of this invisible structure. According to Ross (1969), Lasnik (2007), and Merchant (2001, 2008) among others, the sluiced clause has the syntactic structure of a wh-question and is derived by wh-movement plus TP deletion, as illustrated in (4).

(3) Joan met someone, but I don't know who.

(4) Joan met someone, but I don't know [*CP* who$_i$ [*TP* ~~*Joan met*~~ t_i.]]

However, there is another analysis advocated by Pollman (1975) and Erteschik-Shir (1977) who argue that sluicing derives from an underlying copular clause, as in (5).

(5) John bought something, but I don't know what [it was].

The sluice in (5) arguably occurs by deletion of the subject "it" and the copula "was". Merchant (2001) points out that Erteschik-Shir (1977) is concerned with island-ameliorating and that in deriving sluicing from such a copular structure, island effects become irrelevant. Furthermore, he argues that such a structure is a type of cleft, or more precisely a type of reduced cleft whose pivot is an extracted wh-phrase. Merchant (2001) calls this type of ellipsis "pseudosluicing," and he states that such a structure is different from true sluicing, as shown in (6).

(6) a. Someone left. Guess who [it was that left]. Pseudosluicing
b. Guess who [left]. Sluicing

The two arguments above sound plausible, and they lead to a valid question: to what extent is the sluiced clause's (invisible) structure isomorphic or identical to the structure of the antecedent clause? The first question I intend to address in this chapter is to determine whether sluicing in Libyan Arabic derives from regular wh-questions or from a copular source (that is, a cleft).

Sluicing in Libyan Arabic

Sluicing exists in Libyan Arabic. As in other languages, sluicing is only licensed by interrogative complementizers, and it occurs in main and embedded contexts. Main-clause sluices occur as mere wh-phrases in contexts in which the antecedent is a main wh-question, as in (8); embedded-clause sluices occur in asyndetically conjoined constructions, as in (7). Moreover, embedded-clause sluices are introduced by verbs that select CP complements such as "know," "guess," "remember," etc."

(7) waḥəd zār Ali, lakən miš ʕarəf man.
someone visited.3MS Ali but NEG know.1MS who
"Someone visited Ali, but I don't know who."

(8) a: Ali ʕzəm waḥəd. b: man?
Ali invited.3MS someone who
"Ali invited someone." "Who?"

Sluicing Typology

Sluicing constructions fall into four subtypes: (a) sluices with adjunct wh-phrases, (b) sluices with overt correlates, (c) sluices with implicit arguments, and (d) contrast sluices (Chung, Ladusaw, and McCloskey 1995; Merchant 2001). The sluiced wh-phrase in the first type is an adjunct corresponding to nothing in the antecedent clause, as in (9); in the second type, the wh-phrase corresponds to an overt correlate in the antecedent; the correlate has to be either an indefinite pronoun or noun, as in (10).

(9) Ali sāfər, lakən miš ʕarəf lēš/əmta /la-wēn.
Ali left.3MS but NEG know.1MS why/when/to-where
"Ali left, but I don't know why/when/to where."

(10) Ali zār waḥəd/ražəl /*r-ražəl, lakən miš
Ali visited.3MS someone /man/the-man but NEG
ʕarəf man.
know.1MS who
"Ali visited someone/a man/*the man, but I don't know who."

The wh-phrase in the third type of sluicing corresponds to an implicit argument licensed by argument structure; this sprouted argument can be a direct object or a non-direct-object argument, as in (11) and (12), respectively.

(11) Ali yəggra, lakən miš ʕarəf šenu/šeni.
Ali reading.3MS but NEG know.1MS what
"Ali is reading, but I don't know what."

(12) baaʕ l-hoš, lakən miš məʕruf l-man.
sold.3MS the-house but NEG known to whom
"He sold the house, but it is not known to whom."

Finally, contrast sluices are those sluices in which "the descriptive content in the sluiced wh-phrase clashes with that of its correlate" (Merchant 2001, 150). Contrast sluices in Libyan Arabic are acceptable as demonstrated by the example (14).

(13) There were nine girls in the party, but I don't know how many boys.

(14) ʕənd-ha tlata wlād, lakən miš ʕarəf kam
has.3FS three sons but NEG know.1MS how many
bent.
daughter
"She has three sons, but I don't know how many daughters."

Form Identity Effects in Libyan Arabic Sluicing

Crosslinguistically, sluicing constructions display some morphosyntactic features referred to as form identity effects; these include case matching, preposition stranding, and binding effects. Form-identity effects argue in favor of the PF deletion analysis of sluicing as an elliptical wh-question derived by wh-movement and TP deletion.

FORM-IDENTITY GENERALIZATION I: CASE-MATCHING

> The sluiced wh-phrase must bear the case that its correlate bears.
>
> (Merchant 2001, 91)

In case-marking languages, the sluiced wh-phrase displays only the case of its correlate in the antecedent clause. The sluiced wh-phrase in (15) requires nominative and not accusative case which is assigned by the verb *ksero* "know" (16); therefore, it cannot be a direct argument to the embedding predicate, that is, the verb "know." The absence of internal structure in the ellipsis site makes this case-marking unexplained (Aelbrecht 2010).

(15) Greek
Kapjos irthe, alla dhe ksero {pjos/*pjon}
someone came, but not know.Isg who.NOM/who.ACC
"Someone came, but I don't know who."

(16) Dhe ksero {* i apantisi/tin apantisi}.
not know.Isg the answer.NOM/the answer.ACC
"I don't know the answer."
(Merchant 2001, 43)

Modern Arabic dialects including LA are not case-marking languages; therefore, the case-marking effect cannot be taken as evidence that LA sluicing derives from wh-questions.

(17) Ali grē riwaya, lakən miš ʕarəf ʔyya
Ali read.3MS novel but NEG know.1MS which
riwaya.
novel
"Ali read a novel, but I don't know which novel."

FORM IDENTITY GENERALIZATION II: PREPOSITION-STRANDING

> A language *L* will allow preposition stranding under sluicing if *L* allows preposition stranding under regular wh-movement.
>
> (Merchant 2001, 92)

English allows p-stranding under wh-movement, as in (18); therefore, p-stranding under sluicing is permitted, as shown in (19). Libyan Arabic does not permit p-stranding under regular wh-movement (20), thus the p-stranding generalization predicts that p-standing is not permitted in sluicing either. Unexpectedly, this prediction is not correct, as evidenced in (21). This suggests that the language is a counterexample to the p-stranding generalization; therefore, the latter cannot be strictly taken as evidence that sluicing stems from regular wh-questions.

(18) a. Who did John talk to?
b. To whom did John talk?

(19) John talked to someone, but I don't know who.

(20) a.

*man	təkəllem	Sami	mʕə?
who	talked.3MS	Sami	with

"Who did Sami talk with?" (Intended reading)

b.

mʕə	man	təkəllem	Sami?
With	who	talked.3MS	Sami

"With whom did Sami talk?"

(21)

Sami	təkəllem	mʕə	waḥəd,	lakən	miš	ʕarəf
Sami	talked.3MS	with	someone	but	NEG	know.1MS
(mʕə)	man.					
with	who					

"Sami talked with someone, but I don't know (with) who(m)."

ISLAND CONSTRAINTS AND SLUICING

If it is the case that sluicing stems from wh-questions and is derived by wh-movement, then sluicing should obey movement constraints. However, sluicing shows insensitivity to syntactic islands, as in (22) (see, for example, Ross 1969; Merchant 2001, 2008). Consequently, what appears as grammatical sluicing could be derived from island-violating constructions. Sluicing in LA is insensitive to islands. The sluiced wh-phrase can have an overt correlate in the antecedent clause located within an island, as in (23a); this is not permissible in non-elliptical wh-questions due to island effects, as illustrated in (23b).

(22) Coordinate Structure Constraint Island
a. Irv and someone were dancing together, but I don't know who.
b. * . . . but I don't know whoi Irv and ti were dancing together.
(Chung, Ladusow, and McCloskey 1995, 273)

(23) Adjunct island

a.

Omar	kan	ḥazīn	liʔna	xṣr	mubara,
Omar	was.3MS	sad	because	lost.3MS	game
lakən	miš	ʕarəf	ʔyya	mubara.	
but	NEG	know.1MS	which	game	

b.

*ʔyya	$mubara_i$	Omar	kan	ḥazīn	liʔna
which	game	Omar	was.3MS	sad	because
xṣr	t_i?				
lost.3MS					

To sum up, it seems that form-identity effects do not provide evidence that sluicing in LA derives from regular wh-questions. First, as a non-case-marking language, LA is not subject to the case-matching generalization; second, sluicing seems to falsify the p-stranding generalization, which casts further doubts on the underlying source of sluicing. Finally, island insensitivity indicates that sluicing could indeed have an alternative underlying structure. Based on these initial findings, the next section examines the underlying structure of sluicing by implementing some sluicing-defining diagnostics.

Libyan Arabic Sluicing: Sluicing or Pseudosluicing?

Crosslinguistically, there have been controversies in analyzing sluicing in null subject languages with covert copula. Japanese sluicing, for instance, has been identified as sluicing (Takahashi 1993, 1994) and pseudo-sluicing (Shimoyama 1995; Kuwabara 1996). Merchant (1998) attributes this confusion to two main facts about Japanese: first, Japanese is a null subject language (thus null-expletive); second, it optionally permits copula omission in embedded clauses. In response to Takahashi's (1993, 1994) analysis, a number of researchers (Shimoyama 1995; Kuwabara 1996; Nishiyama, Whitman, and Yi 1996; Kizu 1997) have proposed that Japanese sluicing is a type of reduced cleft, which is dubbed by Merchant (1998, 91) as pseudosluicing and defined as follows:

> A pseudosluice is an elliptical construction that resembles a sluice in having only a wh-XP as remnant, but has the structure of a cleft, not of a regular embedded question.

Libyan Arabic also has some features that make sluicing and pseudosluicing indistinguishable. First, Libyan Arabic is a null subject language, and it has no equivalent to the expletive subject "it"; second, it has no present-tense copulas in cleft constructions. Finally, Libyan Arabic is not a case-marking language, so there is no indication whether the case of the sluiced wh-phrase is identical to that of its correlate. In this regard, Merchant (2001, 101n11) remarks that "in those languages without overt morphological case, we may be dealing with a truncation of something like 'who it is'."

Since pseudosluicing is a type of cleft structure, it is expected that pseudosluicing will display cleft properties. In order to substantiate the presence of sluicing or pseudosluicing in LA, I implement a number of sluicing-defining diagnostics to differentiate the behavior of the wh-phrase in sluicing and pseudosluicing/clefting. Prior to implementing these tests, it is worthwhile to introduce cleft structure in LA. Cleft constructions consist of a focused constituent, an optional pronominal copula,[2] and a relative clause, as in (24).

(24) a. Nadia (hiyya) illi safrət.
Nadia (PRON.she) that traveled.3FS
"It is Nadia who traveled."

b. man (hiyya) illi safrət?
who (PRON.she) that traveled.3FS
"Who is it that traveled?"

It is worth noting that a restriction applies to the type of grammatical category that can be clefted; only nominal constituents, but not phrases of adverbial functions, can be clefted, as in (25) and (26).

(25) Ali (huwwa) illi b-yəmši l-ṭrabləs.
Ali (PRON.he) that FUT-go.3MS to-Tripoli
"It is Ali that will go to Tripoli."

(26) *l-ṭrabləs (hiyya) illi Ali b-yəmši.
to-Tripoli (PRON.she) that Ali FUT-go.3MS
"It is to Tripoli that Ali will go." (Intended reading)

Merchant's Diagnostics

Merchant (2001) proposes a set of diagnostics to differentiate the behavior of the wh-phrase in sluicing and pseudosluicing. Some of these tests will be applied to LA data in order to determine whether sluicing derives from regular or cleft wh-questions.

ADJUNCTS AND IMPLICIT ARGUMENTS

English sluicing is grammatical with adjuncts and implicit arguments, whereas pseudo-sluicing is not, as in (27)[3]. Similarly, the LA elliptical structure in (28) cannot be pseudosluicing since the adjunct wh-phrases are incompatible with cleft wh-questions, as shown in (29). This indicates that sluicing with adjunct wh-remnants is genuine sluicing and not pseudosluicing.

(27) a. He fixed the car, but I don't know how (*it was).
b. They served the guests, but I don't know what (*it was).
(Merchant 2001, 121)

(28) Ali ṣəlləḥ s-siyyara, lakən miš ʕarəf
Ali fixed.3MS the-car but NEG know.1MS
kēf/əmta.
how/when
"Ali fixed the car, but I don't know how."

(29) *əmta/kēf hiyya illi Ali ṣəlləḥ s-siyyara?
when/how PRON.she that Ali fixed.3MS the-car
"When/how was it that Ali fixed the car?" (Intended reading)

Sluicing is grammatical with implicit arguments, as in (30), and so are cleft wh-questions, as in (31), indicating that sluicing with implicit arguments can derive from a regular or cleft wh-question.

(30) Ali kan yəggra, lakən miš ʕarəf šenu.[4]
Ali was.3MS reading.3MS but NEG know.1MS what
"Ali was reading, but I don't know what."

(31) miš ʕarəf šenu (hu) illi Ali kan
NEG know.1MS what PRON.he that Ali was.3MS
yəggra fi-h.
reading.3MS in-it
"I don't know what it is that Ali was reading."

AGGRESSIVELY NON-D-LINKED WH-PHRASES

In English, aggressively non-D-linked wh-phrases, for example, "who the hell" or "who the devil," cannot occur in sluicing, but they are acceptable as pivots of clefts, as in (32).

(32) Someone dented my car last night.
a. I wish I knew who!
b. I wish I knew who the hell it was!
c. *I wish I knew who the hell.
(Merchant 2001, 122)

As for LA, aggressively non-D-linked wh-expressions are compatible with cleft wh-questions, as in (33), but not with sluicing and regular wh-questions, as in (34) and (35), respectively. This diagnostic shows that sluicing and clefting should be considered two distinct structures.

(33) man (hu) š-šiṭan illi xədē s-siyyara?[5]
Who PRON.he the-devil that took.3MS the-car
"Who the hell was it who took the car?"

(34) *waḥəd xədē s-siyyara, lakən miš ʕarəf
Someone took.3MS the-car but NEG know.1MS
man š-šiṭan.
who the-devil
"*Someone took the car, but I didn't know who the hell."

(35) *man š-šiṭan xədē s-siyyara?
who the-devil took.3MS the-car
"Who the hell took the car?" (Intended reading)

MENTION-SOME MODIFICATION

Mention-some modification is compatible with sluicing and wh-questions, but not with clefts since the wh-pivot of a cleft is only compatible with mention-all interpretation. This means that a cleft wh-pivot is incompatible with modifiers such as "for example" that enforce mention-some interpretation, as in (36).

(36) a: You should talk to somebody in the legal department for help with that.
b1: Could you tell me who (*it is), for example?
b2: Who (*is it), for example?

(Merchant 2001, 122)

As for LA, mention-some modification with "mətallən," literal translation of "for example," is acceptable in sluicing and regular wh-questions, as in (37b1) and (37b2), respectively. It is also compatible with cleft wh-questions, as in (38). This suggests that sluicing with mention-some modification can derive from regular or cleft wh-questions.

(37) a:

enta	təgder	tətkəllem	mʕə	waħəd	ʕən
you	can.3MS	speak.2MS	with	someone	about

l-muškla	hadi.
the-problem	this

"You can speak to someone about this problem."

b1:

mʕa	man,	mətallən?
with	who,	for example

b2:

mʕə	man	mətallən	nəgder	tətkəllem	ʕən
with	who	for example	can.1MS	speak.1MS	about

l-muškla	hadi?
the-problem	this?

(38)

man	(hu)	mətallən	illi	nəgder	nətkəllem
who	(PRON.he)	for example	that	can.1MS	talk.1MS

mʕ-əh?
with-him
"Who is it, for example, that I can speak with?"

MENTION-ALL MODIFICATION

Mention-all modification has the opposite distribution of "mention-some" in English; it is compatible with clefts, but not with sluicing, as shown in (39). This fact is seen by Merchant (2001) as an indication that sluicing is not an elliptical cleft. The claim is that if the underlying structure of sluicing is a cleft, the former is then expected to display cleft properties with respect to the modifier "all."

(39) A bunch of students were protesting,
a. sluicing: *and the FBI is trying to find out who all.
b. cleft: and the FBI is trying to find out who all it was.

(Merchant 2001, 122)

In Libyan Arabic, the wh-modifier *kul* "all" is degraded in both sluicing (40) and wh-questions (41). This degradation, however, does not affect cleft wh-questions, as in (42).

Merchant (2001) considers these facts as supporting the argument that sluicing derives from wh-questions and not clefts; that is, if the underlying structure of sluicing is a cleft, then the former is expected to exhibit cleft properties.

(40) məžmuʕa min ṭ-ṭalaba kanu yəḍahru.
a group of the-students were.3MP demonstrating.3MP
"a group of students were demonstrating . . ."

*w š-šurta təbbi təʕrəf man kul-hum
and the-police want.3FS know.3FS who all-they
"*and the police wants to know who all."

(41) *man kul-hum kanu yəḍahru?
Who all-they were.3MP demonstrating.3MP
"Who all were demonstrating?" (Intended reading)

(42) man (humma) kul-hum illi kanu
who PRON.they all-they that were.3MP
yəḍahru?
demonstrating.3MP
"Who is it all that was demonstrating?"

MENTION-ELSE MODIFICATION

The modifier "else" in English can only modify wh-phrases occurring in wh-questions and sluicing, but not in clefts, as in (43). The distribution of "else-modification" is not straightforward in Libyan Arabic. The word *tani*, literally "second" but also having the interpretation "else," is used in sluicing and wh-questions as in (44) and (45); however, it cannot modify wh-expressions in clefts, as in (46).

(43) a. *Harry was there, but I don't know who else it was.
b. Harry was there, but I don't know who else.
(Merchant 2001, 122)

(44) man ʕədda l-l-ḥəfla?
who went.3MS to-the-party
"Who went to the party?"

Ali ʕədda, lakən miš ʕarəf man tani.
Ali went.3MS but NEG know.1MS who else
"Ali went, but I don't know who else."

(45) man tani ʕədda l-l-ḥafla?
who else went.3MS to-the-party
"Who else went to the party?"

(46)

*man	tani	(huwwa)	illi	ʕdda	l-l-ḥafla?
who	else	(PRON.he)	that	went.3MS	to-the-party

"Who else is it who went to the party?" (Intended reading)

CASE MARKING

Case marking is used as a diagnostic for distinguishing sluicing from pseudosluicing. In sluicing, the case of the sluiced wh-phrase has to match the case of its correlate in the antecedent, whereas in clefting (pseudosluicing), the wh-expression displays only nominative case, as illustrated in the Greek examples in (47) and (48), respectively.

(47)

I	astinomia	anekrine	enan	apo	tous	Kiprious
the	police	interrogated	one.ACC	from	the	Cypriots

prota,	ala	dhen ksero	{* pjos/pjon}	anekrine
first	but	not I.know	who.NOM/who.ACC	interrogated

i	astinomia.
the	police

"The police interrogated one of the Cypriots first, but I don't know who."

(48)

I	astinomia	anekrine	enan	apo	tous	Kiprious
the	police	interrogated	one.ACC	from	the	Cypriots

prota,	ala	dhen	ksero	{pjos/*pjon}	itan.
first	but	not	I.know	who.NOM/who.ACC	it.was

"The police interrogated one of the Cypriots first, but I don't know who (it was)."

(van Craenenbroeck 2010, 1717)

Case is not realized morphologically in LA as mentioned above. Wh-expressions surface in the same form regardless of their position and grammatical function in the clause, as illustrated in (49). Therefore, case marking cannot be used as a test to distinguish sluicing and pseudosluicing.

(49)

Ali	ṭrəd	ṭāləb	lyoum,	lakən	ma-gələ-š
Ali	fired.3MS	student	today	but	NEG-said.3MS-NEG

bi-t-taḥdīd	ʔyya	ṭāləb.
exactly	which	student

"Ali dismissed a student today, but he didn't say exactly which student."

LANGUAGES WITH LIMITED OR NO CLEFT STRATEGY

If sluicing is derived from clefts, then it is expected that sluicing would be unavailable in languages that lack clefts or have a limited clefting strategy. LA has a limited clefting strategy; however, sluicing is used in the language. Cleft structure lacks an expletive "it" and an overt copula, not to mention the restriction on the category that can be clefted (see [3] above). For instance, LA does not allow PP pivots of clefts (50b), though it allows PP wh-phrases as remnants of sluicing, as in (50a).

(50) a. Ali təkəllem mʕə ražəl; gūl mʕə man.
Ali talked.3MS with a man say with whom
"Ali talked with a man; guess with whom."

b. *mʕə man (hu) illi Ali təkəllem?
with who PRON.he that Ali talked-he
"With whom was it that Ali spoke?" (Intended reading)

In sum, the implementation of sluicing-defining diagnostics reveals that sluicing exists in Libyan Arabic and that it patterns with wh-questions. Therefore, it can be analyzed as an elliptical wh-question.

Analysis of Sluicing in Libyan Arabic

Following the PF deletion approach to ellipsis, I propose that sluicing in LA is derived by wh-movement plus TP deletion at PF. Therefore, the derivation of the sluicing example in (51) proceeds as follows. The sluice in (51) is licensed by the interrogative C and is triggered by an ellipsis [E] feature endowed with uninterpretable [*uwh,Q*] features that need to be checked for ellipsis to take place.[6] The E-feature residing in C gets its values checked as soon as the wh-phrase moves to spec CP. Once E is fully checked, it triggers the deletion of its complement, that is, the TP. Eventually, what remains is a sluiced wh-phrase in the left periphery, as represented in figure 1.

(51) Ali ʕədda mʕə waḥəd, lakən miš ʕaraf
Ali went.3MS with someone but NEG know.1MS
mʕə man.
with who
"Ali went with someone, but I don't know with whom."

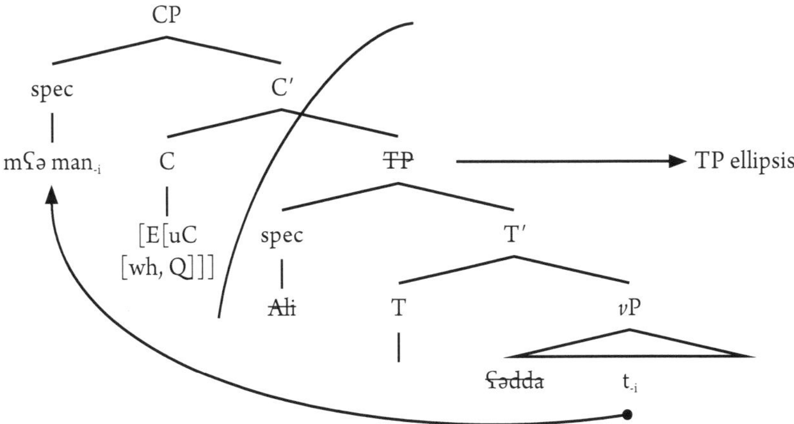

Figure 1.

Preposition Stranding under Sluicing

P-stranding under regular overt wh-movement is allowed in some languages but not in others. Merchant (2001) notices the correlation between p-stranding and wh-movement in full and elliptical wh-questions and claims that such effects are mirrored in sluicing. Based on this correlation, Merchant posits this generalization:

> A language *L* will allow preposition stranding under sluicing if *L* allows preposition stranding under regular wh-movement.
>
> (Merchant 2001, 92)

English allows p-stranding under regular wh-movement; therefore, p-stranding in sluicing is permissible, as in (52). German, on the other hand, disallows p-stranding under regular wh-movement, thus p-stranding is prohibited under sluicing, as in (53).

(52) a. Peter was talking with someone, but I don't know (with) who.
b. Who was he talking with?

(53) a.

Anna	hat mit	jemandem	gesprochen,	aber ich	weiß
Anna	has with	someone	spoken	but I	know
nicht,	*(mit)	wem.			
not	with	who			

b.

*Wem	hat	sie	mit	gesprochen?
who	has	she	with	spoken?

(Merchant 2001, 94–99)

The deletion analysis naturally accounts for the p-stranding effects, suggesting that sluicing is derived by wh-movement plus TP deletion. However, upon closer scrutiny, data from some non-p-stranding languages seem to falsify the p-stranding generalization. Recent research has uncovered cases of non-p-stranding languages that allow p-stranding under sluicing, for example, Polish (Szczegelniak 2006), Brazilian Portuguese (BP) (Almeida and Yoshida 2007), and Spanish (Rodrigues, Nevins, and Vicente 2009).

P-Stranding under Sluicing in Non-P-Stranding Languages

Non-p-stranding languages display p-stranding effects under sluicing differently; whereas in some languages, such as Polish (Szczegelniak 2006) and Spanish (Rodrigues, Nevins, and Vicente 2009), p-stranding is only permitted with d-linked wh-phrases, others display p-stranding effects in both bare and d-linked wh-phrases, for example, Indonesian (Fortin 2007) and BP (Almeida and Yoshida 2007). BP is regarded as a counterexample to the p-stranding generalization (Almeida and Yoshida 2007). Preposition pied-piping in regular wh-questions is obligatory; however, in sluicing it is optional, as in (54).

(54) a. A Maria dançou *com* alguém, mas eu não
the Maria danced with someone but I not
lembro *com* quem$_i$ ~~a Maria dançou t$_i$~~.
remember with who$_i$ ~~the Maria danced t$_i$~~
"Maria danced with someone, but I don't remember with who."

b. A Maria dançou *com* alguém, mas eu não
the Maria danced with someone but I not
lembr quem$_i$ ~~a Maria dançou com t$_i$~~.
remember who$_i$ ~~the Maria danced with t$_i$~~
"Maria danced with someone, but I don't remember who."
(Almeida and Yoshida 2007, 350)

Sluicing in Spanish also exhibits p-stranding effects, as shown in (56). Rodrigues, Nevins, and Vicente (2009) argue that such p-stranding effects are superficial since p-stranding effects in sluicing do not derive from regular wh-questions, but rather from a copular source.

(55) *¿Qué chica ha hablado Juan con?
what girl has talked Juan with

(56) Juan ha hablado con una chica, pero no
Juan has talked with a girl but not
sé cuál.
know which
(Rodrigues, Nevins, and Vicente 2009, 176)

Rodrigues, Nevins, and Vicente (2009) argue that neither BP nor Spanish constitutes a counterexample to the p-stranding generalization. They, instead, propose that both languages have two sources of IP ellipsis, namely, sluicing and pseudosluicing, and that only pseudosluicing exhibits p-stranding effects. The main argument comes from the behavior of multiple sluicing[7]. In English multiple sluicing, p-stranding is only permitted in the first wh-phrase; the preposition of the second wh-remnant cannot be dropped, as in (57).

(57) Peter talked about something to somebody but I can't remember (about) what *(to) whom.
(Martín González 2010, 32)

However, in Spanish and BP multiple sluicing prepositions are obligatory, as in (58) and (59), respectively; preposition drop is not permissible whether in the first or second remnant. As noted by Rodrigues, Nevins, and Vicente (2009, 179), this "is clearly unexpected if the ban on P-stranding is a PF constraint that is avoided only under sluicing by eliding the locus of the violation (as proposed by Almeida and Yoshida 2007)."

(58) Ella habló con alguien sobre algo pero
she talked with someone about something but
no sé *(con) quién *(sobre) qué.
not know-I with who about what

(59) Ela falou sobre alguma coisa para alguém, mas
she talked about some thing to someone but
eu não sei *(sobre) o que *(para) quem
I not know about the what to who
(Rodrigues, Nevins, and Vicente 2009, 179)

Following Lasnik (2006), Rodrigues, Nevins, and Vicente (2009) propose that multiple sluicing can be derived by regular wh-movement of the first wh-expression plus rightward extraposition of the second followed by TP deletion. Given that p-stranding under sluicing derives from a cleft that is a copular bi-clausal structure, the first wh-remnant does not involve any p-stranding; as for the second, this can only escape deletion if it moves out of the embedded relative clause that would constitute violation of the Right Roof Constraint[8] (see Ross 1969). Consequently, the ungrammaticality should not actually be attributed to p-stranding but to the illicit movement of the second wh-remnant (see Rodrigues, Nevins, and Vicente 2009).

P-Stranding under Sluicing in Libyan Arabic

Apparently, LA constitutes a counterexample to the p-stranding generalization. P-stranding is prohibited under regular wh-movement, yet it is allowed under sluicing, as shown in (60). Despite the fact that p-stranding is not allowed under overt wh-movement, as in (61), a preposition can be stranded in a resumptive wh-question[9], as in (62).

(60) Ali ʕədda mʕə waḥəd, lakən miš ʕarəf
Ali went.3MS with someone but NEG know.1MS
(mʕə) man.
with who
"Ali went with someone, but I don't know (with) who(m)."

(61) a. mʕə man$_i$ təkəllem Ali t$_i$?
with whom talked.3MS Ali
"With whom did Ali talk?"

b. *man$_i$ təkəllem Ali mʕə t$_i$?
who talked.3MS Ali with
"Who did Ali talk with?"

(62) man (hu) illi Ali təkəlləm mʕə-h?
who (PRON.he) that Ali talked.3MS with-him
"Who did Ali talk with?"

The data in (60)–(62) indicate that the only possible underlying structure of sluicing under p-stranding is the resumptive wh-questions. Therefore, pursuing the PF deletion approach to sluicing, there are three possible hypotheses to account for the p-stranding effects in sluicing. First, the sluice in (60) is derived by wh-movement plus TP deletion; this is predicted under Wahba's (1984) analysis of Egyptian Arabic (EA) resumptive wh-questions. Wahba (1984) argues that such wh-questions involve overt wh-movement from a clause internal position and that the gap left by the fronted wh-phrase undergoes a morphological rule called 'lexicalization' that transforms the trace into a phonologically realized (resumptive) pronoun, as in (63).

(63) EA
miin illi Mona shaafit-uh ?
who that Mona saw-him
"Who did Mona see?"
(Cheng 1997, 54)

Despite the similarities between LA and EA resumptive wh-questions, I argue that this analysis cannot account for LA resumptive wh-questions. Such an analysis, when extended to the sluicing case in (60), would predict that a wh-phrase can be extracted from within a PP, leaving behind a trace spelled out as a resumptive pronoun. Another unexpected result is the fact that, unlike other non-p-stranding languages that display p-stranding only in cleft constructions that involve no wh-movement from a clause internal position, Libyan Arabic patterns differ in the sense that a sluiced wh-phrase can be extracted from a PP and moved to a clause initial position. The second possibility is that wh-questions that allow p-stranding are not formed by wh-movement as Cheng's (1997) analysis predicts; instead, they are cleft structures in which the wh-phrase is base-generated in some TP external position. The wh-phrase is base-generated in its surface position, that is, spec CP; while in that position, the wh-phrase is co-indexed with a null (relative) operator that moves to spec CP (spec *illi*) to form an operator-variable structure, as illustrated in (64).

(64) EA
[CP[DP $miin_i$] [CP OP_i illi [IP Mona $shaafit\text{-}uh_i$]]]
[CP[DP who_i] [CP OP_i that [IP Mona $saw\text{-}him_i$]]]
"Who did Mona see?"
(Cheng 1997, 53)

This analysis predicts that there is no p-stranding in resumptive wh-questions, since the wh-phrase is base-generated in spec CP. It also patterns with the crosslinguistic evidence that p-stranding effects in non-p-stranding languages derive from a copular source. However, it is not evident how sluicing is licensed and derived under the deletion analysis, which assumes movement of the sluiced wh-phrase to spec CP, given the fact that LA is a wh-movement language, that is, the wh-phrase is argued to undergo movement from spec TP to spec CP.

Finally, p-stranded sluices derive from copular clauses by wh-movement plus TP deletion. This is predicted under Shlonsky's (2002) analysis of Class II (resumptive) wh-questions in Palestinian Arabic (PA). Shlonsky (2002) proposes that such wh-questions are copular clauses consisting of a subject DP and a free relative clause functioning as a nominal predicate. The wh-phrase is base-generated in spec TP, and it undergoes movement to spec CP, as shown in (65).

(65)	[CP man_i	[TP t_i	(hu)	illi	Ali	šāff-ah]]?
	[CP who	[TP	(PRON.he)	that	Ali	saw.3MS-him]]

"Who is it that Ali saw?"

Shlonsky's (2002) analysis is similar to Cheng's (1997) in some aspects. In principle, both analyses consider resumptive wh-questions copular clauses, and both assume no movement from a clause-internal position. However, while Cheng (1997) argues that the wh-phrase is base-generated in its surface position, Shlonsky (2002) proposes that it moves to the CP domain.

Analysis of Sluicing under P-Stranding

Building on Shlonsky's (2002) analysis, I propose that resumptive wh-questions in LA are copular clauses derived by movement. Sluicing can have a copular and noncopular source as an underlying structure (see Martín González 2010; van Craenenbroeck 2010), which indicates that there are two sources of TP ellipsis in the language: sluicing and pseudosluicing. Despite the fact that sluicing and pseudosluicing can be derived by wh-movement and TP deletion, only pseudosluicing displays apparent p-stranding effects.

The fact that wh-clefts, as opposed to regular wh-questions, cannot be headed by a preposition indicates that the former allows neither pied-piping nor stranding a preposition. The preposition in an *illi*-clause does not undergo any movement. Therefore, it is argued that the structure in (66), despite its superficial appearance as sluicing, is derived from a cleft source and thus is an instance of pseudosluicing. Like sluicing, pseudosluicing is derived by wh-movement plus TP deletion. Sluicing under p-stranding is licensed by an interrogative C and triggered by an E feature endowed with uninterpretable [*uwh,Q*] features that need to be checked. Once the wh-phrase has moved to spec CP, the [*u*E] feature is checked; as a result, its complement, the TP, is sent for non-pronunciation at PF.

(66) a: Ali təkəllem mʕə waḥəd, lakən miš
Ali went.3MS with someone but NEG
ʕarəf man.
know.1MS who
"Ali talked with someone, but I don't know who."

b: man?
who
"Who?"

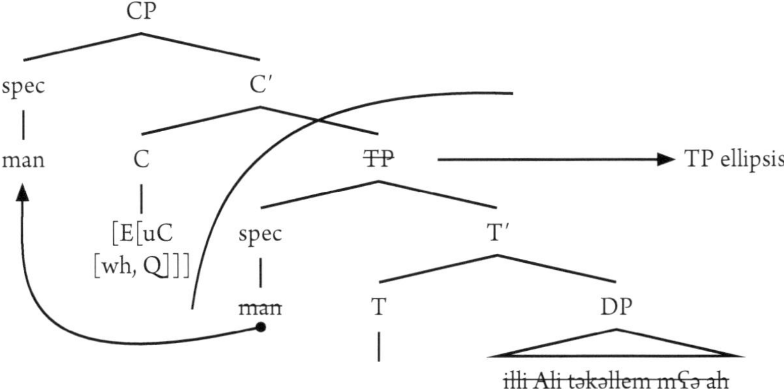

Figure 2.

The fact that resumptive wh-questions allow neither pied-piping nor the stranding of a preposition could be ascribed to the properties of the relativiser "illi," which is compatible with nominal constituents only, as illustrated in (67) and (68).

(67) *(r-ražəl) mʕə illi Ali təkəllem.
the-man with whom Ali talked.3MS

(68) (r-ražəl) illi Ali təkəllem mʕə-***ah***.
the-man that Ali talked.3MS with him
"The man who Ali talked with."

[*DP* (r-ražəl) [*CP* Op_i. C illi[~~WH, EPP, N~~] [*TP* Ali təkəllem
the-man that Ali talked
mʕə ~~Op_i~~]]]
with

It is proposed that "illi" has uninterpretable [*u*WH, *u*N, EEP] features that need to be valued. The [*u*N] feature is valuated via agreement with a nominal goal bearing the same feature; the [*u*WH, EEP] features attract a wh-operator to move to spec CP, as in (68)[10]. Thus, as an active probe, C attracts only nominal constituents to move to spec CP; hence, the incompatibility of nonnominal constituents with "illi" is accounted for (67). The nominal operator is bound by the head DP of the relative (see Shlonsky 2002). The pronominal clitic –*ah* "him" in (68) is the spell-out of the trace (or copy) of the null wh-operator, which is realized on the preposition as a pronominal clitic.

In sum, the apparent cases of sluicing under p-stranding derive from a cleft source; therefore, they are instances of pseudosluicing. This confirms that sluicing in the language conforms to the p-stranding generalization. The fact that the preposition in resumptive wh-questions resides in the relative clause, which eventually gets deleted at PF in pseudosluicing, yields the illusion that such wh-constructions involve p-stranding.

Conclusion

This study concludes that sluicing exists in Libyan Arabic and that it can be derived by wh-movement and TP deletion. The study also argues that sluicing under p-stranding derives from a copular source, which indicates that there are two sources of TP ellipsis: sluicing and pseudosluicing. Sluicing derives from regular wh-questions, and it obeys the p-stranding generalization; pseudosluicing is an elliptical wh-cleft resulting from deletion of a clefted TP whose pivot is an extracted wh-phrase. Finally, the analysis proposed for sluicing under p-stranding provides novel evidence for Shlonsky's (2002) analysis of Arabic Class II (resumptive) wh-questions as copular clauses.

Notes

1. There are three main dialects spoken in Libya: eastern, western and transitional-zone dialects (see Pereira 2008). The data in this paper were collected from and judged by native speakers of different varieties of western Libyan Arabic, referred to herein as Libyan Arabic (LA).

2. The literature normally refers to these pronouns as 'pronominal copula' (PRON) since they can be used to realize copula function in present-tense copular structures (see Doron 1983, 1986; Eid 1983, 1991; Fassi Fehri 1993).

3. However, van Craenenbroeck (2010) points out in a footnote that a full cleft version of the examples in (27) is acceptable, as in (a) and (b).

(a) He fixed the car, but I don't know how it was that he fixed the car.
(b) They served the guests, but I don't know what it was that they served the guests.
(van Craenenbroeck 2010, 1715)

4. The wh-phrases *šen* 'what' and *man* 'who' have other gender-specified variants, namely *šen-u, šen-i, man-u* and *man-i*. The "*-u*" ending is used for masculine and the "*-i*" for feminine. Ouhalla (1996, 683) points out that the Iraqi Arabic wh-phrase *men-o* "who" might have evolved from the combination *man huwwa* found in Classical Arabic reduced clefts, as in (a).

(a) man huwwa → men o
who he who he

5. As can be seen from example (33), the wh-phrase and the aggressively non-D-lined wh-expression do not constitute one unit as is the case in English due to the fact that cleft structure is different in the two languages, i.e., English and Arabic. However, this diagnostic can be used to distinguish regular from cleft wh-questions in Libyan Arabic.

6. Merchant (2001, 2004) proposes that ellipsis is licensed by an ellipsis feature. This feature is the locus of the properties distinguishing elliptical from nonelliptical constructions. The E feature has specific syntactic, semantic, and phonological requirements that need to be satisfied

in order for ellipsis to take place. In sluicing, the syntax of [E] stipulates that E occurs only on an interrogative C [*wh,Q*], whereas its phonology "issues instruction to the PF system to skip its complement for purposes of parsing and production" (Merchant 2001, 60). Finally, for recoverability, the semantics of E ensures mutual semantic entailment between the antecedent clause and elided clause. For further discussion on the nature of the E feature, see Merchant (2001, 2004), Gengel (2007), and Aelbrecht (2010).

7. For further discussion on p-stranding under sluicing in Spanish and BP, see Rodrigues, Nevins and Vicente (2009).

8. Right Roof Constraint: "An element cannot move rightward out of the clause in which it originates." (Citko 2005, 70).

9. I use the term resumptive wh-questions to refer to wh-questions that involve resumptive pronouns. Resumptive wh-questions are characterized by some features: (i) the presence of the relative complementizer illi, (ii) a resumptive pronoun filling (apparently) the gap left by the wh-phrase, and (iii) an optional pronominal copula, as in (62).

10. Unlike its LA counterpart, the relative complementizer *allaði* in Standard Arabic has uninterpretable φ-features, rather than an unspecified [*u*N], in addition to [*u*WH, EEP] features. Thus, in (a), as an active probe with unvalued uφ-features, C probes for a (nominal) goal for feature valuation. The [EEP, *u*WH] are satisfied via movement of the null relative-operator to spec-CP, just as in LA. The difference is that the relative complementizer in Standard Arabic agrees overtly with the head of the relative (via Op). Since PPs and adverbs don't bear φ-features, they are barred from spec-CP, and hence the presence of any non-nominal constituents in spec-CP results in ungrammaticality.

(a) l-kitab-u alllðdi štarytu-hu
the-book-NOM that.3MS bought.1S-it
[*DP* (l-kitab-u) [*CP* Op_i. *C* alllðdi [~~*WH*~~, ~~*EPP*~~, ~~uφ~~, ~~*N*~~] [*TP* štarytu ~~Op_i~~]]]

References

Aelbrecht, Lobke. *The Syntactic Licensing of Ellipsis*. Amsterdam: John Benjamins, 2010.

Almeida, Diogo A. de A., and Masaya Yoshida. "A Problem for the Preposition Stranding Generalization." *Linguistic Inquiry* 38 (2007): 349–62.

Cheng, L. Lisa. *On the Typology of Wh-Questions*. New York: Garland Publishing, 1997.

Chomsky, Noam, and Howard Lasnik. 1993. "Principles and Parameters Theory." In *Syntax: An International Handbook of Contemporary Research*, edited by Joachim Jacobs, Arnim von Stechow, Wolfgang Sternefeld, and Theo Vennemann, 506–69. Berlin: de Gruyter, 1993.

Chung, Sandra, William Ladusaw, and James McCloskey. "Sluicing and Logical Form". *Natural Language Semantics* 3 (1995): 239–82.

Citko, Barbara. *Symmetry in Syntax: Merge, Move & Labels*. Cambridge: Cambridge University Press, 2005.

Culicover, Peter, and Ray Jackendoff. *Simpler Syntax*. Oxford: Oxford University Press, 2005.

Doron, Edit. "The Pronominal Copula as Agreement Clitic." In *The Syntax of Pronominal Clitics*. Vol. 19 of *Syntax and Semantics* by Hagit Borer, 313–32. New York: Academic Press, 1986.

———. "Verbless predicates in Hebrew." Ph.D diss., University of Texas, 1983.

Eid, Mushira. "Verbless Sentences in Arabic and Hebrew." In *Perspectives on Arabic Linguistics III. Papers from the Third Annual Symposium on Arabic Linguistics*, edited by Mushira Eid and Bernard Comrie, 31–61. Amsterdam: John Benjamins, 1991.

Eid, Mushira. "The Copula Functions of Pronouns." *Lingua* 59 (1983): 197–207.

Erteshik-Shir, Nomi. *On the Nature of Island Constraints*. Bloomington, IN: Indiana University Linguistics Club, 1977.

Fassi Fehri, Abdelkader. *Issues in the Structure of Arabic Clauses and Words*. Dordrecht: Kluwer Academic Publishers, 1993.

Fortin, Catherine. *Indonesian Sluicing and Verb Phrase Ellipsis*. Ph.D diss., University of Michigan, 2007.

Gengel, Kristen. *Focus and Ellipsis: A Generative Analysis of Pseudogapping and Other Elliptical Structures*. Ph.D diss., University of Stuttgart, 2007.

Kizu, Mika. "A Note on Sluicing in WH-in-situ Languages". *MIT Working Papers in Linguistics*, 36 (1997): 143–59.

Kuwabara, Kazuki. "Multiple Wh-Phrases in Elliptical Clauses and Some Aspects of Clefts with Multiple Foci." *Formal Approaches to Japanese Linguistics* 2, no. 29 (1996): 97–116.

Lasnik, Howard. "On Ellipsis: The PF Approach to Missing Constituents." *University of Maryland Working Papers in Linguistics* 15 (2007): 143–53.

———. "Multiple Sluicing in English." Master's thesis, University of Maryland, College Park, 2006.

———. "When Can You Save a Structure By Destroying It?" In *Proceedings of NELS 31*, Minjoo Kim and Uri Strauss, Vol. 2, 301–20. University of Massachusetts, Amherst: GLSA Publications, 2001.

Lobeck, Anne. *Ellipsis: Functional Heads, Licensing, and Identification*. Oxford: Oxford University Press, 1995.

———. "The Phrase Structure of Ellipsis." In *Perspectives on Phrase Structure*, edited by Susan Rothstein, 81–103. San Diego: Academic Press, 1991.

Martín González, Javier. "Voice Mismatches in English and Spanish Sluicing." *Iberia: An International Journal of Theoretical Linguistics* 2, no. 2 (2010): 23–44.

Merchant, Jason. "Fragments and Ellipsis." *Linguistics and Philosophy* 27 (2004): 661–738.

———. "Pseudosluicing: Elliptical Clefts in Japanese and English." In *ZAS Working Papers in Linguistics 10*, edited by Artemis Alexiadou, Nanna Fuhrhop, Paul Law, and Ursula Kleinhenz, 88–112. Berlin: Zentrum für Allgemeine Sprachwissenschaft, 1998.

———. *The Syntax of Silence: Sluicing, Islands, and the Theory of Ellipsis*. Oxford: Oxford University Press, 2001.

———. "Variable Island Repair under Ellipsis." In *Topics in Ellipsis*, edited by Kyle Johnson, 132–53. Cambridge: Cambridge University Press, 2008.

Nishiyama, Kunio, John Whitman, and Eun-Young Yi. "Syntactic Movement of Overt Wh-Phrases in Japanese and Korean." *Japanese/Korean Linguistics* 5 (1996) 337–51. CSLI: Stanford.

Ouhalla, Jamal. "Remarks on the Binding Properties of Wh-Pronouns." *Linguistic Inquiry* 27, no. 4 (1996): 676–707.

Paul, Ileana. "Concealed Pseudo-clefts." *Lingua* 111, no. 10 (2001): 707–27.

Pereira, Christopher. "Libya." In *Encyclopaedia of Arabic Language and Linguistics III*, edited by Kess Versteegh, 52–58. Leiden: Brill, 2008.

Pollman, T. "Een regel die subject en copula deleert?" *Spektator* 5 (1975): 282–92.

Rodrigues, Cilene, Andrew Nevins, and Luis Vicente. "Cleaving the Interactions between Sluicing and p-Stranding." In *Romance Languages and Linguistic Theory 2006: Selected Papers from 'Going Romance'*, edited by Danièle Torck and W. Leo Wetzels, Amsterdam, December 2006, 175–98. Amsterdam: John Benjamins, 2009.

Ross, John. R. "Guess who?" In *Papers from the Fifth Regional Meeting of the Chicago Linguistic Society*, edited by Robert I. Binnick, Alice Davison, Georgia M. Green, and Jerry L. Morgan, 252–86, Chicago Linguistic Society, 1969.

Shimoyama, Junko. "On 'Sluicing' in Japanese." Master's thesis, University of Massachusetts, Amherst, 1995.

Shlonsky, Ur. "Constituent Questions in Palestinian Arabic." In *Themes in Arabic and Hebrew Syntax*, edited by Jamal Ouhalla and Ur Shlonsky, 137–55. Dordrecht: Kluwer Academic Publishers, 2002.

Szczegelniak, Adam. "All Sluiced Up, but No Alleviation in Sight." Master's thesis, Boston College, 2006.

Takahashi, Daiko. "Movement of Wh-Phrases in Japanese." NLLT 11 (1993): 655–78.

———. "Sluicing in Japanese". *Journal of East Asian Linguistics* 3 (1994): 265–300.

van Craenenbroeck, Jeroen. "Invisible Last Resort: A Note on Clefts as the Underlying Source for Sluicing". *Lingua* 120 (2010): 1714–26.

van Reimsdijk, Henk. *A Case Study in Syntactic Markedness: The Binding Nature of Prepositional Phrases*. Dordrecht: Foris, 1978.

Wahba, Wafaa Abdel-Faheem Batran. *Wh-Constructions in Egyptian Arabic*. Ph.D diss., University of Illinois, Urbana, 1984.

Rhetorical Properties and Generic Structure Analysis of Christian and Muslim Obituaries

THE CASE OF THE EGYPTIAN DAILY NEWSPAPER *AL-AHRĀM*

■

Sadam Issa, University of Wisconsin–Madison
Ghazi Abuhakema, College of Charleston

Abstract

This study provides an extensive analysis of the rhetorical properties used in Muslim and Christian obituaries in *Al-Ahrām*, the prominent Egyptian daily newspaper. It also provides linguistic and cultural interpretations for the occurrence of these rhetorical features. A sample of two hundred Muslim death announcements (MDAs), and another one hundred Christian death announcements (CDAs) were collected, analyzed, and contrasted. Since death announcements are classified as a genre, the study uses the Swalesian model that profitably illuminates the relationship between social practice and discourse. The study demonstrates that twelve (two mandatory and ten optional) communicative moves exist in both types of obituary, with some variation in frequency and content. The study also shows that the overall rhetorical structure of the two types of death announcements is largely similar and that the religious and social status of either the deceased or his or her family affect the structure. By examining the generic structure of the obituaries, the study also highlights what the obituaries convey about significant and insignificant aspects of the life of the deceased through information about his or her socioeconomic status and career.

Introduction

Obituaries or death notices are classified as a journalistic genre. They include death announcements, condolences, and thank-you notices that are usually published by the family of the deceased (Nwoye 1992). Obituaries are very important and highly informative. They include the names of the deceased, announcers of the death, surviving relatives, and the place and time of the funeral and burial ceremony. Some include those who take part in the funeral and burial arrangements and those who express their condolences through e-mails, telegraphs, telephone calls, and so forth. In addition, death notices reveal, to a certain extent, the social status of the deceased and their survivors by highlighting their professional occupations and academic credentials. According to Moses and Marelli (2004, 124), obituaries "are a window that provides a view into a culture. They are one of the elements out of which literate cultures are built." Jarboe (1989) argues that obituaries are a good source of documentation of facts about both ordinary and famous people. Knutson adds that obituaries are "formal pieces, designed to eulogize important community and national figures" (1981, 11).

Egyptian Christians and Muslims have lived side by side since the Arabs/Muslims invaded Egypt in 641 CE. The relationship between them has been plagued by animosity during certain historical periods. For example, in the last few years, tensions between Christians and Muslims have intensified, resulting in an increase in sectarian disputes and violence. Despite many efforts by the two groups to improve their relationship with one another, it is clear that they have not resolved their differences. As a consequence, religious identity remains a salient aspect of Egyptian life, with religious discourse as one method by which religious identity is expressed in Egyptian society. Because of these long-standing religious divisions, it is important to understand the cultural similarities and differences between the two religious groups as they are invoked and expressed through obituaries. Examining the literary tradition of obituaries and the surrounding written discourse may reveal further insights into this conflicting relationship.[1]

While Christians constitute approximately 10 percent of the Egyptian population, they play a significant role in the social fabric of Egyptian society (Central Intelligence Agency, 2008). A preliminary data check in *Al-Ahrām* shows that death announcements are of two types: Christian death announcements (CDAs) and Muslim death announcements (MDAs). To our knowledge, this study represents the first investigation of the rhetorical structure of MDAs and CDAs in an Arabic newspaper. Analyzing the rhetorical structure of Muslim and Christian death announcements is intended to reveal any differences and similarities between the two and to discover their significance and cultural implications within Egyptian society. The language used in these obituaries deepens our understanding of Muslim and Christian beliefs, traditions, values, and norms about life and death held by Egyptian society. In addition, the analysis shows to what extent MDAs and CDAs conform to the social and religious values of Egyptian society. This analysis reveals the common generic structures and shared communicative functions articulated by the generic components of MDAs and CDAs. By so doing, it deepens our understanding of the sociocultural factors that influence the generic structure of both the MDAs and CDAs as communicative events.

Theoretical Background and Review of the Related Literature

Rhetorically, death announcements are classified as a genre. Bhatia (1993, 13) defines genre as "a communicative event characterized by a set of communicative purpose(s) identified and mutually understood by the members of the professional or academic community in which it occurs." Johnstone (2008, 184) adds that genre is "a recurrent verbal form" that is linked to "a recurrent purpose or activity." To describe a genre, Johnstone says, one needs to describe the text, context, activities people perform to create the text, and its dynamic interaction. Death announcements, therefore, perform a particular rhetorical task, that is, informing the audience of the death of the deceased. The purpose of obituaries is "to announce a person's death, identify the deceased and his or her family, and provide information about the funeral and other services" (Eid 2002, 25). Further, gathering the participants in the house of the deceased provides, according to the Islamic and Christian traditions, a religious and spiritual reward for the deceased and his or her family. Masqood (2001, 172), a religious scholar, says, "It is always preferable if someone of the dying person's nearest and dearest family or friends, one who will be the gentlest helper, should be at their side to help them turn their thoughts to God the Most High, so that they may feel at peace, and so that they may anticipate the loving grace of their Lord, and also to remind them gently to repent of their sins and make their last requests and farewells." Eid (2002) agrees with Masqood, stating that "obituaries provide a wide range of information and thus lend themselves to various types of research on documentation, social perception, and group identity" (23).

According to Nwogu, a move is "a text segment made up of a bundle of linguistic features which give the segment a uniform orientation and signal the content of discourse in it" (1997, 122).

Researchers have tackled the generic structure of death announcements in different contexts. Al-Ali (2005), for example, identifies the types of death announcements published in Jordanian newspapers. He finds the following nine-move structure in his analysis: opening, heading, announcing the occasion, identifying the deceased, specifying the surviving relatives, situating circumstances of the death, outlining funeral and burial arrangements, outlining arrangements for receiving condolences or congratulations, and closing.

In his comparative study of English and German obituaries, Fries (1990a) points out that such announcements convey information about the name of the deceased, which is considered an obligatory element. He also notices that there are optional elements such as announcing the death, time and place of death, age of the deceased, and the announcer. Nwoye (1992), on the other hand, analyzes the death notices in Nigerian newspapers written in English and compares them with similar death notices in English and German investigated by Fries (1990a). Nwoye finds that there are obligatory features such as "introduction," "the name of deceased," "date, place, and manner of death," "burial arrangement," "survivors," and some "identification of the announcer/sender."

Moses and Marelli (2004) argue that the language of obituaries reveals important understandings of the beliefs the society holds about life and death, especially with respect to the causes of death, life expectancy, and gender differences in the society's life stories. With regard to the relationship between the cause of death and age of the deceased, Moses and Marelli propose that the cause of death is not optional if the person is young. Additionally, they observe that no cause is given for decedents over the age of eighty-seven, and all obituaries for people under fifty have a cause listed. If the death occurs away from the decedent's home, the death place and home are clearly stated.

The size of death announcements is an important social indicator; it communicates information about the deceased and those who compose obituaries. Nwoye (1992) states that the size of the newspaper insertion ranges from a full page to a fraction of a page. Announcements can be placed once or multiple times, sometimes running several days consecutively or intermittently. This, according to Nwoye, reflects the social status of the deceased or the people left behind. He further proposes that the same phenomenon is present in electronic media, where the length of the announcement is indicative of the social status and economic power of the announcer. Analyzing German and English death notices, Fries (1990b) points out that there are some differences between the two, for example, the layout. While English death notices appear as smaller items in the personal columns of the newspaper, German death notices are printed in boxes in different sizes. In general, the cost of the announcement varies according to the place of the announcement in the newspaper (front page, middle of the newspaper, etc.), the size of the announcement (the longer the announcement is, the more it costs), and the presence of a photograph, to mention some factors. From a sociolinguistic perspective, the more expensive the announcement is, the more indebted and appreciative the deceased family feels toward the announcement composer. Such indebtedness and social appreciation grant social status and veneration to the composer. Eid (2002), however, associates obituary size with religious beliefs. She says, "Arabic obituaries occupy the most space because of the relatively greater status orientation of obituaries in that culture and the historical importance of death rituals in Egypt since ancient times. From the gender perspective, men occupy more obituary space partly because public—including obituary—space is perceived as being more pertinent to men than women" (80). So, the size of an obituary is motivated by socioeconomic and religious factors.

In some societies, death is regarded as a taboo. Fernandez (2006) says in his study of euphemisms used in two Irish newspapers (*The Connaught* and *The Cork*) in the mid-nineteenth century that the taboo of death cannot be appropriately understood without taking into account the role religion plays in sad occasions. He argues that there are some semantic devices in death announcements used to mitigate the taboo of death. Hyperbole, Fernandez goes on to say, is a semantic resource that aims at both complimenting the deceased and praising the biological act of dying by means of overstatement of some of the Christian beliefs. For instance, in the newspapers mentioned above, the deceased is said to be "in a kingdom or enjoying a holy and uninterrupted communion with God" (111).

In addition, there is a significant difference between English and German obituaries in word choice. Whereas English death notices mention only the word "dying" in the headline of the entire section, in German death notices, there are no limits on inventing new expressions for dying (Fries 1990b, 58). In his contrastive study of German and English death announcements, Fries (1990a) notes that the place of death in both the German and English papers is not specified.

This study identifies the underlying genre components of Muslim and Christian death announcements. We hypothesize that these announcements conform to a particular format that reflects the social and religious values of the society to which the announcers belong. While Al-Ali (2005) and Eid (2002) offer analysis of the generic structure of obituaries in Jordanian newspapers, and generic analysis of gender-related differences in obituaries in *Al-Ahrām*, respectively, we know little about the generic structure differences among Muslim and Christian death notices.

Methodology

Prior to selecting the sample, researchers examined death announcements in a number of issues of *Al-Ahrām*. They noticed that there were two types of death notices: Muslim death announcements (MDAs, see appendix 1) and Christian death announcements (CDAs, see appendix 2). A preliminary textual analysis of the collected samples did not reveal significant differences in the generic structures of such notices. The study used 300 random obituaries (200 MDAs and 100 CDAs) from *Al-Ahrām*, the prominent Egyptian daily newspaper. After classifying obituaries into MDAs and CDAs, researchers used simple random design, by which every notice had a chance of being selected for study. The sampled announcements were published over a period of six months, from April 2007 to September 2007. This period is, we believe, long enough to reflect any variation in the announcements. We believe that the number of issues chosen is sufficient to accomplish the objectives of this study.

The death announcements appear on the third to last page of the newspaper and sometimes on the penultimate page. To ensure anonymity, we omitted names of both the announcer and the deceased and anything else that would reveal the identity of the people concerned. The size of death notices varies from a whole-page announcement to smaller ones. We analyzed the content of these notices and examined them to identify the different generic structures employed, their frequencies and significance.

We chose *Al-Ahrām* as the subject of the study based on the following factors. It is one of the oldest national newspapers in Egypt. *Al-Ahrām* also has a prestigious reputation and wide circulation inside and outside Egypt. The newspaper has no religious affiliation, and it was the first Arab newspaper to introduce obituaries. Finally, the paper is available through the archive division at the University of Wisconsin-Madison Memorial Library, a place easily accessible to one of the researchers as his academic affiliation. *Al-Ahrām* can be accessed online; however, the online version has no section devoted to death announcements. The death page includes various communicative events: death announcements; condolences given by colleagues, friends, and relatives; and *shukr* announcements (thank-you notices) that are usually published by the family of the deceased.

Procedure

The announcements were identified as CDAs and MDAs based on the following criteria. First, the names of the announcer and the deceased in obituaries indicate the type of announcement. Second, CDAs and MDAs have exclusive religious expressions. There are certain specific expressions used by Muslims but not by Christians for religious beliefs, and vice versa. When there was ambiguity about the religious identity of a death announcement, we excluded it from the sample and replaced it with another one. With regard to age, the data analyzed gave no indication of the age of the deceased.

To identify the genre components that are used to articulate the communicative purposes of the death announcements, the researchers adopted the Swalesian genre-move-analysis approach, which draws insights from the schema-theory model. Rumelhart defines schema as "a structure in semantic memory that specifies the expected sequence of events" (cited in Yu-hui, Li-rong, and Yue, 2010, 61). Yu-hui, Li-rong, and Yue (2010) suggest that "there are various kinds of schemata in man's mind, such as car schemata, teacher schemata, building schemata and so on. The main point of schema theory is that one needs to connect new things with those known concepts, past experiences, or background knowledge, to understand new things. Understanding and interpretation of new things depend on the existing schema in mind and the input information must match existing schema." (61) We adopted the Swalesian model because it "has been profitably extended to a study of the schematic structure of different types of communicative events" (Al-Ali 2005, 10), and it "is more powerful in interpreting the move structures of texts" (Kong 1998, 104). Kong also emphasizes that this model "demonstrates how a set of writing conventions can influence the logical sequence of ideas that are linguistically signaled" (1998, 110). Al-Ali (2005) adds that this theoretical framework can be used to investigate and identify the various communicative functions that interact to create the genre system of a class of written texts that serve similar functions.

Analysis and Discussion

Analyzing the generic structure of the obituaries in *Al-Ahrām* reveals that there are twelve communicative moves. Most of the identified moves appear regularly in the texts. The order by which these moves appear here is the most prevalent order found in the sample notices. We identify the boundaries of these moves using linguistic instruments (lexical, phrasal, functional, etc.) and content.

We also observe that some structural features (size, font, photographs, etc.) of death announcements appear in different formats: Some occupy the entire page and some take less space. Financial considerations determine these variations, which consequently reflect the social standing of the deceased or their families. This conclusion is in line with that of Nwoye (1992), who argues that the length of the announcement is indicative of the economic power and social standing of the announcer.

The study finds that the death notices that announce the death of the deceased are titled *na'y* (obituary), *ta'āzī* (condolences), *dhikrā* (remembrance or commemoration), and *shukr* (thank you). The last two communicative events are included because they share the rhetorical structure of the death announcements. Table 1 displays the number of occurrences of each move found in Muslim and Christian death announcements.

The most frequent moves in both types of announcements are announcing the occasion and identifying the deceased, signaling the importance of these moves to the

Table 1. Percentage of occurrences of communicative moves in MDAs and CDAs in *Al-Ahram*

No.	Type of Move	MDAs (%)	CDAs (%)
1.	Opening	26	38
2.	Heading (obituary, thanking and obligation)	12	58
3.	Announcing the occasion	100	100
4.	Identifying the deceased	100	100
5.	Specifying surviving relatives	74	40
6.	Situating the circumstances of death	1	1
7.	Outlining funeral and burial arrangements	5	8
8.	Outlining arrangements for receiving condolences	17	15
9.	Specifying the announcer(s)	93	35
10.	Identifying people who participated in funeral and condolences ceremonies	5	19
11.	Situating the commemoration arrangements	3	58
12.	Closing	94	6

composers. Without them, the announcements would be odd, as demonstrated by Fries (1990a). The occurrence of "situating the circumstances of the death" in both MDAs and CDAs shows the same frequency, 1 percent each. Accordingly, "situating the circumstances of the death" is not an obligatory move; its absence will not defeat the overall communicative purpose of death announcements. This may explain why it occurs in very few instances in this data. Moreover, "specifying the surviving relative(s)" comes at the same rank, but with different frequency in the two types of announcements.

The study reveals that two obligatory and ten optional communicative moves are used in Muslim and Christian obituaries. While obligatory moves appear in all instances, optional moves occur in some but not in others, with varying frequencies.

Obligatory Moves

ANNOUNCING THE OCCASION

This obligatory communicative move occurs in every sample notice. It publicizes the death of the departed. The announcer is a member of the family or tribe of the deceased, a friend, a colleague, a governmental or private organization or company, or an official body.

Announcing the occasion takes different forms. It may announce the death of the deceased, commemorate the anniversary of the death, or thank people who participated in the funeral and burial services. Occasions also involve inviting friends and relatives to participate in the different religious prayers and practices when the mourning period has ended.

Text composers use different formulaic expressions with religious connotations to announce the purpose of the death notices in both CDAs and MDAs. Typical examples of these expressions included in the CDAs are "*wad-da'ūna ilas-samā'*" (they bid us farewell to heaven); "*yazif-fu ilas-samā'*" (present as a gift to heaven); "*tuqīmul-usrah al-qud-dās al-illāhī*" (the family will hold the mass); and "*intaqalat ilal-amjādis-samawiy-yah*" (she has moved to the noblest of heavens).

These expressions reflect Christian religious beliefs about life and what follows. Some expressions like "*yazif-fu ilas-samā'*" (bring glad tidings to heaven) denote happiness and pleasure on the part of the announcers. Likewise, MDAs use numerous religious expressions; however, these are different. A typical expression reads "*intaqala ilá raḥmatil-lāhi ta'ālá*" (moved to the mercy of Allah the Great). This expression reveals that Muslims believe that death is a transition into another life, and the deceased is now under the mercy of Allah (God).

Interestingly, all major religions, including Islam and Christianity, subscribe to the notion of an eternal life of tranquility and peace known as the hereafter (Sherry 2004). Just like Christians, some Islamic traditions also believe that the afterlife affects Muslims' behaviors, practices, and interactions with other people in several ways (Segal 2004). Heather (2001) says that Islam does not look at death as the end. In fact, Islam has a well-developed belief about the afterlife, from the tomb of corporeal death to the day of resurrection. The purpose of the worldly life is to prepare for the eternal life (Kramer 1988). Death announcements, therefore, are fraught with religious expressions. While Muslims, for example, use the nomenclature of *Allāh,* Christians use *God,* and they make reference to "Christ" on many occasions. Other expressions involve phrases that express the integrity and solidarity of the announcer with the family of the deceased, such as "*al-akh a ṣ-ṣadīq*" (the brother, the friend). This notion is discussed below.

IDENTIFYING THE DECEASED

This is the second obligatory move in both types of announcements. The move is obligatory in that it would be odd to announce the death of a particular person without mentioning his or her name. The manners of identifying the deceased are quite diverse: Some are mentioned by their full names, and some with full names and titles. Fries (1990b) argues that mentioning the name of the deceased is obligatory since the texts would make no sense without it. Milde (1994) adds that mentioning the name of the deceased is important because it perpetuates his or her personality.

A plethora of academic and professional titles pervade the samples. Academic titles include phrases such as *duktūr* (doctor), *ustādh* (professor), *muhandis* (engineer), and *mu'al-lim* (teacher). Professional titles include *rajul al-a'māl*" (businessman), *al-iqtiṣādi al-kabīr* (the great economist), and *muḥāsib* (accountant). These titles help identify the professional, academic, and social status of the deceased. There are plenty of religious titles, too. In MDAs, announcers use *ḥajj* (male pilgrim), *ḥaj-jah* (female pilgrim), and *sheikh* (male religious leader), whereas in CDAs, announcers use *qid-dīs* (priest), and sometimes *muqad-das* (holy). Announcement composers use religious, professional, and academic titles abundantly, since they denote respect and trustworthiness as well as social prestige on the part of the deceased and his or her family. They also serve as an affiliation with his or her social networks. This finding seems to be in agreement with those of Nwoye (1992) and Al-Ali (2005), who demonstrate that Nigerians and Jordanians value highly the social status of the individual, even the dead. In very few examples, the names of the deceased are not explicitly mentioned, but instead a third-person singular accusative pronoun is included. Whenever that happens, the pronoun is printed in bold using a different font size.

This only occurs in obituaries published by people other than the family of the deceased, in which the purpose is to express condolences to the family of the deceased or a member of it. Instead of the name of the deceased, a member of the family is usually mentioned on a separate line using a different size font along with his or her titles, if he or she has any.

Optional Moves

OPENING

The opening is the first optional communicative move noticed in the death announcements we investigated. It occurs in 26 percent of MDAs and 38 percent of CDAs. In MDAs, the opening varies from the use of Qur'anic verses such as "*bismil-lāhi ar-raḥmān ar-raḥīm*" (In the name of God, the most gracious, and the most merciful) to "*in-nā lillāh wa in-na ilayhi rāji'ūn*" (We belong to God and to him we shall return). While the latter is a verse that shows the predetermined end of everyone's life, the former is the opening verse in every Qur'anic chapter, 114 chapters in total, except for one. Due to the influence of Islamic traditions on people's daily life, people in the Arab world in general and Muslims in particular use it as a saying appropriate to many events, most notably death. The cited Qur'anic verses found in the data communicate different religious functions such as praying for the deceased, showing his or her place in paradise, and showing the true end of people's life, death. The use of the same Qur'anic verses in the death notices indicates that these verses suit the occasion of death more than other expressions. In addition to these verses, announcers use others, such as "*yā ay-yatuhannafsul-muṭma'i n-nah 'irji'ī' ilá rab-biki rāḍiyatan marḍiy-yah fadkhulī fī 'ibadī wadkhjulī jan-natī*" (It will be said to the pious believers of Islamic monotheism: 'O [you] the one in [complete] rest and satisfaction! Come back to your Lord well-pleased [yourself] and well-pleasing [unto Him]! Enter you then among My [honored] slaves, and enter you My Paradise,' Qur'an 89:27–30). This finding seems to agree with that of Eid (2002), who suggested that Arabic obituaries "tend to quote a verse from a holy book or introduce the obituary in language borrowed from religious ceremony" (45). This verse shows the rewards God promises that righteous Muslims will receive on the Day of Judgment. Abdul Hal and Husain (2000) maintain that this belief is shared by Christians.

Careful scrutiny of the data shows that there is no relationship between the type of Qur'anic verse used as an opening move and the manner of death. This is perhaps due to the following two reasons. First, situating circumstances of death is rarely used in the data analyzed. Such circumstances are explicitly mentioned only on one occasion in both types of announcements (this is discussed later). Second, there is no special occasion in Egypt that might correlate the Qur'anic verses used as opening move with the manner of death. In Palestine, for instance, and because of the long-standing Palestinian-Israeli conflict, we see causalities from both sides quite frequently. Whenever that happens, Palestinians regard those killed by Israeli forces as martyrs, and according to the Islamic traditions, martyrs are promised paradise. Qur'anic verses cited thus match the occasion and the manner of death in obituary announcements in the Jordanian newspapers (Al-Ali 2005), where a large percentage of the population comes from a Palestinian origin or has relatives living in Palestine.

Likewise, CDAs use a lot of religious expressions. These expressions vary from "*Tubá liman ikhtartahu waqabiltahu liyaskuna diyaraka ilal-abad*" (Blessed is he whom you have chosen to abide in your company for eternity); "*thikraṣ ṣadīq tadūm ʾilalʾabad*" (The memory of a friend lasts an eternity); "*ḥabīburrab-bi yaskunu āminan ladayhī*" (The beloved of the Lord abides with him in peace, Mt 13:41). This biblical verse shows God's rewards toward the righteous people. These expressions embody Christians' beliefs about death. Their use also reflects the religious backgrounds of the announcer. Some of these expressions are borrowed from religious texts but formulated differently.

Overall, the Egyptian community, both Christians and Muslims, seems to be religiously oriented, and religion influences the language used in both types of death announcements since both share some beliefs about the predetermined end of the deceased. This finding supports our assumption that both types of announcements are influenced by religion.

According to some Christian beliefs, Jesus Christ is the second member of the Triune God, the Son of the first part of the Triune God, but at the same time fully God in every respect, and thus trustworthy. Because Christians respect, love, and believe in Jesus, they make reference to him on many occasions. The following is an example: "*maʿal-masīḥ thāka afḍal*" (It is better to be with Christ). Since Christians believe that Jesus is the prince of peace, they are eager to be with him. To be with someone forever indicates that he or she is (or becomes) a member of the family with whom he or she is staying. Thus, to be staying with Jesus Christ means to be incorporated with him into his family. Some Christians believe that Jesus is in heaven preparing a place for them to reside in peace and pleasure. In this respect, Rowell (2000, 151) points out that some Christians assert, based on scripture, "the fundamental dignity of the human person, created in the image and likeness of God (Genesis 1:26), saved by Jesus Christ (Ephesians 1:10), and destined for eternal life with God (1 Corinthians 15:42-57)." Moreover, some CDAs' openings include the following format: "*Aynal-abarār yuḍīʾūna kash-shamsi fī malakūti abīhim?*" (Where are the righteous who shine like the sun in the dominion of their Father?) Christians believe that candles are sometimes lit to remind people that Jesus is the light of the world, and that because of him, Christians can be saved from their sins and go to heaven.

Variations occur in both types of announcements. At the word level, for example, Christians used the term "heaven," whereas Muslims used the term "paradise" to refer to the place in which righteous people will finally reside. Wheeler (1990) states that although "heaven" is used as a periphrasis for God in the Judeo-Christian tradition, it is generally taken to be God's realm, created by him, subject to him, and thus distinguished from him. Moreover, Christians use the word "priest" in every death announcement, whereas Muslims do not. For Muslims, the counterpart for "priest" is *imām*, a learned member of the community who leads prayer sessions at mosques. No single MDA mentions the word *imām* in announcing a death.

HEADING

Heading refers to the title of the announcement that the announcer, usually, chooses for his or her announcement. The title seems to be in harmony with the purpose of the announcement. Some death announcements are titled *shukr* (thank you) because the purpose of these announcements is to thank those who participated in the funeral, burial, and condolence services. On the other hand, some death notices are titled *na'y* or *ta' ziyah* (obituary) and the purpose is either to have a member of the deceased's family or, on certain occasions, the whole family, announce the death or to convey condolences by friends, colleagues, or relatives of the deceased or his or her family. In this study, CDAs use the heading in 58 percent of the samples. However, MDAs use it in only 12 percent. This observation indicates that heading is an optional communicative move. However, this move is communicated implicitly by relying on other moves such as the type of Qur'anic verse placed at the top and sometimes at the bottom of death announcements. For example, some Qur'anic verses read "*in-nā lil-lāhi wa in-na ilayhi rāji'ūn*" (We are to God and to him we shall return, Qur'an 2:156). Using this quotation shows that the purpose of the text is to announce a death. Thus the words of the announcements indicate the nature of the announcements. In addition, the communicative function of the heading is bolstered by the location of death notices in the newspaper, namely in the obituary section.

Some headings are titled *shukr* (thank you) and *dhikral'arba'īn* (forty-day commemoration) to indicate a commemoration announcement thanking people who consoled the family of the deceased. Death announcements designed to thank people have the following generic structure: announcing the occasion, identifying the deceased, and thanking all those who participated in the death arrangements. They do not, however, have a closing move. Eid (2002, 50) says that *shukr* is often used to "make specific mention of important figures (possibly government officials or representatives) who may have attended the funeral." In such an announcement, the family of the deceased is perhaps attempting to convey a prestigious social position on their part.

On the fortieth day after the death of the deceased, there are usually religious services held by the family of the deceased, ranging from reciting Qur'anic verses to praying for the deceased to visiting his or her tomb, as well as having a feast to which friends and relatives are invited. Muslims choose the period of forty days because, according to Islamic tradition, it is the end of the customary period of mourning. The forty-day prayer in MDAs and the "outing service" in CDAs are used as an indication of the end of the mourning period (Nwoye 1992).

Some announcements also commemorate the anniversary of a death. This type of announcement is not only a celebration of the end of mourning but also a social practice carried out by families to remember their beloved ones. Thus, death announcements might facilitate the sentiment of social unity. Halevi (2007) argues that Muslim funerals could bring community mourners together since hundreds would attend the death rituals and ceremonies.

SPECIFYING SURVIVING RELATIVES

MDAs mention the surviving relatives of the deceased 74 percent of the time, whereas only 40 percent of the CDAs mention them. This is perhaps because mentioning the surviving relatives is slightly less significant in CDAs than in MDAs. Also, it is possible that Muslims have more surviving relatives than do Christians and, therefore, deceased surviving relatives are mentioned more frequently. Whenever surviving relatives are mentioned, their academic achievements and social and professional titles accompany their names. Such expressions may include *as-say-yid* (Mr.), *ma'ali ash-sheikh* (His Excellency), *ash-shaykh*, and *ad-duktūr* (Dr.). By using these titles, announcers perhaps try to glorify the family members' achievements as well as highlight their academic and economic status. This, in turn, communicates a prestigious social status for both the deceased and his or her family.

SITUATING CIRCUMSTANCES OF DEATH

This communicative move informs the audience of the circumstances of the death in terms of date, place, time, and cause. The circumstances of death are optionally included in the death announcements in *Al-Ahrām*. In this study, only 1 percent of the samples of both MDAs and CDAs situate the circumstances of the death. Informing the audiences of these details seems to be of less importance compared to the information included in other moves, particularly when there are no special circumstances surrounding the death. In both instances, the cause of death is a serious automobile accident while the deceased was on duty. Dying on duty promotes a good reputation for the deceased, and communicates a sense of pride on the part of his or her family. It denotes good qualities such as loyalty and sincerity. Additionally, writers refrain from stating sensitive information to avoid offending the reader or infringing on others' privacy or interest (Huckin 2002). Swales (2004) refers to this tendency as "discoursal silence," while Huckin calls it "textual silence."

The time of death is never mentioned in the data investigated. For Fries (1990b), this is "vague," since death date and time cannot be inferred from the announcement. Time is of less importance than the place of death. During the whole period investigated, there were few references to the place, and no reference to the time. This runs against Fries's (1990a) findings of fewer references to place than to time of death in his contrastive study of German and English death notices. Additionally, there is no indication of the age of the deceased because it is possibly less significant than indicating the cause and the place of death. The data also show that the place of death is mentioned if the death takes place outside the country of the deceased.

OUTLINING FUNERAL AND BURIAL ARRANGEMENTS

The purpose of this move is to enable relatives, colleagues, and friends of the deceased to attend the burial and funeral services. This occurs in 5 percent of the MDAs and 8 percent of the CDAs. Egyptian Muslims' burial services begin by washing the deceased, taking him or her to the mosque, and performing prayer for his or her soul. Masqood (2001, 185) argues that funeral prayer is "a religious duty, and a collective obligation that has to be performed by at least one Muslim." After that the deceased is taken to the cemetery to be buried. Egyptian Christian burial services, similarly, begin by taking the dead to the church where prayers for the soul of the deceased are offered, enabling the relatives as well as the well-wishers to pay their last respects. After that, the deceased is taken to the cemetery and buried. It seems that both Muslims and Christians in Egypt have almost the same basic rituals for burial. Halevi (2007) proposes that Muslims share some burial practices with Jews and Christians, and that these practices date back to the dawn of humanity. Mentioning the funeral and burial arrangements involves giving a detailed description of the address of the deceased and the time of the different services. By including this move, text composers publicize the arrangements to as many people as possible through the wide circulation of the newspaper. Habenstein and Lamers (1963) argue that most cultures believe that the religious and spiritual aspects of the ceremonies help the departed on the journey through various rituals, which often require the participation of family and friends. Funeral prayer was introduced for this very purpose (Shehab 1988).

In our examination of death announcements, we found that both types give very little information about burial arrangements. This could be related to the fact that the announcements were published after the burials had taken place, so there is no need to mention them. Usually, such arrangements are mentioned to allow relatives and friends, especially those who are not in the household of the deceased, to come and participate in the different burial and funeral ceremonies. In addition, such arrangements are rarely communicated in the samples investigated because many of the death notices are either commemorating the occasion or thanking those who already conveyed condolences and participated in the burial and funeral arrangements.

OUTLINING ARRANGEMENTS FOR RECEIVING CONDOLENCES

This move communicates some information about the place and time for those close to the deceased to receive condolences. It includes telegraph, telephone, and fax numbers as well as e-mail addresses through which condolences can be conveyed. E-mail addresses are mentioned when the death has occurred in Western countries such as the United States.

In the Arab world, the traditional condolence formula is "May God make your reward abundant and your solace great, and grant forgiveness to the departed." To which the reply is "May God hear your prayer, and have mercy upon us and you."

This move occurs in 17 percent of the MDAs and 15 percent of the CDAs. In MDAs the condolences are held in the local mosque of the deceased. There is a distinct place for men and women to convey condolences. This emphasizes that not only men can convey condolences but also women. The place—usually a big hall—in which men can convey condolences is usually separate from the women's place. Yet both are situated in the same location. According to Islamic law, mingling men and women (who are allowed by the Islamic law to marry) in the same place on such a private occasion is forbidden. In this connection, Ask and Tjomsland (1998) argue that the social organization in Muslim countries is based on the sexual division of space. Men and women, they further argue, spend their daily lives in relatively separate spheres, according to the Islamic moral-legal code. A "woman should go out for her needs, but must be courteous, dress properly when in the public, and avoid vulgar expressions and intermingling with men unnecessarily" (Ansar-Ud-Deen Society of Nigeria 1983, 31). However, there is no gender indication for the place in which condolences will be received in the CDAs. According to the Christian tradition, men and women may convey condolences in the same place. Moreover, they can perform their rituals and prayers at the same church.

Linguistic choices are another variation between CDAs and MDAs. Muslims tend to use, for example, the expression "*sa-yuqāmul-'azā' fī* [place, time, and/or date]" (Condolences will be received at [place, time, and/or date]," as a way to announce the arrangements for receiving the condolences. Christians may use either this expression or "*yuqāmal-qud-dāsul'ilāhī fī* [place, time, and/or date]" (the mass will be held in [place, time and/or date]) to announce the condolences arrangements.

To sum up, this move is rarely included in the death notices because many of the notices are published by announcers (friends and colleagues) who are not part of the deceased's immediate family. However, when the family announces the death of their deceased, outlining the condolences services is included.

SITUATING THE COMMEMORATING ARRANGEMENTS

This move presents the place, time, and other special details for commemorating the anniversary of the death. The move was present in only 3 percent of the instances in the MDAs and 58 percent in the CDAs. It is thus evident that commemorating the anniversary of the death is more significant for Christians than for Muslims. In the commemoration, the family, friends, and relatives of the deceased and other invitees gather either at the local mosque or the house of the deceased in the case of MDAs, and at the church or the house of the deceased in the case of CDAs. Prayers for the deceased, reciting the Qur'an, supplication to God for mercy on the soul of the deceased, preaching, and singing of hymns, choruses, and psalms are offered. Commemorations occur at different intervals, ranging from forty days—the end of the customary period of mourning—to a year, and in other places two,- five-, and ten-year intervals.

SPECIFYING THE ANNOUNCER

This move is intended to specify the names of the announcers who place the death notices. Specifying the announcers' names occurs in 93 percent of the instances in MDAs but in only 33 percent in the CDAs. This variation shows that Muslim announcers are more likely to place their names in the death announcement than Christians. A typical example reads "*al-mustashār* [name of the announcer] *yan'ā bi-bālighil-ḥuzni wal-asá 'am-mahūl-mustashār*" [name of the deceased]" (The consultant [name of the announcer] announces with sadness and grief the death of his uncle the consultant [name of the deceased]). Christians use more generic names, like "the family" to express this function, "*usrah* [name of the family tribe] *yan'awn bibālighil-ḥuzni wal-asá al-marḥūm* [name of the deceased]" (The family of [name of the tribe] announces with sadness and grief the death of [name of the deceased]). In general, using this move can be interpreted as an attempt to inform the family of the deceased who places the death announcements.

We found that this move occurs when the death notice is either a commemoration of the death anniversary, a thank-you announcement, or a conveyance of condolences by friends, colleagues, or relatives. This reflects the high social status of the text composers. These seem to be keen about showing their identity to the deceased family. Specifying the names of the announcers satisfies the readers' curiosity about the announcer's identity because it would be vague to have an announcement without specifying the announcer or at least a hint that would lead to an identity.

In her investigation of three samples of obituaries from three different languages (Egyptian Arabic, Iranian Persian, and American English), Eid (2002) finds that *Al-Ahrām*'s obituaries do not communicate women's first or last names. She postulates that this loss of women's identity "means invisibility and obliteration of (basic) individual identity. These women are identified through a male relative, whose name, title, and occupation may all be mentioned" (128). She further argues that marriage is the major reason for their "loss of public identity" (130). While we recognize the importance of Eid's gender analysis in the domain of obituary, this aspect is beyond the scope of this study.

IDENTIFYING PEOPLE WHO PARTICIPATED IN FUNERAL AND CONDOLENCES CEREMONIES

This move states the name of friends, colleagues, relatives, and some important figures who participated in the funeral and burial arrangements. This also includes those who conveyed their condolences either by their presence or through telephone calls, faxes, or telegrams. The data show that this move is only used when the type of the announcement is a thank-you announcement. Although only 5 percent of the instances in the MDAs and 19 percent in CDAs include this move, they still have a social message to convey: showing gratitude on the part of the family of the deceased toward those who shared their sadness and grief over the loss of a family member. Acknowledging people in this way communicates a higher social status for the family of the departed. It also shows that the family is well connected and reputable. Generally, people positively evaluate and look admiringly at those who have connections with members of various social networks. These judgments are heightened by inclusion of the name of the country's former President, Hosni Mubarak, and other political and religious figures. Moreover, some thank-you announcements tend to thank those who participated in the condolences on behalf of the bereaved tribe that has roots in different Arab and Western countries by mentioning the name of these countries: "The tribe [name of the tribe] and family of the deceased in Cairo, Alexandria, Ba'quuba, Bagdad, Turkey, Jordan, Syria, Germany, France, Spain, America is extending its gratitude and thanks to all those who conveyed their condolences during the mourning of [name of the deceased]."

Acknowledging the family network outside Egypt serves to promote a higher, more prestigious social status of the family. Having relatives and friends residing in different parts of the world is evidence of the family's higher socioeconomic status.

CLOSING

This communicative move is employed predominantly in the MDAs. It is used in 94 percent of the instances, whereas it is only used in 6 percent of the instances in CDAs. Eid (2002, 22) finds that *Al-Ahrām* incorporates a "one or two-line statement at the end of an obituary to express condolences to the families." In MDAs, closings are rounded off by various rhetorical expressions including Qur'anic verses, invocation, calling for God's mercy upon the deceased, appealing to God's (Allah) benevolence, and requesting for *Fātiḥa* (the opening chapter of the Qur'an) to be recited. The following are some prevailing expressions used as closing expressions: "*nas'alukum al-Fātiḥa*" (We ask you for

Fātiḥa); *"lil-faqīd ar-raḥmah walil-usrah khāliṣul-ʿazāʾ"* (May God bestow his mercy on the departed and to the deceased family we express our deepest condolences); *"in-na lil-lāh wa in-na ilayhi rajiʿūn"* (We are to God and to Him we shall return) (al-Baqarah, v. 156).

In the CDAs, various rhetorical expressions are also utilized as closing components. The following are some examples: *"niyāḥa li-rūḥihit-ṭāhirah"* (Mourning for his pure soul); *"wa li-yakūn dhikruhū mu-abadan"* (May he be remembered for eternity); *"lil-ʿazīz ar-raḥmah walil-usrah taʿziyāt as-samāʾ"* (For the departed we ask for God's mercy and for the family we express our deepest condolences); and *"al-masīḥ qāma ḥaq-qan qāma"* (Christ has truly risen).

Several religious expressions and phrases in general, and Qurʾanic and biblical verses in particular, are used as closing components in the death announcements under investigation. This reflects the religious background and orientation of the Christian and Muslim societies in the Arab world. Having religious expressions in death announcements performs two communicative acts; illocutionary and perlocutionary. In particular, they indirectly invite the addressees to come and participate in the different funeral and condolence arrangements by religiously appealing to the people's emotions through the use of some religious expressions (illocutionary act). Further, these religious expressions serve as mitigating tools aiming at softening the imposition of the face-threatening act (death) on the addressees (perlocutionary act).

In addition, this communicative move shows how religion intervenes in every aspect of people's lives: social, economic, and political, among others. Many of the Christian and Muslim verses mentioned express the announcers' deepest feelings of sorrow and affiliation. The communicative purpose of these verses might be seen as mitigating the effect of the occasion (death) on the reader. These religious overtones perform a phatic function; they convey feelings of solidarity and express unity with the deceased and the survivors.

Euphemism is also used in the components of this communicative move. For example, the announcers tend to replace words like "the deceased" by "his pure soul" or "the dear" as in the Christian case, and "departed" as in the Muslim examples. Another mitigating device used extensively in the MDAs is the use of the following Qurʾanic verse: *"in-nālil-lāhi wa in-nā ilayhi rajiʿūn"* (We are to God and to him we shall return). This belief is also shared by Egyptian Christians. For example, *"aynal-abrār yuḍīʾūna kash-shamsi fī malakūti abīhim?"* (Where are the righteous who shine like the sun in the dominion of their Father?). These expressions show the theologically determined end of all creatures, in which everybody is treated equally. The verse states that everybody is going to die regardless of their age, gender, or socioeconomic status. This goes along with the proverb which says "Death is a great leveler." So what happened is not strange or new at all. God said that and we should expect it. In other words, this Qurʾanic verse serves as a regressive strategy attempting to alleviate the imposition of a face-threatening act (death) on the hearers' positive/negative face.

The term "death" is described in a flowery language. Instead of using "death," the term "eulogy" is used by both Al-Ali (2005) and Nwoye (1992). They use it as a formulaic expression to enhance the deceased's value. Wikipedia defines "eulogy" as "a speech or writing in praise of a person or thing." The word is derived from two Greek words, ευ (pronounced "you") meaning good or well, and λογος (pronounced "logos") meaning word, phrase, speech, etc.

The purpose of using eulogy in death announcements is to express the love of the text composers for the departed. Psychologically, it makes the reader relax, and it softens the pain of death for the reader as well. In other words, eulogy functions in this context as a mitigating tool the announcer sometimes uses to reduce the effect of the occasion on the reader. There are numerous expressions used as eulogies such as "*ruḥihi al-ṭāhirah*" (his pure soul); "*a'azz wa aghlash-shabāb*" (the dearest youth); "*al-faqīd al-'adhīm*" (the great departed); "*ash-shaqīq wal-akh al-ghāli*" (my dear brother and friend); "*al-khawājah, ma'āli ash-shaykh*" (his excellency sheikh); and religious titles such "*ḥajj*," "*shaykh*," "*qiss*" (priest), to name a few. Honorifics also appear, such as "*ḥaḍratuka*" (Your Excellence) and "*say-yid*" (Sir), and descriptions of the profession of the deceased, such as "*al-ustādh al-kabīr*" (the great teacher). Some titles are modified by epithets like "*al-baṭal*" (the hero). The data show that Christians, in their announcements, use more eulogies than Muslim do.

A careful look at the above expressions indicates that the announcer tries to acknowledge the departed in a positive manner by indicating his or her professional and personal attributes. Eulogy is also an attempt to glorify the achievements of the deceased, if he or she has any, which, again, serves as a softening strategy to alleviate the passing of a beloved person.

Conclusion

In this study we identify and describe the components of Egyptian Muslim and Christian death announcements published in *Al-Ahrām* newspaper. We conclude that there are two obligatory and ten optional communicative moves, and that these moves have similar basic features. Although these notices communicate the same type of communicative moves, some moves are more salient for a particular group than others, and they are used at varying frequencies. For instance, while MDAs tend to list the surviving relatives and announcers as well as having a closing, CDAs exhibit more interest in the opening, heading, and situating of the commemorative arrangement. This distinction implies that Muslims are preoccupied with the survivors more than they are with the deceased or the idea of death, while Christians take death as an opportunity to celebrate life, and hence commemorative arrangements are more important than who survived or who announced the death.

We also find that the rhetorical structure and format in both MDAs and CDAs is similar to a great extent. The similarity may be due to the fact that Egyptian Muslims and Christians speak the same language, interact with each other on a daily basis, and therefore share similar values, traditions, and social practices including the death announcement. The similarity may also result from the fact that death notices are usually written by independent newspaper staff with a particular format to follow. What they may change, in this regard, is specific information such as the name of the deceased, funeral and burial arrangements, and circumstances of the death. Enkvist (1987, 211) observes that death notices are texts "whose macrostructure is set in advance where the text producer, so to say, enters new data into preexisting page, as when filling a hotel-registration card or an income-tax return." We are unable to determine which of these explanations is responsible for such similarity. In addition, we do not quantify or rate the degree of occurrence of the various formulae or expressions within each move.

We observe that the obituaries investigated are set in a frame of religious jargon that plays an important role in shaping the social identity of the announcers. Also, the face-threatening nature of the subject (death) may account for the deployment of some euphemistic religious expressions in communicating the death. Finally, the study shows that obituaries are personal and contextualized in that they communicate personal information about the deceased and his or her family, and achieve particular illocutionary acts such as calling people to come and attend the different funeral and burial arrangements. In addition, these announcements communicate information about the sociocultural norms and practices that are encoded in the rhetorical and organizational components of the notices. It is interesting to note that age is not mentioned in any of these moves.

Our observations have several implications. First, Egyptian obituaries join those of other cultures in reflecting fear and prejudice about death. Thus age and cause of death are rarely mentioned. Second, despite the different religious beliefs among Muslims and Christians in Egypt and the sectarian tensions they experience, death announcements, as a cultural practice, seem to unify them and diminish such tensions as both MDAs and CDAs deploy similar rhetorical structures and include similar communicative moves. On the other hand, as an expression of religious identity, religious discourse has the potential to lead to more hatred and animosity through engraving that identity into people's minds. The first page many Egyptians, particularly older individuals, read is obituaries. Finally, it seems that there could be confusion between cultural and religious identity as two different paradigms, since Muslims and Christians share some cultural aspects although they have distinct religious identities.

While the present study presents an extensive analysis of the generic structure of obituaries, it does not account for gender-related differences (if any) among either the deceased or the announcers. Moreover, the study examines samples over a six-month period in one newspaper. Examining obituaries over a longer period of time and in several newspapers might reveal the use of other communicative moves or structural differences and the way obituaries evolve over time. This study also investigates death announcements as they are used in written discourse. Investigating death announcements in spoken discourse, through radio, for example, is a promising avenue for future research. Finally, since these obituaries occurred under a political system where all media outlets were censored, it will be interesting to see how death announcements change under other political systems, particularly if sectarian conflicts between Muslims and Christian continue to exist.

Note

1. While we recognize that there are various religious groups among Egyptian Christians (Coptic, Roman Catholic, Greek Coptic, etc.), we have not noticed any indication of these religious groups within the CDAs. We believe that no religion-based communal varieties have developed in Egypt, which might have affected the generic structure of the CDAs, unlike those that exist in some neighboring countries such as Syria, Lebanon, and Iraq.

References

Abdul Hal, H., and A. Husain. "Muslim Perspectives Regarding Death, Dying, and End-of-Life Decision Making." In *Cultural Issues in End-of-Life Decision Making*, edited by K. L. Braun, L. H. Pietsch, and P. L. Blanchette, 199–212. London: Sage Publications, 2000.

Al-Ali, M. "Communicating Messages of Solidarity, Promotion and Pride in Death Announcements Genre in Jordanian Newspapers." *Discourse and Society* 16, no. 1 (2005): 5–31.

Al-Hilali, M., and M. Khan. *The Noble Qur'an in the English Language* (Trans.). Riyadh, Saudi Arabia: Maktoba Dur-us-Salam, 1993.

Ansar-Ud-Deen Society of Nigeria. *Women*. Lagos: Islamic Publication Committee, Lagos Branch, 1983.

Ask, K., and M. Tjomsland. *Women and Islamization: Contemporary Dimension of Discourse on Gender Relations*. Oxford: Berg Publishers, 1998.

Bhatia, V. K. *Analyzing Genre Language Use in Professional Settings*. London: Longman, 1993.

Brody, L. R. "Gender and Emotion: Beyond Stereotypes." *Journal of Social Issues* 53 (1997): 369–94.

Central Intelligence Agency. *The World Factbook*. Last modified 2008, www.cia.gov/library/publications/the-world-factbook/geos/eg.html.

Eid, M. *The World of Obituaries: Gender across Cultures and over Time*. Detroit: Wayne State University Press, 2002.

Enkvist, N. E. "Text Strategies: Single, Dual, Multiple." In *Language Topics: Essays in Honor of Michael Halliday*, edited by R. Steele and T. Threadgold, 203–11. Amsterdam: John Benjamins, 1987.

"Eulogy." *Wikipedia*, http://en.wikipedia.org/wiki/Eulogy.

Fernandez, E. C. "The Language of Death: Euphemism and Conceptual Metaphorization in Victorian Obituaries." *Journal of Linguistics*, 19 (2006): 101–30.

Fries, U. "A Contrastive Analysis of German and English Death Notices." In *Further Insights into Contrastive Analysis*, edited by J. Fisiak, 541–60. Amsterdam, Holland: Benjamins. 1990a.

———. "Two Hundred Years of English Death Notices." In *On Strangeness*, edited by M. Bridges, 57–71. Tubingen: Guntar Naar. 1990b.

Habenstein, R. W., and W. M. Lamers. *Funeral Customs the World Over*. Milwaukee, WI: National Funeral Directors Association of the United States, 1963.

Halevi, L. *Muhammad's Grave: Death Rites and the Making of Islamic Society*. New York: Columbia University Press, 2007.

Heather, M. R. "Islamic Tradition at the End of Life." *Medsurg Nursing* 10, no. 2 (2001): 83–87.

Huckin, T. "Textual Silence and the Discourse of Homelessness." *Discourse and Society* 13, no. 3 (2002): 347–72.

Jarboe, B. *Obituaries: A Guide to Sources*. Boston: G. K. Hall, 1989.

Johnstone, B. *Discourse Analysis*. Malden: Blackwell Publishing, 2008.

Knutson, G. "Content Analysis of Obituaries of Prominent Librarians in the New York Times, 1984–1976." Master's thesis, University of Chicago, 1981.

Kong, K. C. C. "Are Simple Business Request Letters Really Simple? A Comparison of Chinese and English Business Request Letters." *Text* 18, no. 1 (1998): 103–41.

Kramer, K. P. *The Sacred Art of Dying: How World Religions Understand Death*. New York: Paulist Press, 1988.

Masqood, W. R. *After Death, Life: Thoughts to Alleviate the Grief of All Muslims Facing Death and Bereavement*. Lahore: Talha Publication, 2001.

Mazid, B. "Decomstructing a Contemporary Egyptian Newspaper Caricature." *Applied Linguistics* 4, no. 9 (2000): 45–53.

Milde, H. "Going Out into the Day: Ancient Egyptian Beliefs and Practices Concerning Death." In *Hidden Futures: Death and Immortality in Ancient Egypt, Anatolia, the Classical, Biblical and Arabic-Islamic World*, edited by J. M. Bremer, T. P. J. Van Den Hout., and R. Peters, 15–35. Amsterdam: Amsterdam University Press. 1994.

Moses. R., and G. Marelli. "Obituaries and the Discursive Construction of Dying and Living." *Texas Linguistic Forum* 47 (2004): 123–30.

Nwogu, Kevin. "The Medical Research Paper: Structure and Functions." *English for Specific Purposes* 16, no. 2 (1997): 119–38.

Nwoye, O. G. "Obituary Announcements as Communicative Events in Nigerian English." *World Englishes* 11, no. 1 (1992): 15–27.

Rowell, M. "Christian Perspectives on End-of-Life Decision Making: Faith in a Community." In *Cultural Issues in End-of-Life Decision Making*, edited by K. Braun, J. H. Pietsch, and P. L. Blanchette, 147–63. London: Sage Publications, 2000.

Segal, A. F. *Life after Death: A History of the Afterlife in the Religions of the West*. New York: Doubleday, 2004.

Shehab, U. R. *Islamic Festivals and Rituals*. Lahore: Maqbool Academy, 1988.

Sherry, N. "Is There Life after Death?" Modified 2004. www.opednews.com/sherry032004_life_after_death.htm.

Swales, J. *Research Genres: Exploration and Applications*. Cambridge, UK: Cambridge University Press, 2004.

Wheeler, M. *Death and the Future Life in Victorian Literature and Theology*. Cambridge, UK: Cambridge University Press, 1990.

Yu-hui, L., Z. Li-rong, and Z. Yue. "Application of Schema Theory in Teaching College English Reading." *Canadian Social Science* 6, no. 1 (2010): 59–65.

Appendix 1: A Muslim Death Announcement (MDA) Sample

Moves	MDA Text
Opening	*bismil-lāhi al-raḥmān al-raḥīm* In the Name of God the most Passionate the most Merciful *"wabash-shir al-sābirīn al-lathīna itha aṣābathummuṣībahqalū in-nalillhāwa in-na'laihiraji'ūn"* "O (you) the one in (complete) rest and satisfaction! Come back to your Lord well-pleased (yourself) and well-pleasing (unto Him)! Enter you then among My (honored) slaves, and enter you My Paradise." *Sadaqa'al-lāhū'al-'athīm* God Almighty has spoken the truth
Specifying the announcer	*al-multaqal-'arabi lil-istithmār* Arab Investment Forum *'uḍw majmū'at dal-lat al-barakah al-qābiḍah* a member of Dallah Al-Baraka Holding Group [Name of the announcer] *'uḍw majlis al-idārah al-muntadab* a member of the elected board of directors *wakul al-muwath-thafīn* and all the employees
Announcing the occasion. Specifying surviving relatives	*yushāṭirūna* share *Ma'ālī al-shaykh* His Excellency Sheikh [Name of one of the family members of the deceased] *wasa'ādat al-shaykh* and His Excellency Sheikh [Name of another member of the family of the deceased] *wajamī' usrat ālkāmil wa 'qāribihum wa arhāmiḥim* all members of the family of [name of the tribe of the deceased] and all their relatives *al-'ḥzān f ī wafāt al-maghfūr lahū bi-ithinil-lāhi ta'ālá* the sadness for the death of late, God willing
Identifying the deceased	*Ma'ālī ash-shaykh* His Excellency Sheikh [Name of the deceased]
Closing	*Dā'īnal-mawlá'az-za wajal-la an yataghamadahū bi-raḥmatihī* praying for God Almighty to bless him with his mercy *wa an yuskinuhū fasīḥa jan-natihī wa li-usratihī al-karīma hkhaliṣ al-'azā'* and dwell him his spacious paradise, and for the noble family our sincere condolences.

Appendix 2: A Christian Death Announcement (CDA) Sample

Moves	CDA Text
Opening	*ʾin-na ḥabībina qad raqad waʾana thāhibun li-ʾūqithuhū li-ʾan-na manʾāmana bī waʾin mata fa-sayaḥaya* *biqulūb malīʾah bilʾīmān bilqiyāmah wal-ḥayāh al-ʾabadiyah.* Our beloved has rested and I am going to wake him up because who believed in me, and if died, will resurrect with hearts full of faith in the resurrection and the absolute life
Specify- ing the announcers	*ʾal-madglisʾal- ṭāʾf al-ʿāmlir-rūmʾalʾarthuduxʾal-miṣry* General Council of the Greek Orthodox in Egypt *kanīsat ruʾasāʾ al-malāʾkah bit-tahrir* Church of Archangels in Tahrir Square *kanīsat ʾal-qid-dīs niqulāws bi-miṣr ʾal-jadīdah* Saint Nicolas Church in *Misir ʾal-jadīdah* *jamʿiy-yat mār girisʾal-khayriy-yah bil-qāhirah* mārgiris Charitable Society in Cairo *ʾal-Jamʿiyahal-khairiyah lir-rūm ʾal-ʾorthudux bil-qāhirah* The Orthodox Charitable Society in Cairo *jamʿiy-yat (Name of the society's owner) fī miṣr ʾal-jadīdah* Society of (Name of the society's owner) in *miṣr ʾal-jadīdah* *dārʾal-qid-dīs niqulās lir-riʿāyatʾal-musin-nīn bi-misr ʾal-jadīdah* Cathedral of Saint Nicolas for Elderly Home in *misrʾal-jadīdah*
Announcing the occasion. Specifying surviving relatives	*yushārikūn* share *ʾas-say-yed (Name of the deceased father)* Mr. (Name of the deceased father) *wal-ʿāʾilah* and the family (i.e. family of deceased) *ʾa ṣ-ṣalāh bi-ruqād najlihim* the Prayer for the death of their son
Identifying the deceased	*(Name of the deceased)*
Closing	*wal-yakun thikruhūmuʾabadan* And let his mentioning be eternal *ʾal-masīḥ qāma ḥaq-qan qāma* Christ had truly risen

Arabic-Teacher Training and Professional Development

A VIEW FROM STARTALK

■

Mouna Mana , National Foreign Language Center, University of Maryland

Abstract

While more professional development opportunities for teachers of Arabic exist today than in the past, a shortage of training for Arabic-language teachers persists. Further, the field does not have a complete picture of what Arabic teachers feel they need in terms of professional development of knowledge and skills. This study examines professional development opportunities by reviewing program curricula from STARTALK Arabic-teacher training programs. It also explores Arabic teachers' views on their own training needs using a survey questionnaire. Findings suggest that programs tend to emphasize pedagogical knowledge and skills over content knowledge and that some Arabic teachers approach professional development with the principal goal of gaining knowledge and skills rather than earning a degree or certification.

Introduction

To date, fewer than a half dozen colleges and universities provide training and preparation opportunities for Arabic-language teachers. This situation exists in spite of numerous studies over the past decade reporting that Arabic-language education in the United States has experienced a marked growth at both K–12 and postsecondary levels (Allen

2007; Furman, Goldman, and Lusin 2010; Greer and Johnson 2009; Welles 2004). The rapid increase of Arabic enrollments over the past dozen years has highlighted the continuing and growing need for more well-trained Arabic teachers. However, as the number of programs and enrollments in Arabic courses continue to increase, the scarcity of qualified Arabic teachers becomes more apparent. The United States simply lacks the number of skilled teachers of less commonly taught languages (LCTLs) it requires (Ingold and Wang 2010), and Arabic is probably the clearest example of the shortage.

Over the past five years, however, institutions have made efforts to increase professional development opportunities for teachers of some LCTLs, including Arabic. In particular, the STARTALK program has for the past five years served as a unique resource to train teachers of critical languages such as Arabic. Many of STARTALK's programs lead to or facilitate participants' progress toward certification; all programs are designed to ensure high-quality teacher training aligned with field-supported educational best practices. However, while the intensive training programs offered through STARTALK provide an avenue otherwise unavailable to teachers, many STARTALK programs focus on generic principles of language teaching with instruction delivered in English to teachers who are native speakers of a language other than English, in this case, usually Arabic.

The aim of this study is to illustrate the current status of professional development activities within the LCTL teacher community, looking specifically at the professional development experiences of Arabic teachers during the past four years of STARTALK teacher-training programs. While STARTALK has been in implementation for five years and is now entering its sixth year, we examine only the four years between 2008 and 2011, excluding 2007 because data collection procedures on program curricula were under development during that year.

The study asks the following questions:

- What professional development opportunities have STARTALK programs provided?
- What gaps exist?
- What are the perspectives of participants in STARTALK teacher workshops regarding their professional development experiences and needs?
- What implications for improving professional development and training can be drawn from the answers to these questions?

A survey of about twenty-seven teachers of Arabic enrolled in two of the STARTALK programs offered in 2011 addresses the third question.

LCTL Teachers and Arabic-Language Teachers

An area of concern in training Arabic teachers and LCTL teachers in general is providing appropriate professional development opportunities that address distinct language-learning needs. LCTL teachers face greater challenges than teachers of more commonly taught languages because LCTLs typically have less in common with English than languages like French, Spanish, and Italian. Early in the history of world language education, experts identified basic principles for teaching LCTLs. They recognized that the broadest challenge facing LCTL teachers is to enable learners "to interact in and with the culture being studied" (McGinnis 1994; Walker and McGinnis 1995). Scarce resources, primarily the human resource of qualified instructors, however, remain a key obstacle in overcoming this challenge. Teachers who are not equipped with adequate professional training may fall short of the mission of enabling learners to become active participants in a very different culture. STARTALK, a federally funded initiative established in 2006 designed to increase the nation's capacity in LCTLs, particularly critical languages such as Arabic and Chinese, seeks to address this challenge head-on. By providing funding for teacher-training programs and student programs, STARTALK builds and develops the professional knowledge of LCTL teachers in order to move them from novice to expert teachers.

Rather than recruiting language teachers from abroad, a strategy that some people have posed as a potential solution (Van Houten 2009), experts increasingly view training teachers here in the United States as a more sustainable way to build the supply of qualified LCTL teachers. Training LCTL teachers includes a combination of theory and practice that is both language specific and aligned with general principles of effective teaching (Brecht and Walton 1994; Walker and McGinnis 1995). Effective training results in teachers who feel that the training has transformed their approach to teaching and who can apply what they have learned in a variety of contexts (Walker and McGinnis 1995; Oleksak 2009). This is particularly true for teachers of LCTLs such as Arabic, which has been designated as a category IV language by the Defense Language Institute and a category III language by the Foreign Service Institute. These categories indicate how difficult a language is and how long it takes for a native speaker of American English to learn it.

Arabic-Language Education in the United States

Arabic has historically been taught in the United States mainly for scholarly rather than everyday-life purposes. In the past ten years or more, however, Arabic has been increasingly taught and studied for more functional and practical purposes, prompting a move from more traditional pedagogical methods (grammar-based) to more communicative approaches (Ryding 2006, 13–16). This shift calls for a different cadre of teachers prepared to privilege and emphasize spoken Arabic (with its diglossic nature) alongside Modern Standard Arabic (MSA). Preparing teachers to use such a fundamentally different approach remains a challenge to the field since, as Ryding explains, most Arabic teachers are taught to privilege written Arabic rather than the spoken varieties, which are viewed as degenerate forms of the source, MSA (2006, 16).

STARTALK Arabic-Teacher Training Programs

STARTALK's core mission is to increase the foreign language capacity of US citizens via intensive summer programs. These summer programs teach critical languages as well as train teachers of these languages. From 2008 to 2011 there have been a total of thirty-three STARTALK workshops designed specifically for training Arabic-language teachers, and over 1,130 Arabic teachers across the United States have enrolled in these workshops. The teacher participants have come from K–12 private and public schools as well as undergraduate institutions. While several multilanguage STARTALK teacher-training programs have included Arabic teachers, this study focuses on programs designed for Arabic teachers only and tailored to their particular professional and pedagogical needs.

One of STARTALK's unique features is that it requires program grant awardees to align their program curricula with a set of field-recognized principles and best practices in language education. To that end, it endorses the following six principles that guide the selection of teacher-training workshop topics:

- Implement a standards-based and thematically organized curriculum
- Facilitate a learner-centered classroom
- Use the target language and provide comprehensible input for instruction
- Integrate culture, content, and language in a world language classroom
- Adapt and use age-appropriate authentic materials
- Conduct performance-based assessments

By design, teacher-training programs often provide participants with professional knowledge and experience in relation to these six principles in order to help teachers integrate them into practice. The following sections illustrate to what extent four years of STARKTALK programs have addressed these principles in their training of Arabic-language teachers.

Professional Development Topics

The first two questions this study poses are the following: What professional development opportunities have STARTALK programs provided? What gaps exist? A close investigation of STARTALK curricular materials responds to these questions. The study includes only curricula for programs that were designed solely for Arabic teachers, and they served as the first source of data for this section.

Program protocols require every STARTALK teacher-training program to follow a template designed by STARTALK that details the components of a workshop curriculum. The template asks programs to describe what participants should know and be able to do by the end of the program. The template also requests a detailed outline of the topics to be addressed in the workshop. A content analysis of the curricula was conducted. Analysis shows that over the past four years, programs offered the following topics:

- National standards/standards-based teaching; the five Cs
- Curriculum design, lesson planning, backward design, thematic unit design
- Language, culture, and content

- Materials design and adaptation
- Second-language acquisition/theory
- Technology in the world-language classroom
- Assessment/oral proficiency interview (OPI)/language testing
- Pathways to certification/certification related
- Observation, practice, microteaching, mentorship
- Language-specific issues
- Instructional strategies and best practices (communicative or learner-centered approach)
- Maintenance of target language/comprehensible input
- Language proficiency/proficiency guidelines
- Other (including heritage-language education and leadership)

Programs are not required to state one topic, although some do. Programs often list multiple topics and themes within the same workshop's curriculum even if the curriculum indicates that their program has one main topic. For example, a program may state that it focuses on incorporating technology in language teaching, but closer examination of the curriculum reveals that the program also addresses other topics, such as the national standards of the American Council on the Teaching of Foreign Languages (ACTFL), using authentic materials, or lesson planning. This study looks at curricula for in-depth information about program content, not just a main topic or theme. Figure 1 shows the distribution of topics and their frequency of occurrence over the past four years in STARTALK Arabic-teacher training programs.

Figure 1 captures the frequency with which certain topics were addressed in STARTALK Arabic-teacher training programs. The x-axis details the topics; the y-axis details the number of times programs addressed a particular topic. (There are far fewer indicators in 2010 because of an unexpected drop in the number of programs offering topics.) As the figure shows, the two most frequently addressed topics are pedagogical ones: the ACTFL national standards for teaching foreign languages; and curriculum, lesson design, and planning (linked to the standards). Less frequently addressed topics include assessment; observation, practice, and microteaching; and instructional strategies and best practices, which address communicative as well as learner-centered approaches in teaching languages. In stark contrast, certification is one of the least frequently addressed topics during the past four years. Recalling the six principles, we can see that the least frequently addressed principles are integrating cultural content and language, using the target language and providing comprehensible input for instruction, and adapting and using age-appropriate authentic materials. Of special interest as well is how often language-specific issues, or issues specific to teaching Arabic, are addressed. This topic apparently garnered a great deal of attention during the first two years of STARTALK Arabic-teacher training programs, but less during the most recent two years.

While explaining why certain professional development topics are so frequently covered may be possible (programs may believe these topics are required or that they constitute fundamental knowledge), addressing why the least frequently offered topics

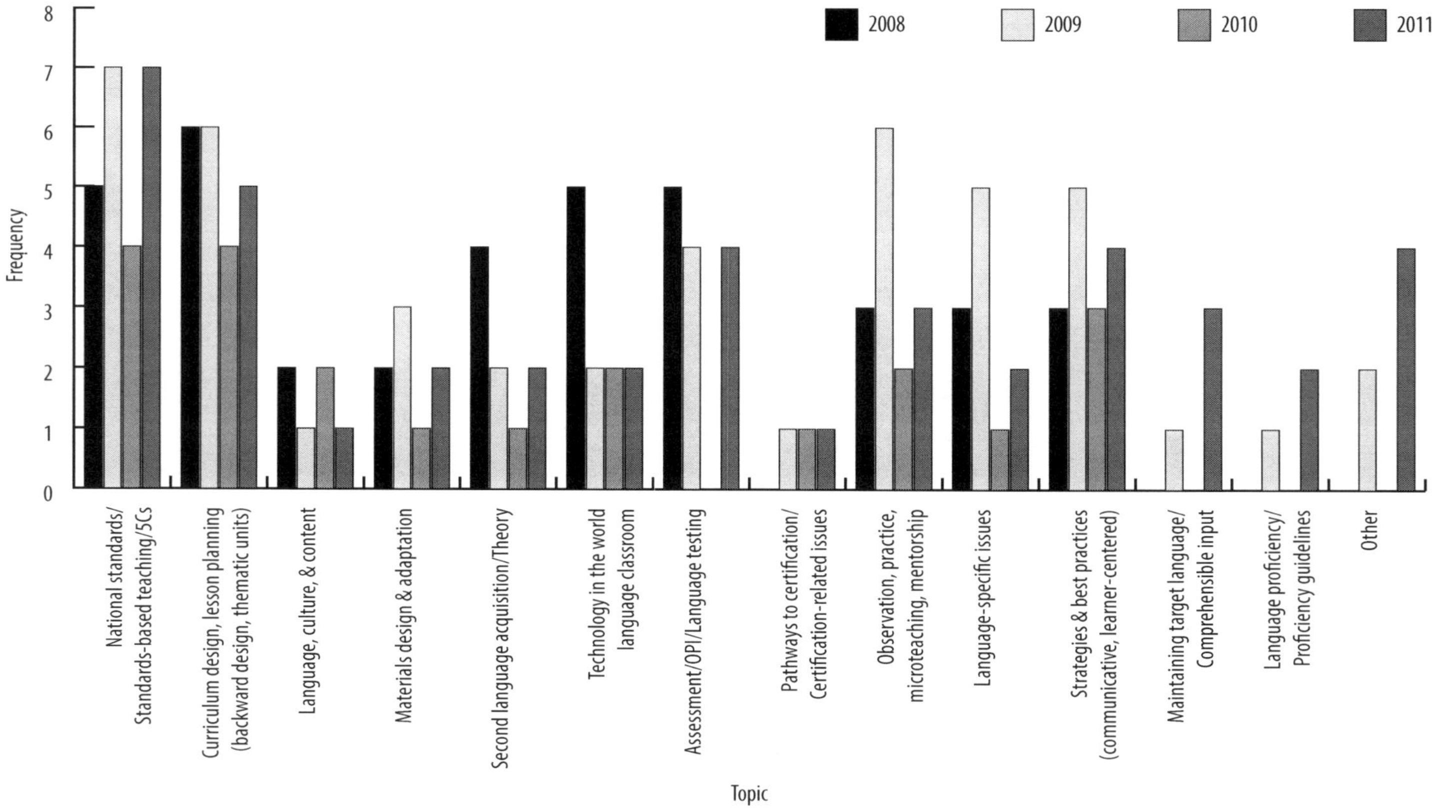

Figure 1. Topics addressed in STARTALK Arabic teacher-training programs

are so rarely presented is more challenging. These findings as well as their implications are discussed in detail in a later section.

STARTALK Arabic Teacher Trainees' Perspectives

A third question this study asks is, "What are the perspectives of teacher participants regarding their professional development experiences and needs?"

Examining professional development offerings provides us with a window into what experts and trainers believe teachers need. It does not, however, shed light on what Arabic teachers believe they need or what they feel they struggle with professionally. To explore these areas, a total of twenty-seven teachers from two 2011 STARTALK Arabic-teacher training programs participated in a brief survey that asked about their professional experiences, needs, challenges, and preferences. The survey, designed specifically for this study, serves as the second source of data.

We begin with demographic information about the teacher trainees who participated in the survey. All but one of the teachers are native speakers of Arabic, and all but two have immigrant backgrounds. Consistent with other studies (Wang 2009), the majority are women (female n=21; male n=6) and most hold bachelor's degrees (n=14) and master's degrees (n=10), with a few possessing only high school diplomas (n=2). One teacher holds an associate of arts degree (n=1), and none has an advanced graduate degree such as the Ph.D. The survey does not ask at what types of institutions participants teach, for example public schools, private schools, after-school programs, or colleges. Only two are certified. Data about how many are in the process of becoming certified were not collected, but participants came from two programs, one of which placed an emphasis on enrolling participants who are pursuing certification in accredited programs.

The majority of these teachers have taught Arabic for over five years in the United States (n=12). Seven of the teachers are new to the profession of teaching Arabic, having taught one year (n=6) or never having taught at all and listing themselves as prospective teachers (n=1). The rest of the teachers have between two and four years of experience teaching Arabic (n=7). One teacher did not respond to this question. Of the teachers surveyed, a dozen have taught Arabic overseas (n=12) and slightly more have not taught Arabic overseas (n=14). One teacher did not respond to this question.

The survey asks teachers to indicate all the grade levels they currently teach. Most provided multiple responses, indicating that they teach several different grade levels simultaneously. The vast majority (62%) teach across the various K–8 grade levels, 22% teach high school, 11% teach undergraduates, and nearly 5% teach students at the graduate level. Likewise, the survey asks teachers to indicate all of the levels of language proficiency they currently teach. Teachers' responses cluster around the beginner/novice level (31%), intermediate level (29%), or all levels simultaneously (29%). Only a few teach strictly at the advanced level (11%).

Professional Development Goals of STARTALK Arabic Teacher Trainees

When asked what their main professional goals were for participating in STARTALK Arabic-teacher training programs, teachers overwhelmingly indicate that their goals were to increase their professional knowledge (31%) and to gain new skills (29%). Only 16% indicate a goal of becoming certified, and only 10% indicate that one of their main goals was to earn a master's degree. Some teachers also indicate that their goal was to network (7%), or to train for working in a future STARTALK student program (7%). Figure 2 shows the distribution of teacher responses.

The figure reveals that teachers seem to focus on the two practical goals of enriching their professional knowledge and gaining new skills. The third most frequently selected goal is earning certification. This may indicate that addressing teachers' needs regarding their current practice (for example, gaining professional knowledge or skills they can immediately use) may be much more pressing or important to teachers than future professional aspirations such as certification.

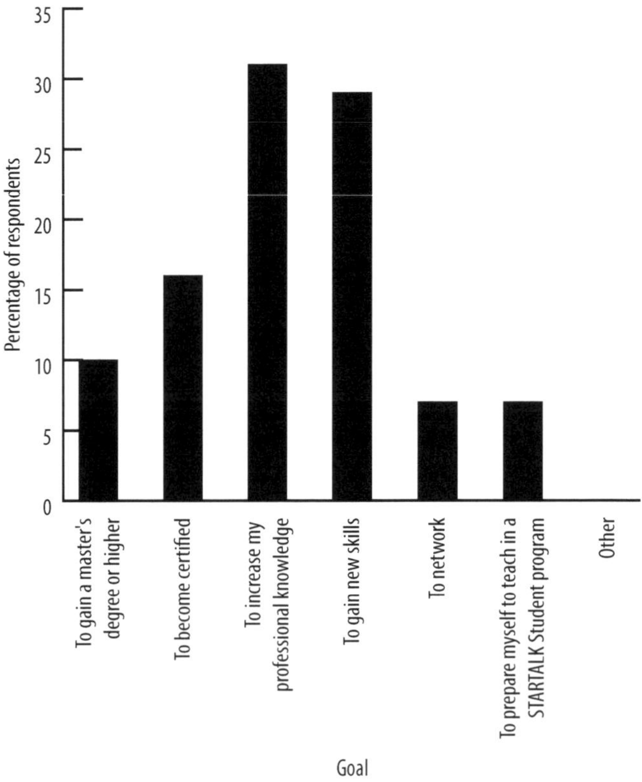

Figure 2. Arabic teachers' goals for professional development

Arabic Teachers' Professional Development Needs

The survey asks teachers what they feel they need most in terms of professional development. Their responses are presented in figure 3.

The figure shows that teachers feel they most need professional development on the topic of differentiated instruction. Briefly, differentiated instruction is an approach in education that attempts to provide individual students with different ways to learn, thereby building on commonalities among students in a class while responding to their individual differences in prior knowledge and particular learning needs and styles (Tomlinson 2001). The number of responses indicating the need for professional development in differentiated instruction far exceeds other needs related to topics emphasized strongly in the STARTALK-endorsed principles, such as implementing a standards-based curriculum; using a learner-centered approach; or integrating culture, content, and language.

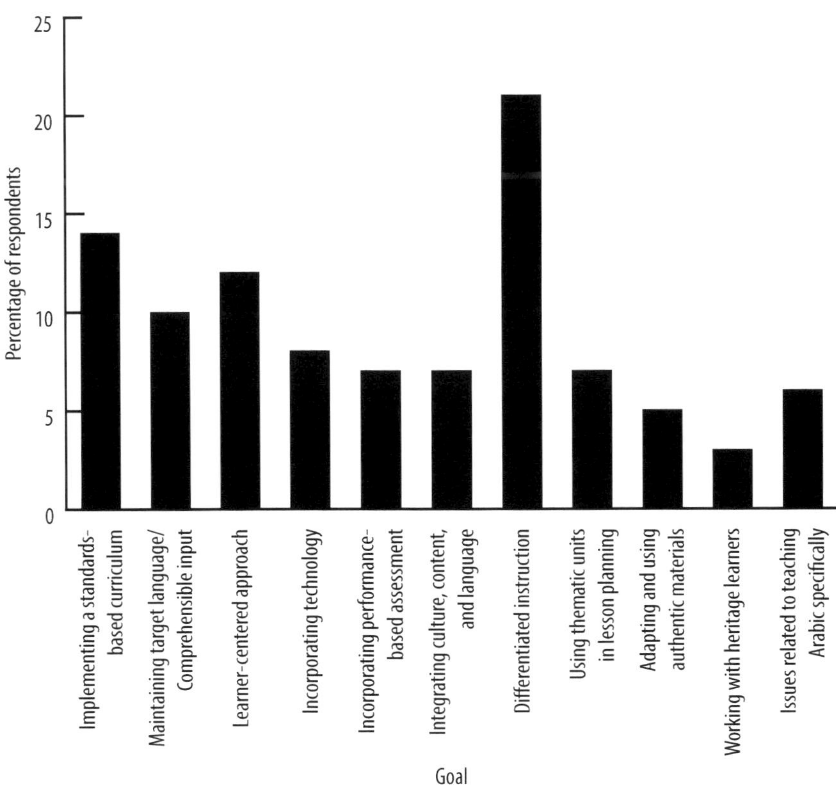

Figure 3. Topics in professional development that Arabic teachers feel they need most

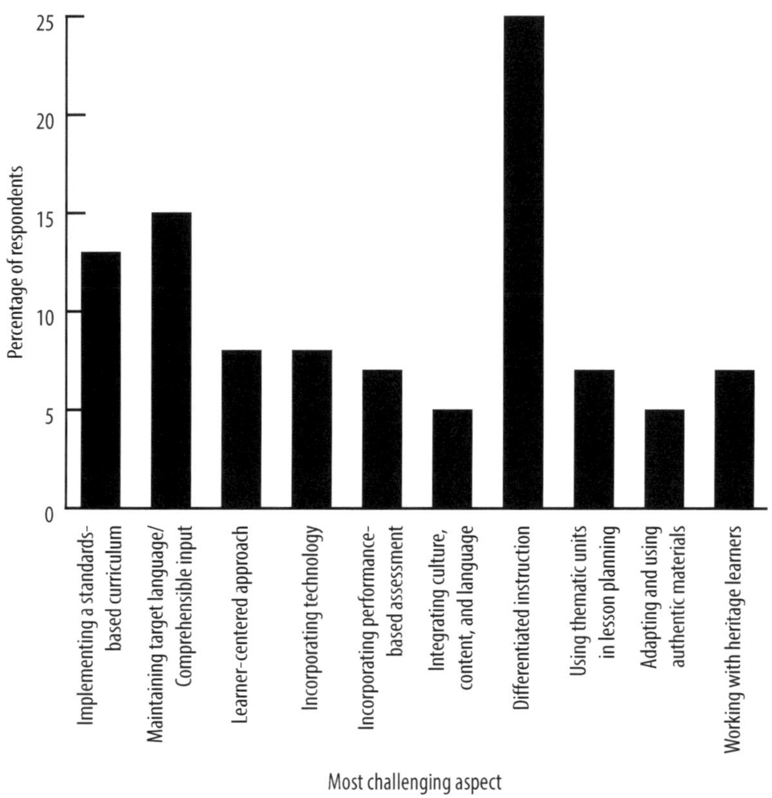

Figure 4. What teachers find most challenging in teaching Arabic

What Arabic Teachers Find Most Challenging in Teaching Arabic

In an effort to compare what teachers feel they lack in terms of professional knowledge and skills with what they feel they struggle with in teaching Arabic, figure 4 indicates the teachers' responses to the latter. Differentiated instruction is the most frequently selected challenge in teaching Arabic, which mirrors what teachers feel they need most in professional development. All other areas are selected much less frequently, although maintaining target language use seems to be the next most commonly reported challenge for some teachers.

Arabic Teachers' Preferred Language for Professional Development

Pedagogical and professional concepts can be difficult to grasp even in one's own native language. The survey asks teachers for their preferred language for professional development activities. Their answers are reflected in figure 5.

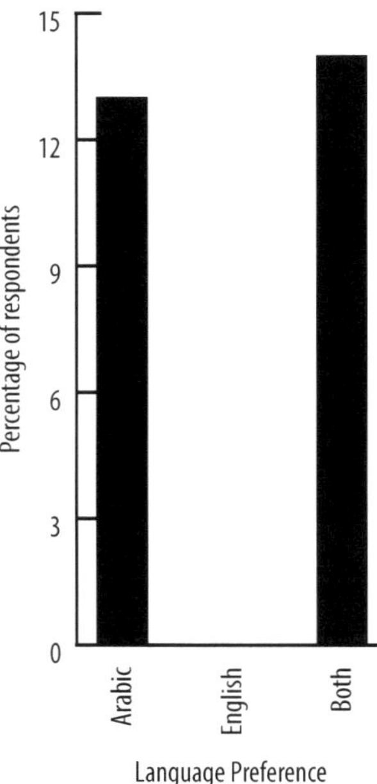

Figure 5. Language preference for professional development

As the figure shows, a slightly higher number of teachers prefer to have their training in both Arabic and English. Others indicate that they prefer to have it only in Arabic. None of the teachers prefers professional development to be delivered only in English. Open-ended questions asking teachers to explain their rationale for their language preference reveal that teachers are eager to master professional knowledge in both languages. Teachers who say that they would prefer to have their professional development in both languages mainly indicate that it is useful for them to use and learn terminology related to teaching in both languages or to have concepts clarified in both languages. Teachers who select only Arabic as their preferred language of professional development indicate in their open-ended responses that they prefer Arabic because of frustration with translations, because of greater comfort with their native language, or because of the importance of proficiency in professional Arabic to their confidence as Arabic-language teachers. Many simply state that their preference is based on their professional identity: "Because I'm an Arabic teacher."

Discussion and Implications

In a chapter from the *Handbook for Arabic Language Teaching Professionals in the 21st Century,* several experts discuss areas for Arabic teachers' professional development (Alosh, ElKhafaifi, and Hammoud 2006; England 2006). While Alosh, ElKhafaifi, and

Hammoud detail a holistic set of dimensions including knowledge of cognitive theory, the teaching profession, Arabic-specific issues, culture, pedagogy, curriculum design, and assessment, England focuses on the content of a complete program for teaching Arabic as a foreign language. She discusses four main content areas: language and research competencies, knowledge and language skills pedagogy, professional development activities, and assessment criteria for Arabic teachers' progress as professionals.

While experts have thoroughly explained ideal models for professional development for Arabic teachers, we have seen that immediate practical needs are what tend to concern teachers of Arabic (Alosh, ElKhafaifi, and Hammoud 2006, 414), for example, how to differentiate instruction for all the students in a class. We have also seen that professional development programs tend to focus on a rather narrow slice of experts' recommendations. For example, most STARTALK teacher programs focus on standards (a guiding principle) and related methodology, such as designing curricula or lesson plans based on these standards, and devote little time to other recommended areas of professional growth that teachers may not immediately identify as needs. In fact, this point emerges somewhat indirectly in teachers' responses about their professional needs and challenges.

As we have seen, a large majority of teachers report that they feel they need professional development on differentiated instruction (an aspect of pedagogical knowledge) and that this is a particularly challenging area for them in teaching Arabic. We can interpret this finding in a number of ways; it may reflect underlying challenges related to the implementation of differentiated instruction. For instance, the finding may reflect a struggle with assessment and knowing how to implement effective placement tests. It may also reflect teachers' need to understand strategies for teaching heritage and nonheritage speakers, who are often in the same classroom, or varieties of Arabic heritage speakers, which then implies a need to understand the different cultures of Arabic heritage students, their Arabic histories, their experiences with the Arabic language, and so on. Furthermore, the struggle with differentiated instruction could point to teachers' need to understand ways of structuring lesson plans based on language proficiency. Yet another professional need revealed by this challenge is the issue of adjusting comprehensible input, which inevitably relates to needs for Arabic-language knowledge (also referred to as language-content knowledge).

The findings of this study show that most Arabic-language teachers surveyed from STARTALK programs are in-service teachers, taking workshops such as those offered by STARTALK programs because they feel a need to enrich themselves and to address specific challenges they face in their daily practice. The second largest group consists of novice teachers who are teaching Arabic largely for the first time, so the gap between the two groups' professional experiences and needs is presumably quite large. The first group may have a great deal of experience in the classroom but insufficient pedagogical knowledge, whereas the second may lack both experience and knowledge. Experts in the field responsible for training would have to emphasize both basics (such as the ACTFL standards, lesson planning, etc.) and more nuanced and conceptual needs such as those related to differentiated instruction.

The findings, however, do not lead us to recognize the systemic professional development needs that continue to exist in the field of Arabic-language education. Even if the field identifies all the areas of professional growth needed in teaching Arabic as a foreign language, we nevertheless face a shortage of institutions of higher education invested in rigorous training of these teachers, as Wang aptly points out (2009). Likewise, we face a shortage of qualified trainers who understand the issues and needs pertaining to specific communities of LCTL teachers, and who are able and equipped to address these needs in a language-specific manner. Therefore, tackling the issues of content and structure of professional development programs wins only half the battle of establishing sustainable and effective language-teacher training and professional development.

Closing Thoughts and Future Directions

We have seen that even a single reported challenge for language teachers can indicate a web of more intricate professional needs. Because the teachers surveyed are largely in-service, after gaining a set of basic professional and pedagogical principles and skills, they may realize their need for a more theoretical understanding of language learning that will, in turn, have an impact on instructional practices such as differentiated instruction. Also, although programs such as STARTALK and, more recently, the professional development programs of Qatar Foundation International, address key areas of pedagogical and professional development for Arabic teachers, programs clearly need to implement more strategic and consistent efforts to address issues that are specific to the Arabic language and to provide support for teachers' ongoing professional growth. This is particularly true for the majority of teacher trainees who come from across the K–12 spectrum and who have traditionally been ignored because of experts' focus on postsecondary instructors. While such a focus is understandable considering the rising enrollment rates in college-level Arabic courses, it is largely not teachers from these institutions who seek professional development opportunities. It is unclear what this means for the design and implementation of Arabic-teacher training programs.

Of equal concern is Arabic teachers' relatively low interest in pursuing degree and certification options when compared to interest in increasing professional skills. Why is this the case and what can be done about it? While many programs offer credit toward certification, certification does not receive much emphasis in professional development programs. This may reflect what teachers seek from professional development, or it may be symptomatic of a more complex situation. Experts must devote serious attention to and deeper investigation of these questions. Additionally, programs offering professional development would do well to survey their incoming trainees in order to determine the gaps and areas of future growth that can be addressed. Investigation by both researchers and trainers is in order if the LCTL field and that of teaching Arabic as a foreign language are truly to make progress in overcoming the shortage of qualified Arabic-language instructors and in building the national capacity of people proficient in the Arabic language.

Limitations of this exploratory study are largely related to the small sample size for the survey. The field needs more incisive analyses of teachers' responses regarding their challenges and professional development needs. Specifically, it would be helpful to know which teachers of which backgrounds report facing challenges in differentiated instruction, and what their professional, linguistic, and pedagogical experiences are. A further limitation is that we did not investigate which of our teacher-survey participants are currently in the process of acquiring certification and how this may affect their professional development needs.

Future studies extending from this one would do well to include more contextual information about professional development workshops as well as more in-depth interviews with teachers. At present, however, this overview serves as a stepping-stone for future inquiry.

References

Allen, Roger. "Arabic—Flavor of the Moment: Whence, Why, and How?" *The Modern Language Journal* 91, no. 2 (2007): 258–61.

Alosh, Mahdi, Hussein M. ElKhafaifi, and Salah-Dine Hammoud. "Professional Standards for Teachers of Arabic." In Wahba, Taha, and England, *Handbook*, 2006, 409–18.

Brecht, Richard D., and A. Ronald Walton. "National Strategic Planning in the Less Commonly Taught Languages." *The Annals of the American Academy of Political and Social Science* 532, no. 1 (1994): 190–212.

England, Liz. "Methodology in Arabic Language Teacher Education." In Wahba, Taha, and England, *Handbook*, 2006, 409–18.

Furman, Nelly, David Goldberg, and Natalia Lusin. "Enrollments in Languages Other Than English in United States Institutions of Higher Education, Fall 2009." Web publication: The Modern Language Association of America, 2010. www.mla.org/pdf/2009_enrollment_survey.pdf.

Greer, Michael, and Dora Johnson. "National Survey of Schools Teaching Arabic as a Core Course." Paper presented at the Annual Convention of the American Council on Teaching Foreign Languages, San Diego, CA, 2009.

Ingold, C. W., and S. Wang. *The Teachers We Need: Transforming World Language Education in the United States.* College Park, MD: National Foreign Language Center at the University of Maryland, 2010.

McGinnis, Scott. "The Less Common Alternative: A Report from the Task Force for Teacher Training in the Less Commonly Taught Languages." *ADFL Bulletin* 25, no. 2 (1994):17–22.

Oleksak, Rita. "Building Capacity, Shaping the Future." *The Modern Language Journal* 93, no. 2 (2009): 278–80.

Ryding, Karin C. "Teaching Arabic in the United States." In Wahba, Taha, and England, *Handbook*, 2006, 13–20.

Tomlinson, C. A. *How to Differentiate Instruction in Mixed-Ability Classrooms.* Alexandria, VA: ASCD, 2001.

Van Houten, Jaqueline Bott. "The State Perspective on Teacher Shortage, Certification, and Recruitment." *The Modern Language Journal* 93, no. 2 (2009): 274–77.

Wahba, Kassem M., Zeinab A. Taha, and Liz England, eds. *Handbook for Arabic Language Teaching Professionals in the 21st Century.* Berlin: Lawrence Erlbaum Associates, 2006.

Walker, Galal, and Scott McGinnis. *Learning Less Commonly Taught Languages: An Agreement on the Bases for the Training of Teachers.* The Ohio State University: Foreign Language Publications, 1995.

Wang, Shuhan. "Preparing and Supporting Teachers of Less Commonly Taught Languages." *The Modern Language Journal* 93, no. 2 (2009): 282–87.

Welles, Elizabeth B. "Foreign Language Enrollments in United States Institutions of Higher Education, Fall 2002." *ADFL Bulletin* 35, no. 2–3 (2004): 7–26.

Destructive Genesis

THE DIALOGISM OF NAJĪB SURŪR'S *LUZŪM MĀ YALZAM*

■

Hala Ghoneim, University of Wisconsin-Whitewater

Abstract

The development of Arabic literary genres has been shaped by the tensions, negotiations, and alliances between Arabic poetics and Western modernism. The former bears and preserves national identity but could engender fossilization and buttress many hegemonic practices of the postcolonial state; the latter may sustain resisting and reversing the hegemonic in the traditionalist but could jeopardize authenticity and reinforce cultural colonization. The development of genres with questionable or nonexistent indigenous ancestry, like drama and the novel, has been characterized by a relentless search for indigenous roots. Modernist poetry, conversely, has been characterized by curbing the hegemonic influence of established poetics. This article conducts a close reading of Najīb Surūr's poem *Luzūm mā Yalzam,* using intertextuality as a framework to illuminate modernist poets' interrogation of their Arab and Western poetic precursors. Surūr's drawing from and interruption of these ancestors interestingly represent the dialectic of the Self and Other in modernist poetry.

Al-'Arabiyya, 44–45 (2011–2012), 103–118

> In the beginning was repetition, and no matter how far back into the past we go, we find old words being taken up again and again. In this matter nothing distinguishes the moderns from the ancients. The heir need not feel dependent on his predecessors, for he owes them no more than they owed those people who came before them.
>
> Abdelfattah Kilito (2001, 12)

> [In the structures of Dialogical discourses], writing reads another writing, reads itself and constructs itself through a process of destructive genesis.
>
> Julia Kristeva (1980, 77)

Authenticity has been a central issue for Arab poets and critics since pre-Islamic time. It is curious that modernist poets feel obligated to safeguard their poetry against inauthenticity vis-à-vis their own indigenous ancestors more than they do against their Western ones. Unlike drama and narrative, Arabic poetry has more urgently needed to break free from the hegemonic literary heritage, whose immutability has been at the core of the Arab-Islamic nationalist agendas of the postcolonial states. Western poetics of modernism and postmodernism have played a liberating role, providing an example of transcending one's own ancestry and, by extension, any aesthetic ancestry including the very sources of one's own inspiration. Most avant-garde Arabic poetry is an arena of contests and negotiations among poets and texts that go beyond the aesthetic and extend to the social and political.

Intertextuality is a fitting approach to reading Surūr's *Luzūm mā Yalzam*,[1] not only because it could elucidate the overwhelming presence of Abū al-ʿAlāʾ al-Maʿarrī (973–1057) and other poetic ancestors in the collection, but also because the collection is a site for clamorous dialogic negotiations among many texts. I use the term "text" here in its broadest sense, adopting the culture-as-text semiotic view, which sees every aspect of culture as textual. Cultural-textual analysis is "not an experimental science in search of law but an interpretive one in search of meaning" (Geertz 1973, 5). In the twenty-fifth poem in *Luzūm*, "A Dialogue with Abū al-ʿAlāʾ al-Maʿarrī," Surūr summons a giant poetic ancestor and engages in a dialogue with him. The dialogue turns the poem into an interrogation of poetics and politics, traditionalism and modernism, Self and Other, genre boundaries, and language. The collection validates Kristeva's contention that "the 'literary word' is an *intersection of textual surfaces* rather than a *point* (a fixed meaning), as a dialogue among several writings: that of the writer, the addressee (or the character), and the contemporary or earlier cultural context" (1980, 65).

The concept of intertextuality sheds light on modernist Arab poets' problematic relationship with their indigenous and Western ancestors and the "mosaic of texts" with which their texts engage. It addresses the concern about authenticity on which modern and ancient Arab poets and critics have been fixated and sheds light on their strategies of indigenizing the Other.[2] It can also offer critical and theoretical elucidation of the presence of diverse linguistic registers, genres, and hypertextual practices.

Many contemporary Arab critics have been interested in the concept of intertextuality, probably because a text's relationships to earlier texts and authors' relationships to earlier authors have been a central issue in medieval Arabic criticism. It has also been of importance to contemporary critics who concern themselves with issues of modernism, texts' derivation or divergence from canonical texts. Many critical elucidations by medieval Arabic critics could be considered early reflections on what is now called intertextuality (or transtextuality)[3]. Medieval Arab critics investigated ways in which texts relate, alter, derive from, or comment on earlier texts. However, until recently, most of these investigations were mainly concerned with a text's authorship, ownership, and sources rather than its interpretation. The former approach investigates a given text's constituent parts, whereas the latter investigates its overall meaning with regard to its context, author, readers, and the texts with which it engages in a dialogue.

Ibn Rashīq (999–1063), the author of *Al-'Umdah,* dedicates an entire section in his book to enlisting and defining different ways poets appropriate meanings, words, and tropes from other poets. He labels all these practices *sariqāt* (plagiarism), but he makes a clear statement that "[plagiarism] is a wide-ranging practice to which no poet can claim to be immune"[4] (1972, 280). Ibn Rashīq presents an avalanche of terms, some of his own and others belonging to earlier critics, for example, al-Jurjānī.[5] The terms describe different modes, degrees, and purposes of plagiarism: plagiarizing meanings, words, phrases, lines, metaphors, and so on; with no, little, subtle, or major alterations. He also describes plagiarism by means of changing genre: *naẓm al-nathr* (versification) and *ḥall al-shi'r* (prosification), which he considers the gravest brands of plagiarism.[6] Two important terms that relate to plagiarism are *iqtibās* (citing a Qur'ānic verse in a work of literature and using Qur'ānic imagery, style, and vocabulary), *taḍmīn* (citing a known poetry line in a work of literature), and *talmīḥ* (allusion to a text without directly citing it). *Mu'āraḍāt* and *naqā'iḍ* are two important genres of Arabic poetry that have been considered representative of intertextuality in Arabic literature.

Mu'āraḍāt, poems that replicate the themes and form of earlier poems, and *naqā'iḍ,* satirical poems representing a quarrel between two poets but following the same meter and rhyme scheme, are prominent examples of intertextuality in Arabic poetry. The poet of the *mu'āraḍah* (singular form of *mu'āraḍāt*) is so appreciative of and influenced by a given canonical poem that he or she models his or her poem after it, paying tribute to the parent poem (and poet) and signaling continuation of the literary and cultural tradition. However, the poet of the derivative poem consciously or unconsciously attempts to create for his or her poem a space in the canon comparable to that of the precursor's poem. When Shawqī writes his "Sīniyyah," modeled after the "Sīniyyah" of al-Buḥturī, his "Nūniyyah," modeled after the "Nūniyyah" of Ibn Zaydūn, and his many other *mu'āraḍāt,* he is claiming a contemporary poetic status comparable to the poetic status these mentors occupied in their respective eras. The status of the parent poem is never challenged; its affirmation is what gives value to the derivative poem. The writing of *naqā'ḍ,* on the other hand, is in fact an erasure of the opponents' poems, a refuting and ridiculing of their claims. The identical meter and rhyme of the *naqā'ḍ* is not tributary; it merely signals that the poems are a part of the same quarrel.[7]

Arab critics have disagreed on whether or not *mu'āraḍāt* are considered representative of intertextuality. Rajā' 'Īd (2000) dismisses these arguments, for all allusions are by definition forms of intertextuality. He raises a more important question about the value of intertextual practices. ʿĪd argues that intertextuality is of little value if the hypertext is a pale imitation of the hypotext, a mere expression of approval or admiration of it, or a repetition of its themes or message. Valued intertextual practices are creative and transformative; they add, delete, alter, combine, and generate new meanings. Thus ʿĪd considers the *muʿāraḍāt* of al-Barūdī and Ḥāfiẓ to be "valueless imitations" and Shawqī's as "so distinctive, unique, and idiosyncratic that it is inconceivable to call them *'muʿāraḍāt'*" (2000, 229).

The task of the contemporary critics, in ʾĪd's opinion, should transcend medieval critics' obsession with tracing hypertexts back to an original text and dividing poets into antecedents and mimics. In other words, the term *sariqāt* must be redefined so that intertextual practices that have long been regarded by Arab critics as plagiarism can be analyzed in more productive ways. The focus of this analysis should aim at revealing the transformations the hypotext undergoes in the process of the creation of the hypertext:

لا نترصد (شظايا هذه التناصّات) المتناثرة على ساحة النص المتناص، لنقع في خطأ النقد القديم تحت مصطلحه السابق: السرقة، وإنما لنتتبع تحوّلات تلك النصوص واستكشاف قيم تحرّكها ومدى توظيفها وما تضيفه في إعادة إبداع جيدي وتشكيل مخالف.

> I will not locate [fragments of hypotexts] scattered on the surface of the hypertext, which would be a repetition of the mistake traditionalist criticism made under its old rubric "plagiarism." I will trace the transformations of these hypotexts, discover the measure of their movement, the extent to which they are utilized, and what they contribute to the re-creation of excellent innovations and distinct configurations. (ʿĪd 2000, 230)

Such critical revisions of medieval terminologies and practices are of importance to Arab modernism. On the one hand, they enable a rethinking of heritage without ultimately destroying it and a utilization of Western notions more oriented toward catering to indigenous needs than fetishizing the Other. A bridge is established between the past and the present, between modernist and traditionalist poetry and criticism: "Modernist poetry guards [*yarʿā*] traditionalist poetry; both meanings [of the Arabic verb *yarʿā*] are intended: 'preserve' and 'mock'. The two meanings are inseparable. Modernist poetry is an interpretation of traditionalist poetry" (Nāṣif 2000, 234).

One can immediately infer from the title of Surūr's collection and the ten epigraphs he cites that the poet is mainly concerned with the authenticity and utility of the poetic utterance. On the one hand, he subscribes to the acknowledged fact that poets are bound to take up again and again the ideas, words, and tropes of their forbears. He insists, on the other hand, that poets are capable of making an authentic contribution to life and art. The title of the collection *Luzūm mā Yalzam* (The necessity of the necessary)[8] misreads the title of al-Maʿarrī's famous collection *Luzūm mā lā Yalzam* (The necessity of the unnecessary), known as *Luzūmiyyāt* or "Necessity verses" (singular, *Luzūmiyyah*). Al-Maʿarrī's *Luzūmiyyāt* is a unique yet paradoxical text. It introduces to Arabic poetry new and unique philosophical themes, elegantly written in traditionalist verse. Al-Maʿarrī not only commits to the already strict traditionalist poetics but voluntarily imposes on himself additional restrictions. He resolves to use all letters of the alphabet as letters of *rawī* in his collection, which consists of more than ten thousand lines. The letter of *rawī* is the essential element—among other less important elements—the rhyme scheme on which a traditionalist Arabic poem is built. It has to be repeated in every line, and it often gives classical poems their titles: *mīmiyyah, sīniyyyah, lāmiyyah,* and so forth. Al-Maʿarrī also insists that every letter be represented in *Luzūmiyyāt* four times: three times with the three short vowels of Arabic and once with the *sukūn* (absence of vowels). Moreover, he resolves on using an unnecessary additional letter (besides the letter of *rawī*) in each rhyme scheme. Al-Maʿarrī never deviates from these additional, unnecessary restrictions that give his poems their name.

Critics and poets have always been fascinated by al-Maʿarrī's ability to express complex philosophical ideas so lucidly and effortlessly in spite of these restrictions. *Luzūmiyyāt* remains one of the most significant, most quoted masterpieces of Arabic literature that have called into question the political and religious institutions of their eras. One of Surūr's ten epigraphs is a line by al-Maʿarrī: "Although I am among the moderns, I shall achieve what the ancients could not."[9] This epigraph stands out because it is the only one that challenges the ancients, while the other nine—written by such authors as ʿAntarah, Voltaire, Jean de La Bruyère, ʿAlī ibn abī Ṭālib, an anonymous ancient Egyptian author, Abū Tammām, and others—give in to the idea of the inevitability of repetition. Surūr accepts al-Maʿarrī's genius but questions the difficult and strange way he chooses to challenge other poets:

__ سيدي كم حرت في أمرك..حقًا لست أفهم..
كيف يغدو ثائر القوم ولوعًا بالقيود !
__ كنت أهفو للخلود .
__ كان يغنيك الذي يلزم عما ليس يلزم !

- Sir, I am confused. I truly do not understand;
How does an avant-garde [poet] become captivated by restrictions!
- I sought immortality.
- You should have given up the unnecessary for the necessary!
(1996, 148)

Al-Maʿarrī reminds Surūr that a poet's quest for immortality justifies any practices to which he may choose to adhere as long as he is talented enough to observe them. He goes on to accuse Surūr and his fellow modernist poets of renouncing the restrictions prescribed by al-Khalīl, the founder of Arabic prosody (d. 789), because of their inability to adhere to them. This accusation echoes familiar accusations by traditionalist critics and poets that free-verse poets are incapable of rather than unwilling to follow traditionalist prosody. Surūr defends modernist poets by pointing out to al- Maʿarrī that almost all of these poets had written traditionalist poetry before they self-consciously renounced it in favor of free verse. Free verse has been adopted by avant-garde poets because it deliberately distances them from a nationalist agenda of which they do not approve. Moreover, it gives them liberating tools for challenging political, religious, and cultural institutions, which is at the core of their social message. Transgression of aesthetic and linguistic codes, characteristic of free verse and (post)modernist literature in general, is in essence a transgression of power: "There is no equivalence, but rather, identity between challenging official linguistic codes and challenging official laws" (Kristeva 1980, 65). Surūr dedicates *Luzūm* to his father "who taught me poetry and revolution" (1996, 111). The juxtaposition of "poetry" and "revolution" reflects Surūr's, and like-minded poets', view of the two as one and the same.

Surūr concerns himself with the social message of his poetry, but, like ʿAntarah, Zuhayr, and al-Maʿarrī, he is also concerned with his immortality, his place among his precursors and contemporaries. What the precursors said is vividly present in his consciousness when he says his own words: "Hadn't Shakespeare said it before me, I would have said, '[all] the world's a stage'" (1996, 145).[10] Surūr is aware that his poetry will be evaluated in terms of the lingering influence of the ancestors' models, the distorting criteria of contemporary critics, and the distorted judgment of uninformed or misinformed audiences. He is also well aware of the role oppressive political regimes play in establishing the aesthetic and moral criteria for the creation, reception, and evaluation of art. His poetry could be under attack not only by the corrupt regime it satirizes but also by audiences and critics, whose preconceived norms of morality and taste he constantly destabilizes.

Conservative critics and audiences would surely take issue with many of Surūr's poems. The most radical example is his notorious *Mother-Cunt Verses*, banned and condemned on moral grounds. The government's real reason for banning the poem was its unprecedented, blunt assault on state-sponsored corruption. The masses were reassured about their government, which played the same role the caliphate had played in the past: the guardian of morality. Surūr's poetry, like al-Maʿarrī's, could easily offend the religious sensibilities of Muslims and Christians alike. In the tenth poem in *Luzūm* he writes:

وحفظت في الكتّاب آيات الكتاب ،
عن ظهر قلب.
ونسيتها عن قلب ظهر!
إلا علامات على جسمي لضرب.
- بهراوة عمياء—مثل بقية الوشم القديم ،
وغراب هابيل وقابيل ، وفأسًا للخليل ،
والفعل—فعل الأمر—"اقرأ !"

In the Qurānic school, I memorized the verses of the Book,
word-for-word.
And forgot them word by word.
[What I did not forget were] the beating bruises on my body,
the crow of Cain and Abel, the axe of Abraham,
and the verb—the command—"Read!"

(Surūr 1996, 126)

He also writes in the sixteenth poem titled "Fatwā":

__ أعطوا لقيصر ما لقيصر ،
وللاله..
ما للاله !
__ فما الذي تعطي لنا ؟ !
__ ماذا تبقى عندكم ؟
__ لم يبق شيء..
__ فاهنأوا..طوبى لكم !

- Render unto Caesar what is Caesar's
  and unto God
  what is God's!
- What do you render unto us?
- What else is there?
- Nothing!
- Rejoice! Thou art Blessed!
  (Surūr 1996, 134–35)

Surūr misreads the Qur'ān and the Bible. One of the few lingering memories from his Qur'ānic school days is the command "read." The command is a clear allusion to the first revealed verse of the Qur'ān (96:2), in which Prophet Muhammad is commanded by Gabriel to recite the Qur'ān, the word of God. Surūr obeys the divine command, but instead of reading the Qur'ān, he reads poetry: the epics of "Adham, al-Zīr Sālim, al-Hilāli, Ibn Dhi Yazan, and ʿAntarah" (1996, 127). This shifting of the command's context from religious to secular (literary) is significant. It establishes a status for the poetic utterance comparable to that of scripture. In the second stanza above, Surūr misreads a famous biblical statement (Mark 12:17). The verse is turned into a dialogue between Jesus and the masses. The meaning of Jesus's phrase, which is typically understood as a demand to separate material and spiritual matters, is dramatically altered. Surūr's dialogue reorders the hierarchy of God, kings, and masses. The masses are asked by the holy texts to obey God and kings, but not enough emphasis on social justice and human rights exists in them. The poor are left with nothing to inherit but the blessings, which have not alleviated the injustices they have suffered throughout the ages. Poetry fills in the gaps in holy texts by centralizing the needs of the masses here and now.

Surūr judges poetry that does not communicate a clear social message harshly. In "A Dialogue with Abī al- ʿAlā'Al-Maʿarrī," tension between the avant-garde poet and the giant precursor arises as they try to judge each other's aesthetic and ideological inclinations. Al-Maʿarrī is impatient with modern poets' lack of talent, and Surūr is critical of al-Maʿarrī's eluding confrontations and the many restrictions he imposes on himself. However, the dialogue reveals that they are not in any disagreement. Both poets preach revolution, favor rationality, and conflict with power. Al-Maʿarrī's road to revolution is to impose more restrictions, and Surūr's is to break free from all restrictions. Surūr does not believe that al-Maʿarrī's choices are necessarily wrong; he acknowledges his indebtedness to him by choosing him to be his spokesperson:

أنت ما خلفت من شيء لشاعر،
إذ تحديت فأعجزت الأوائل
والأواخر وأنا قد جئت في ذيل الأواخر.

You left nothing for poets [to say];
You challenged the ancients
and the moderns, and I am the very last of the moderns.
(Surūr 1996, 148)

The dialogue between Surūr and al-Maʿarrī leads to a dialogue that goes beyond their two texts, *Luzūm* and *Luzūmiyyāt*. Four stanzas of contemporary poetry are presented to al-Maʿarrī for evaluation. Al-Maʿarrī, once the revolutionary among traditionalists, is now exercising his authority to judge modernist poets. The first of the four is a traditionalist piece, written in the *khafīf* meter, which Surūr wrote when he used to write that kind of poetry:

هيئوا اللحد والكفن ها هنا غاية البدن
ملت النفس عيشها وغدت تطلب السكن

Prepare the grave, the shroud; the body's end is here.
The soul is bored of living, and is [now] seeking tranquility.
(Surūr 1996, 149)

Surūr tells al-Maʿarrī that he decided to renounce al-Khalīl's prosody because it would have necessitated the use of cacophonic, tasteless words like *ʿafan* (rottenness) to keep the rhyme scheme unbroken. Al-Maʿarrī scornfully tells Surūr that rottenness would have plagued his poem with or without al-Khalīl's rhyme scheme. Later in the poem, Surūr proves to be right when al-Maʿarrī is compelled to use the word *maghaṣ* (colic) to maintain his rhyme scheme (1996, 154). On several other occasions, Surūr is irritated by his own choice of words that are only useful for maintaining the rhyme scheme. The exchange reveals al-Maʿarrī's impatience with the traditionalist poetry of others and Surūr's impatience with the remaining restrictions that even free verse has to observe.

Al-Maʿarrī asks Surūr to give him examples of modernist poetry. Surūr presents three examples that reflect the unique flavor of known modernist poets. He does not directly quote from or name them, but parodies the style, images, and overall aura of their poetry. The three parodies are put together in a section titled "*Ṭibq al-aṣl*" (Replica). After each example is recited, al-Maʿarrī renders ambiguous yet clearly unfavorable judgments. These imitations represent an interesting brand of intertextuality, where allusions are made not to particular texts but to text types. The first *muḥākāh* (parody) impersonates the Syrian and Iraqi poets Adonis, al-Sayyāb, and al-Bayyātī, whose poetry heavily capitalizes on Greek, Roman, and Babylonian mythology:

سيزيف قال لشهرزاد..
الصخرة العمياء أدركها الصباح.
وجناح ديدالوس ينشد للرياح . . .
أنشودة الدم والجليد.

Sisyphus said to Shahrazad,
"Morning overtook the blind rock,
and the wing of Daedalus sings to the wind
the song of blood and ice."
(Surūr 1996, 150)

The second imitation invokes the style of the Syrian poet Nizār Qabbānī, especially his fiery love poems, notorious for their blunt references to love, sex, and the female body:

نهداك ومصباح أحمر..
قمعا سكر،
فرخان بعش من مرمر ،
أرنبتان..
قبرتان..
وتران لقيثار أخضر.

Your breasts [in the light of] the red lamp [are]
two cones of sugar,
two little birds in a marble nest,
two does,
two larks,
two strings of a green guitar.
(Surūr 1996, 151)

The third and last replica imitates the aura of the Egyptian free-verse poet Ṣalāḥ ʿAbd al-Ṣabūr, who is known for his incorporation of both erudite and mundane vocabulary:

أحداق تابوت على الأسياخ خفاش يموت :
وسعال برغوث يعوم بقلب حوت ،
والفأرة الحمراء مشنقة المغيب ،
والعنكبوت..
في القدر مثل الثلج يغلي.

The eye-pupils of a casket on the skewers [are] a dying bat:
The cough of a flea, swimming in the heart of a whale,
and the red mouse, the gallows of the sunset,
and the spider
is in the pot, boiling like ice.
(Surūr 1996, 152)

Although Surūr does not issue any explicit evaluative statements about these replicas, it is clear that they parody and critique the poets to whom he is indirectly alluding. He might agree with them regarding taboo transgression and canon deconstruction, but he is still critical of their ambiguity and elitism. The way Surūr constructs the three replicas reflects his unfavorable judgment of some of his contemporaries: They use resonating words but do not communicate comprehensible social messages. He might have been speaking his own mind when he makes al-Maʿarrī's persona say about these poets, "By God, it is they, not I, who cling to the unnecessary" (1996, 153).[11]

Critics, the target of Surūr's repeated assault and resentment, are denied textual space in *Luzūm*. He conceives of them as guardians of the literary and political status quo and blames them for glorifying unworthy poets, whose only talent is to sugarcoat the corrupt practices of oppressive regimes. As a result, dissident poets like Surūr are marginalized, demonized, censored, and forgotten. Surūr alludes to critics when he offers to share with al-Maʿarrī samples of their writing. Al-Maʿarrī refuses, because he predicts that the criticism of modern poetry will be as poorly written as the subject of its inquiry. The silencing of the critics is a condemning pronouncement that reverses the traditional roles of literature and criticism. Surūr's poem critiques criticism and critics and denies them any authority to judge his poetry, having obviously failed in judging the poetry of his contemporaries. The authority and status they enjoy validate a line al-Maʿarrī wrote in his *Luzūmiyyāt*, which Surūr reiterates in the last line of the poem: "Falsehood has prevailed since the beginning of time, and wise men die of anger" (1996, 156).[12]

By using *Luzūmiyyāt* as a hypotext in his collection, Surūr embeds the meaning of al-Maʿarrī's text into his own and claims him as an ideological and poetic ancestor. Al-Maʿarrī's well-known ideological stances as a representative of the clash between the intellectuals and both power and the masses can be assumed to be identical to Surūr's. But this alignment between the two poets and the two texts does not entrap Surūr's text in the tributary function of the *muʿāraḍah*, a text that owes its existence to an earlier text. The *muʿāraḍah* lodges the present text in the past, while Surūr's text brings al-Maʿarrī's *Luzūmiyyāt* to the present by highlighting the contemporaneousness and continuity of the issues it raised. Thus *Luzūm* does not owe its existence to *Luzūmiyyāt*; the latter owes its new life, its rebirth in a different time, and its acquisition of new meanings to the former. Changing into the affirmative the negated title of al-Maʿarrī's text signifies that Surūr's text has a life of its own and that it capitalizes on but does not duplicate the earlier text.[13] *Luzūm* thus can be said to be an *anti-muʿāraḍah*.

Surūr deliberately constructs his poem in a manner quite at odds with the construction of the *muʿāraḍah*. The authors of the *muʿāraḍah* walk in the tracks of earlier authors by duplicating their themes, form, and style; Surūr engages the earlier author in a dialogue and challenges rather than endorses his aesthetic and political choices. Besides objecting to his following unnecessary prosodic restrictions, Surūr also admonishes al-Maʿarrī about his *taqiyyah*, deliberate dissimulation of one's ideas or beliefs to avoid persecution:

"أيها الثائر..لم لذت بدارك؟"
"لِمَ لمْ ترحل.."
"أي سر كنت تعني حين قلت:
ولدي سر ليس يمكن ذكره   يخفى على البصراء وهو نهار."

"Rebellious one, why did you take refuge at your home?" (Surūr 1996, 154)
"Why didn't you emigrate?" (Surūr 1996, 155)
"What secret were you hinting at when you said,
'I have a secret I cannot reveal; those endowed with eyesight cannot
know [it]   although it is crystal clear.'"
(Surūr 1996, 155)

The allusions Surūr makes to al-Maʿarrī (and other poets) do not replicate the traditionalist utilizations of classical heritage, typically inspired by a nationalist agenda. Such utilizations hold utopian, nostalgic views of the past. Surūr, on the other hand, is critical of the past and the present, the forbears and the contemporaries. He alludes to the past because its problems and crises still persist today. When poets like Surūr, Dunqul, and Ḥijāzī look back, they see injustice, irrationality, and intolerance rather than glory and abundance. When they identify with figures from the past, it is usually with dissidents like Abū Nuʾās, al-Mutanabbī, and al-Maʿarrī. The hypotext is not fetishized; the poet enables it to comment on contemporary issues of aesthetic, political, and cultural importance. As they read *Luzūm* (the hypertext), readers' knowledge and memories of *Luzūmiyyāt* are reactivated. Al-Maʿarrī's legacy partially constitutes the meaning of Surūr's text, which it encompasses but also transcends. Lines are often cited from *Luzūmiyyāt*, but one word is usually altered, which creates a new meaning or an irony. Surūr says, "These sects are means to bring earthly [glories] to poets" (1996, 152).[14] He replaces the word "kings" in al-Maʿarrī's original line with "poets." He not only elaborates on the meaning of al-Maʿarrī's line but establishes parallelism between oppressive kings and hypocritical poets, a point Surūr repeatedly makes in his poems.

One strategy modernist Arab poets use to distance themselves from the neoclassicists' full-blown alignment with indigenous ancestors is to claim Western (or non-Arab) poetic ancestors. Surūr uses a number of Western texts as hypotexts in his collection, including *Don Quixote, Hamlet, Julius Caesar, The Waste Land, The Divine Comedy,* and others. In his epigraphs (and repeatedly within the poems of the collection), Surūr names or alludes to a number of Western poetic ancestors whose works shaped his consciousness at the time he wrote *Luzūm*. A bridge of relevance is established among his text and the Arab and Western hypotexts he uses. Surūr identifies al-Maʿarrī with Quixote, "a poet who crosses over all times" (1996, 155).[15] This identification links the two major texts with which Surūr engages in his collection, Cervantes's *Don Quixote* and al-Maʿarrī's *Luzūmiyyāt*. It brings together the different times, spaces, cultures, and meanings of these texts and enables them to contribute to the meaning of the later text. Claiming Western ancestors not only broadens the semiotic and aesthetic horizons of the hypertext but also challenges the hegemony of indigenous tradition when it poses as the sole legitimate source of contemporary poetic inspiration.

Metaphorical union brings together Quixote, al-Maʿarrī, Surūr, and the masses. On one occasion, Surūr identifies al-Maʿarrī with Quixote, who shares his courage, clear conscience, and melancholy: "You are Quixote" (1996, 155).[16] On a different occasion,

Surūr confuses his own story with Quixote's when he refers to the latter's beloved as his own: "Say to the beautiful Dulcinea/[And to] my beloved village Akhṭāb,/'He didn't die like a hero, but, like knights, he died on a quest for heroism'" (1996, 118).[17] Finally, Quixote is depicted as one of the masses, demonstrating against British occupation and shouting the famous slogan "Absolute Independence or Imminent death": "Quixote, you shouted [the slogans] of 'Independence or Imminent Death'" (1996, 130).[18]

In "Poet Laureate" Dante agrees to give Surūr a tour of hell, where they encounter present-day sinners including poets and politicians. Surūr continues discussing the issues related to aesthetics and politics. His discussion with al-Maʿarrī focuses on the dialectic of classical and modern and the relationship between the poet and the ancestors. His dialogue with Dante focuses on the definition of poetry, its relation to politics, and the dialectic of high and low cultures. They conclude that poetry is not sheer manipulation of images and rhythm or a dramatized representation of life; poetry, Dante declares, is whatever a poet creates. Dante (and Surūr) thus give the intention of the poet and the message of poetry primacy over any aesthetic quality poetry may have:

__ ماذا عن الشعراء لو لزموا الحياد..
في زحمة الألوان..ظلوا كالرماد ،
كالماء..لا لون لهم ،
وليذهب الشيطان بالألوان طرا.
فالشعر شيء والسياسة..
شيء سواه.
كالماء والقطران من حيث الكثافة !
__ يا للسخافة !
من قال هذا ؟

- What if poets become unbiased;
if they remain grey amid the range of colors
like colorless water.
Let all the colors go to the devil;
Poetry is one thing, and politics
another.
Like water and tar in density.
- How ridiculous!
Who said that?

(Surūr 1996, 167)

Surūr addresses Dante as a messiah, a saint, and a sheikh, considering him as much a poetic ancestor as al-Maʿarrī. Surūr asks him to evaluate more modern poets. Two poets are chosen, Shawqī, the uncontested poet laureate, and an anonymous popular poet. After listening to the latter's poem, Dante tells Surūr that the anonymous poet is the true poet laureate. Only one line by Shawqī (about a cat that devours its kittens) is cited, and the "Prince of Poetry"[19] is dethroned for his questionable alliance with the aristocratic class. The anonymous colloquial poem is the only hypotext that Surūr cites in its entirety in *Luzūm*. By so doing, Surūr equalizes classical Arabic poetry, canonical European poetry, and marginalized, low-culture texts that traditionalist criticism often ignores. The poet can allude to or transform any hypotext capable of liberating the hypertext aesthetically or ideologically, if necessary. *Luzūm* robustly transcends the limitations and transgresses the boundaries of the Arabic language and the genre of poetry. The embedded colloquial poem and the colloquial words and expressions he frequently uses diversify the linguistic registers from which he draws and systematically violate the rules of language, canonical aesthetic practices, and, by extension, all forms of hegemony in art, religion, and politics.

A central part of *Luzūm*'s intertextual practices is its superimposition on poetry of traits belonging to other literary genres. Bakhtin theorizes about the dialogism of the novel, its conscious awareness of the predominance of heteroglossia, the changing social, historical, and psychological conditions and contexts governing the meaning of a given utterance. Declaring the novel as a genre without a canon, he conceives of it as the literary genre most capable of encompassing multiple voices and languages: "In the majority of poetic genres, the unity of the language system and the unity (and uniqueness) of the poet's individuality as reflected in his language and speech, which is directly realized in this unity, are indispensible prerequisites of poetic style. The novel, however, not only does not require these conditions but . . . even makes the internal stratification of language, of its social heteroglossia and the variety of individual voices in it, the prerequisite for authentic novelistic prose" (1981, 264). In *Luzūm*, Surūr deliberately gives up the unitary and unique voice, characteristic of poetic genres. He orchestrates, to use another of Bakhtin's terms, different voices and languages.

Surūr's poems repeatedly capitalize on dialogue, be it direct, theatrical dialogue between the poet and a poetic persona or an academic, or a dialectical interrogation of competing arguments. Not only do readers hear the distinct voices of individuals, poets, prophets, critics, philosophers, and anonymous popular artists, they also participate in political debates and academic arguments. The collection employs traits borrowed from literary and nonliterary genres, like drama (dialogue), the novel (plot), and the essay (argument, notes, and citations). It also uses different dialects (standard and colloquial), sociolects (educated, peasant, vulgar, etc.), and idiolects (idioms known by his personae, e.g., al-Maʿarrī, Dante, Qabbānī, and Jesus). Moreover, it dispenses with traits traditionally conceived as prerequisites for poetry (poetic diction, lyricism). Surūr's poetry gives up the authority Arabic poetry has enjoyed since time immemorial as "the register of the Arabs,"[20] the reservoir of their science, wisdom, language, and history. This famous saying confers on poetry the sacredness of scripture and the accuracy of science; it idolizes it as the distillation of the finest cultural qualities of the nation, a notion quite central to Arab nationalism.[21] Avant-garde poetry, on the other hand, celebrates fragmentation and denies poets any claim of accessing truth; poetry does not represent what we wish to be remembered about us but what needs to be destabilized in our past and present.

Luzūm is an exploration of the Self-Other relationships wherein the Self is the poet, the nation, or the masses, and the Other is the forbear, the West, or the guardians of tradition, religion, or power. The textual surface of *Luzūm* is punctuated by hypotexts: scripture, popular literature, and classical and contemporary Arabic and Western literary texts. Each text is not simply alluded to but linguistically, semantically, and culturally manipulated and transformed so that it is incorporated in the larger meaning of Surūr's text. Rearticulating these texts is not simply tributary, as in the *muʿāraḍah*'s imitation of an earlier text. An ironic time-space distance separates the hypertext and the hypotexts. It is within this distance that hypotexts are transformed to generate irony, parody, negation, affirmation, deconstruction, or commentary. In order for these processes to be successfully realized, Surūr also employs genre-related intertextual practices. The dialogic nature of the poem entails that many competing voices and languages be given textual space so that meaning emerges through dialogic negotiations among them. Poetry is thus "novelized"[22] through deliberate transcending and transgressing the limitations of its canon and any canon. The postmodernist self-reflexivity of Surūr's poem, its reflections on the conditions of its own production, stretches the poem's intertextuality to include its cultural context as one of its main hypotexts.

Although *Luzūmiyyāt* is the text Surūr directly alludes to in *Luzūm*, the structure of his poem strongly invokes another important text by al-Maʿarrī, *Risālat al-ghufrān* (The epistle of forgiveness). In *Risālat al-ghufrān* al-Maʿarrī and the then recently deceased Ibn al-Qāriḥ (b. 962) visit heaven and hell and, like Surūr and al-Maʿarrī in *Luzūm*, debate literary, linguistic, critical, religious, and philosophical issues and sit in judgment on a number of pre-Islamic master poets. Al-Maʿarrī's questioning of his poetic ancestors inspires Surūr to question his own, especially al-Maʿarrī. Surūr does not only question the canon, he also interrogates modernist poetry, religion, and politics. Aḥmad Fuʾād Nijm (2008, 8) equates poetry with freedom; Surūr equates poetry with revolution. As Egypt continues the struggle for freedom and democracy that began with the overthrow of the Mubarak regime in February 2011, Surūr's serious questioning of the aesthetics and politics of post–1952 Egypt is still as relevant today as it was at the time *Luzūm* was written.

Notes

1. Henceforth referred to as *Luzūm*.
2. Susan Friedman uses the term "indigenization" to refer to the process of "making *native* or *indigenous* something [borrowed] from elsewhere" (2007, 430).
3. Kristeva's term "intertextuality" corresponds to Genette's (1997) "transtextuality." Transtextuality is defined as "all that sets the text in a relationship, whether obvious or concealed, with other texts" (1). Genette presents five different types of textual relationships. Intertextuality is "the actual presence of one text within another" (1997, 2). Paratexts include "a title, subtitle, intertitle; prefaces, postfaces, notices, forwards, etc.; marginal, infrapaginal, terminal notes; epigraphs, illustrations; blurbs . . . and many other kinds of secondary signals, whether allographic or autographic" (1997, 3). Metatextuality is a commentary by a text on an earlier text; it "unites a given text to another, of which it speaks without necessarily citing it . . . even without naming it" (1997, 4). Architextuality refers to the generic status of a text (novel, romance, epic, essay, etc.), and hypertextuality is "a relationship uniting a text B (. . . the *hypertext*) to an earlier text A (the *hypotext*), upon which it is grafted in a manner that is not that of commentary" (1997, 5). Genette's book *Palimpsests: Literature in the Second Degree* focuses mainly on hypertextuality.

4. ”(السرقات) باب متسع جدًا ، لا يقدر أحد من الشعراء أن يدعي السلامة منه.“

5. Some of the terms he mentions are *saraq, ghaṣb, ighārah, ikhtilās, ilmām, mulāḥẓah, mubtad-hal, mukhtaṣṣ, iṣṭrāf, ijtilāb, intiḥāl, ihtidām, murafadah, istilḥāq, muwā*zanah, among many others.

6. "Prosification" and "versification" are among the terms that Genette introduces in *Palimpsests*, which correspond to Ibn Rashīq's "*ḥall*" and "*naẓm*." Other terms introduced by Genette include "excision," "condensation," "extension," "expansion," "digest," "transmetrification," "transtylization," and many others. Many of Genette's terms curiously correspond to Ibn Rashīq's.

7. The Umayyad poets Jarīr and al-Farazdaq authored the most famous collection of *naqā'iḍ* in the eighth century.

8. Another valid translation is "The loyalty to the necessary."

9. ”وإني وإن كنتُ الأخير زمانهُ/لآتٍ بما لم تستطعه الأوائلُ.“ (quoted in Surūr 1996, 114).

10. ”لو لم يقلها شكسبير../قبلي..لقلت الأرض مسرح.“

11. ”هم يلزمون—وحق ربك—لا أنا ما ليس يلزم!“

12. ” غلب المين مذ كان على الخلق وماتت بغيظها الحكماء.“

13. Surūr is fond of giving his poems and collections of poems altered titles of famous texts. Another example is the title of his collection *The Human Tragedy*, which clearly reverses Dante's title *The Divine Comedy*.

14. ”إنما هذه المذاهب أسباب لجلب الدنيا إلى الشعراء“

15. ”شاعر يعبر في كل العصور.“

16. ”أنت كيخوت.“

17. ”قولوا ”لدولسين“ الجميلة../”أخطاب“..قريتي الحبيبة:/هو لم يمت بطلا ولكن مات كالفرسان يبحث عن بطولة..“

18. ”وصرخت يا كيخوت بالموت الزؤام وبالجلاء.“

19. The Arabic term for "poet laureate" literally means "the prince of poets."

20. "Poetry is the register of the Arabs" is a famous statement articulated in many classical Arabic texts. It can be traced back to Ibn ʿAbbās, a prominent transmitter of ḥadīth (quoted in Ibn Rashīq 1972, 30).

21. Pre-Islamic poetry achieved this status mainly because it has been used as an authoritative linguistic tool in the understanding and interpretation of the Qur'ān and the codification of the Arabic language and metrics. This resulted in its fetishization by authors who went as far as treating it as a reliable historical source. Resurrecting traditionalist poetry has always been at the core of any Arabo-Islamic nationalist agenda. Traditionalists have strongly resisted modernist poetry for its alleged damaging impact on Arab culture as have rulers for its blunt challenge to dictatorial regimes.

22. I am adopting Bakhtin's (1981, 39) use of the word "novelization" in the context of the following citation: ". . . the novelization of the other genres does not imply their subjection to an alien generic canon; on the contrary, novelization implies their liberation from all that serves as a brake on their unique development."

References

Bakhtin, Michael. *The Dialogic Imagination: Four Essays by M.M. Bakhtin*. Translated by Caryl Emerson and Michael Holquist. Austin: University of Texas Press, 1981.

Friedman, Susan Stamford. "Periodizing Modernism: Postcolonial Modernities and the Space/Time Borders of Modernist Studies." *Modernism/Modernity* 13, no. 3 (2007): 425–43.

Geertz, Clifford. *The Interpretation of Cultures*. New York: Basic Books, 1973.

Genette, Gerard. *Palimpsests: Literature in the Second Degree.* Translated by Channa Newman and Claude Doubinsky. Lincoln: University of Nebraska Press, 1997.

Ibn Rashīq al-Qayrawānī. *Al-ʿumdah fī maḥāsin al- shiʿr wa ādābih wa naqdih* [The fundament]. Beirut: Dār al-Jīl, 1972.

ʿĪd, Rajāʾ. *Al-qawl al-shiʿri: manẓūrat muʿāṣirah* [Poetic utterance: Contemporary perspectives]. Alexandria: Munshaʾat al-Maʿārif, 2000.

Kilito, Abdelfattah. *The Author and His Doubles: Essays on Classical Arabic Culture.* Translated by Michael Cooperson. Syracuse: Syracuse University Press, 2001.

Kristeva, Julia. *Desire in Language: A Semiotic Approach to Literature and Art.* Edited by Leon Roudiez. Translated by Thomas Gora, Alice Jardine, and Leon Roudiez. New York: Columbia University Press, 1980.

Al-Maʿarrī, Abūl ʿAlāʾ. *Al-Luzūmiyyāt.* Beirut: Maktabat al-Hilāl li al-Ṭibāʿah wa al-Nashr, 1969.

———. *Risālat al-ghufrān* (Epistle of forgiveness). 2 vols. Beirut: Al-Sādir, n.d.

Nāṣif, Muṣṭafā. *Al-naqd al-ʿarabi: naḥwa naẓariyyah thāniyah* (Arabic criticism: Towards a second theory). Kuwait:Al-Majlis al-Waṭani li al-Thaqāfah wa al-Funūn wa al-Ādāb, 2000.

Nijm, Aḥmad Fuʾād. *The Complete Works.* Cairo: Dār al-Aḥmadī li al-Nashr, 2006.

Surūr, Najīb. *Najīb Surūr: The Complete Works.* Cairo: Al-Hayʾah al-Miṣriyyah al-ʿĀmmah lil-Kitāb, 1996.

Arab Studies and the *Miʿraj* of Post-ACTFL Technologies

■

Natalie Khazaal, Georgetown University

Abstract

"Arab Studies and the *Miʿraj* of Post-ACTFL Technologies" addresses the essential role of technology in redefining Arabic away from a skill-based education model towards a comprehensive enterprise involving knowledge, dispositions, and skills. Drawing theoretical models for application in critical languages, the article is meant as a contribution to the discursive practice of redefining the humanities through an emerging critical body of post-ACTFL (American Council on the Teaching of Foreign Languages) scholarship. To implement an assessment-based approach to technologies and address the limitations of ACTFL standards, I propose a five-circle model I call "the *miʿraj* of technologies." Based on the metaphor of the Prophet's journey through circles of heaven (spaces that allow communication between different prophetic traditions), the model represents a blending of in-person and distance technologies to assist a holistic multimodal learning. Arab studies programs can counter the phenomenon of the shrinking humanities by being smart and effective with their use of technology and by becoming unique and valuable to the whole university.

Introduction

On February 5, 2010, Snowmageddon—President Obama's name for the historic snowfall over the mid-Atlantic states—buried the US capital with forty inches of snow, transforming it into a cross-country ski resort and punishing the Potomac Electric Power Company's (Pepco) infrastructure with more than 100,000 residences losing power for up to five days. Georgetown University closed for a week because the snow effectively shut down the streets. In the ensuing months, its administrators headed an initiative that urged faculty to go digital, that is, to redesign their classes to be easily conducted in cyberspace to ensure business continuity in the event of another climatic shock. Rainstorms pounded the region in the summer and parts of the capital lost electricity again for several days. In search of a place to plug in my laptop and cell phone, I found a Starbucks coffee shop with power. I fought the crowd for a socket on a customer's power strip, thinking how Georgetown's business-continuity plan would not work if electricity was unavailable. Despite my perspective, climate change drives a new status for technology, making it ever so difficult to doubt its role in education and enhancing faculty's fears of losing their jobs to distance learning and computer-based tutors.

"Wise Use" Defined

The National Middle Eastern Language Resource Center (NMELRC) encourages the wise use of electronic technology to enhance rather than drive the curriculum along established methodologies and cautions against overwhelming the classroom with technology for technology's sake. Indeed, serious and unresolved debates remain over the wise use of electronic technology as its use evolves.

One divisive issue is whether comparative studies of high-technology (electronic) and low-technology (nonelectronic) classrooms are inherently flawed. These studies have produced mixed results. Some report greater satisfaction and higher test scores in digital classes, whereas others report no statistical differences between high-tech and low-tech learning environments (Blake and Delforge 2005; Cahill and Catanzaro 1997; Chenoweth and Murday 2003; Green and Earnest-Youngs 2001; Loewen and Erlam 2006; Russell 2001; Smith 2003, 2005). The difficulty in defining the effect of electronic technologies comes from the impossibility of isolating the medium by holding all other factors constant (methodology, student composition, and so forth) in real language-learning environments. Hence, some have questioned the legitimacy of such comparisons because they are not rooted in examining different theories of language learning (Burston 2006).

Another divisive issue is whether electronic technologies inhibit or facilitate language acquisition within communicative models, which claim that in-person social interactions are indispensable (Gass 1997; Gass, Mackey, and Pica 1998; Long and Robinson 1998). When computer-mediated communication tools (chats, instant messaging, e-mail, forums, blogs, and so forth) became prominent, researchers observed that these tools afford the same benefits associated with interaction in low-tech language classrooms (Kern and Warschauer 2000). This challenged the conclusion that physical presence in a classroom is indispensable (Blake 2000, 2006; Pellettieri 2000; Smith 2003), yet the debate is far from over.

Another debate is whether electronic technologies increase the input in the target language—quite insufficient in most language sequences, especially for the 97 percent of American college students who do not take advantage of study-abroad programs (Chun 2006). For instance, the average three-year Arabic-language sequence affords learners five times fewer contact hours to receive input in the Arabic language than what is recommended for less commonly taught languages (McGinnis 1994). And even those students who study Arabic abroad do not receive sufficient linguistic input (Al-Batal 2007). Since factors as simple as loss of attention might significantly affect acquisition and retention even in the presence of enough input, scholars now debate which classroom—digital or in-person—provides better opportunities for enhancing input by noticing it (Doughty 1998; Gass 1997; Gass and Selinker 2001; Kern 1995; Krashen 1985; Long 1991; Pica 1994; Schmidt 1990; Swain 2000; Warschauer 1997). The question of whether learners working in digital contexts outperform their low-tech peers due to some advantages of the electronic medium (for example, opportunities to self-correct) or because they spend more time working with it is still unresolved.

There are also widespread doubts that electronic technologies can develop oral proficiency, or whether the ACTFL standards for language acquisition depend disproportionately on oral proficiency (Kramsch 1986) and therefore students need to develop equally other proficiencies, such as different registers of writing.

Electronic Aversion

In March 2010, I presented a conference paper on using e-portfolios in the Arabic curriculum. Shortly afterward, colleagues asked me to present it twice more. While the interest was flattering, the unfortunate result was that none of those interested adapted it to their classes. Cases like this are quite common, and the literature unfairly places blame on what I call the instructor's electronic aversion, a condition that renders an instructor unwilling and therefore unable to master electronic technologies. Arnold and Ducate (2006), for instance, attribute electronic aversion to teachers' resistance to the redefinition of their role in the new digital environment due to personal teaching philosophies and widespread beliefs. Their resistance accusation, however, surely does not apply to Arab studies, judging from the enthusiastic interest in the e-portfolios presentation and from articles published on electronic technologies in the field. Since the publication of the ACTFL guidelines (1985, 1988), two major books on issues of Arabic-language pedagogy feature articles on electronic technologies (*The Teaching of Arabic Language: Issues and Directions* 1995; *Handbook for Arabic Language Teaching Professionals in the 21st Century* 2006). These articles present an enthusiastic belief in the advantages of electronic technologies for learning Arabic. In one of them, Al-Husein Madhany (2005, 297, 300) even claims that the Internet will help students develop "total" proficiency (he does not define "total").

My observation is that faculty motivation, such as electronic aversion, affects the successful or wise use of electronic technologies far less often than institutional factors, such as the effect of ACTFL guidelines on understanding the role of electronic technologies, low commercial returns for developing electronic applications in less commonly taught languages, the small number of professionals authoring electronic tools in Arabic compared with commonly taught languages such as Spanish, and poor collaboration between technical support and Arabic teachers. While Arabic-specific factors such as lack of supported typefaces were fairly important for the failure to use electronic technologies in the 1990s and early 2000s, they are no longer an issue.

Technologies 1.0: Skill-Based Use Rooted in ACTFL Guidelines

Applying ACTFL standards to Arabic has had a profound impact on the way we look at technology and its service for acquiring proficiency.

ACTFL levels rate nonnative speakers' performance against a model "native speaker." While teachers in other languages find it challenging to define the native speaker because there are too many variations (Barnwell 1988; Lantolf and Frawley 1985; Salaberry 2000), Arabic teachers cannot find native speakers because in a narrow technical sense there are no native speakers of Modern Standard Arabic (Wahba, Taha, and England 2006). This has affected the use of technology because the idea of a native speaker model is used to help decide which materials are appropriate, where to look for them, and what technologies should be used to find or develop them. In addition, there is a disconnect between ACTFL standards and the Arabic curriculum. Although, as David Wilmsen (2006) has observed, this situation is not caused by the standards but by the outdated Arabic curriculum, they nonetheless fail to reflect the Arabic multiglossic situation (Winke and Aquil 2005). According to the standards, proficiency is measured by oral performance modeled after the spoken practices of a native speaker. Spoken Arabic consists largely of different varieties of vernacular Arabic, yet the curriculum does not teach any of them (Eisele 2006; Wilmsen 2006). The proliferation of Arabic multimedia, websites, YouTube videos, movies, and music clips allows using them as corpora for oral materials. Unfortunately, as these corpora feature different Arabic vernaculars, their uselessness in the curriculum is a poor incentive for teachers to work with them or to otherwise create oral materials in the vernaculars.

Besides the wasted opportunities caused by the disconnect between the ACTFL standards and the Arabic multiglossic milieu, the standards also perpetuate a schism in Arab studies. At one end are language classes, at the other, content classes. Following the schism, Arabic language is articulated as a set of two active skills (speaking and writing) and two passive (listening and reading); the goal of learning it is mastery of these four skills. By contrast, a content class is articulated as a body of knowledge and its goal is acquiring knowledge and developing critical thinking. Because it is often deemed useless with critical thinking, technology is then relegated to language classes where it is seen as a means for acquiring the four skills more efficiently (Bäbler 2006; Van Mol 2006). Arabic language classes lack enough trained teachers, and as a result untrained native speakers employed at the nontenure levels often teach them (Al-Batal and Belnap 2006). With a demanding teaching load and the absence of financial compensation or course release for any additional work towards developing electronic applications, these teachers have meager incentive to engage with electronic technologies. There are further constraints: ACTFL standards focus on a narrow range of speaking performance (the Oral Proficiency Interview as a "direct" exam, for example, neglects group discussions, reports, unscripted conversations, and so forth); the standards cannot offer a true insight into learners' multiple proficiencies and competencies (for example, while oral guidelines are central, the guidelines for the other three skills are simply a spinoff of the speaking guidelines, Dandonoli and Henning 1990; Henry 1996; Thompson 1995); and the standards give no clear guidelines as to what constitutes culture proficiency (McGinnis 1994). Little has changed in the Arabic curriculum since the revision of ACTFL standards as *Standards for Foreign Language Learning: Preparing for the 21st Century* (1996, 1999) that focus on communication, culture, comparisons, connections, and communities.

The Shrinking Humanities

The phenomenon of the shrinking humanities is linked to the challenges brought by the ACTFL standards. Administrators have started to invest in cheaper online courses that serve higher numbers of students rather than maintain expensive, labor-intensive, low-tech classrooms. All online enrollments are increasing on a much higher rate than those in traditional classrooms—one in every five US students was enrolled in a digital class in the fall of 2005 (Allen and Seaman 2006, 2007). The arguable benefits of online courses are higher faculty-to-student ratios and lower overhead. For example, the US Arabic Distance Learning Network based at Montana State University serves regular students from fifteen small colleges, defining itself as a cheaper alternative that empowers colleges to overcome the prohibitive costs of a regular Arabic program and simultaneously disappointing Arabic faculty who might have liked to be hired there.

In view of the pressures from cheap electronic products (e-books, audio, and study aids) designed to teach languages, some have described traditional language learning as an imploding bubble. Surely the time will come when a universal translator with the functionality of the *Hitchhiker's Guide to the Galaxy's* Babel fish will be improved to perform at least as well as an intermediate language student (the Babel fish instantly translates all languages for those brave enough to insert one in their ear). At such time, without the need to satisfy a language requirement, every American could go abroad and instantly communicate in any language (albeit not necessarily engaging with the culture on a deeper level) while language instructors would not be compensated. Consider how many students and instructors would skip an Arabic classic—the Hans Wehr dictionary—and click on Google Translate to get the benefit of fast and unencumbered, though typically less adequate, digital content.

The devaluation of language and literature studies hit hard in October 2010 when the State University of New York (SUNY) at Albany—"a doctoral university that has prided itself on an international vision"—ironically announced axing its German, Russian, Italian, and Classics programs, where more than two thousand students are enrolled

(De Vise 2010; Jaschik 2010). SUNY president George Philip stated that the 30 percent budget cuts suffered by his university first led to SUNY's elimination of nonessential expenditures before SUNY decided to cut the cord on its language programs (CBS 6 Staff 2010). The administrators found justification in the alleged underperformance of these programs, meaning their difficulty to attract a significant number of students to major in them. Faculty members pointed out that language programs service the whole university community, not just majors, by generating global linguistic and cultural competencies. Some have contradicted the administration, pointing out the university's low administrator-to-student ratio, its continuing financial support for its nineteen Division I sports teams, and its refurbishing and construction projects (Herman 2009). Another example of the shrinking humanities occurred earlier in 2010, when Louisiana State University axed fourteen foreign-language instructors midsemester (Chapman and Kelderman 2011). If ultimately the language instructor can be reduced to a universal translator for a fraction of the cost, then SUNY's administrators are already headed in the right direction, and if SUNY survives any backlash, then the humanities at other universities may worry that the writing is on the wall for them. As George Gollin wrote, "the absurd extrapolation to an organization with an administration, but no faculty, that nonetheless continues to issue degrees, is, alas, not so absurd after all" (Jaschik 2010).

Arabic is not presently at risk of the axe because it is cheaper, financially more independent, arguably more profitable than other programs, and in demand. Programs in commonly taught languages have had over a quarter century to give up the untrained faculty-spouse/native-speaker model and are now heavily invested in trained, tenured faculty members with rich research agendas. That might happen with Arabic if Mahmoud Al-Batal and Kirk Belnap's call for professionalizing Arabic succeeds in a decade or two. For now, the university's financial compensation for the Arabic faculty is lower than that in German, French, and Classics because the Arabic faculty is largely nontenure. Further, Arabic has superior access to external funding such as federal funding for security, defense, and community building, which can sustain an Arab studies program and shield it from budget cuts for a while. Also, enrollments in Arabic continue to rise each semester, justifying salaries.

To avoid the predicament that other language programs face, Arabic programs need to be prepared to address the limitations of the skill-based approach. For technologies, these limitations come from several directions: the profound devaluation of Arabic as a skill, the utility of the electronic medium, the institutionalized barriers to adopting the medium that suppress wise use, and the market disadvantages of less commonly taught languages. In the next section I explore how an assessment-based approach to technologies addresses these limitations and transforms the culture of technology use in Arabic.

Technologies 2.0: Assessment-Based Use

The threats to the humanities led to rethinking their overall contribution to academia. Scholars now envision the humanities as fields that develop students' skills, knowledge, and dispositions. Following this paradigm, the study of Arabic should also involve examining a body of knowledge and developing students' dispositions instead of just imparting the four skills. Diana Laurillard (2002) calls this paradigm shift in education "understanding of the insights of others" (23). It involves learning to analyze the meaning, ambiguity, vagueness, and implications of language as part of learning to critically examine reality (Brooks 2000), interrogating "the very notion of culture" through creating "a third space" of negotiation between the culture students grew up in and the target culture (Kramsch 1993; Kramsch and Anderson 1999), and tolerating ambiguity and leaving room for uncertainty for education to proceed productively (Feito 2007).

If Robert Blake (2008) is correct that language teachers will not go extinct, only those who do not use electronic technologies, then technologies are instrumental in the project of redefining and advertising Arab studies and the value of its curriculum to those engaged in it. Below I show how technologies play a holistic role by being involved in every step of the process of rethinking Arab studies. For that to take place, Arab studies programs need to engage in cyclical in-house assessment of the outcomes, attitudes, and attractiveness of their programs. The crucial value of technology in the cyclical assessment is discussed in the section on the third circle.

The *Mi'raj* of Post-ACTFL Technologies

The Islamic tradition holds that on the twenty-eighth night of the month of Rajab, 621 CE, the winged steed named *Buraq* takes the Prophet Muhammad on a journey from Mecca north to Jerusalem and then up through seven circles of heaven.

Although the distance between Mecca and Jerusalem is 768 miles and the actual journey at the time would have taken a month on horseback or four months on foot,

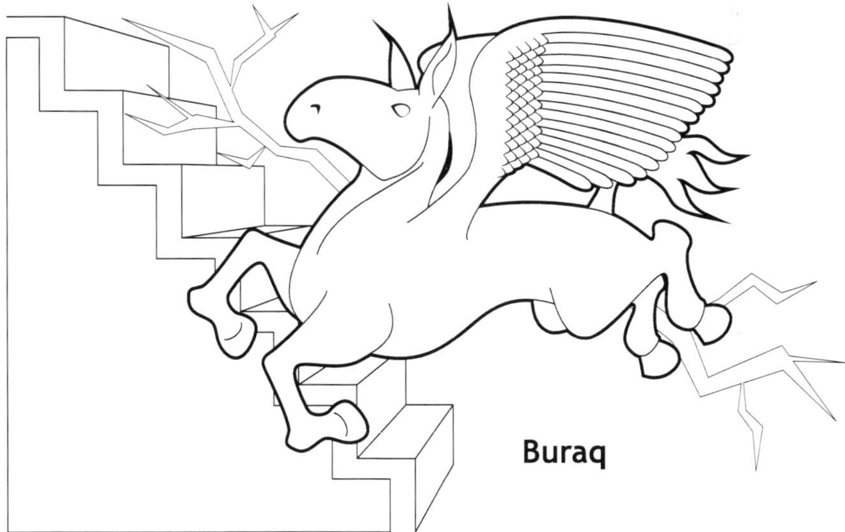

Figure 1. *Buraq*

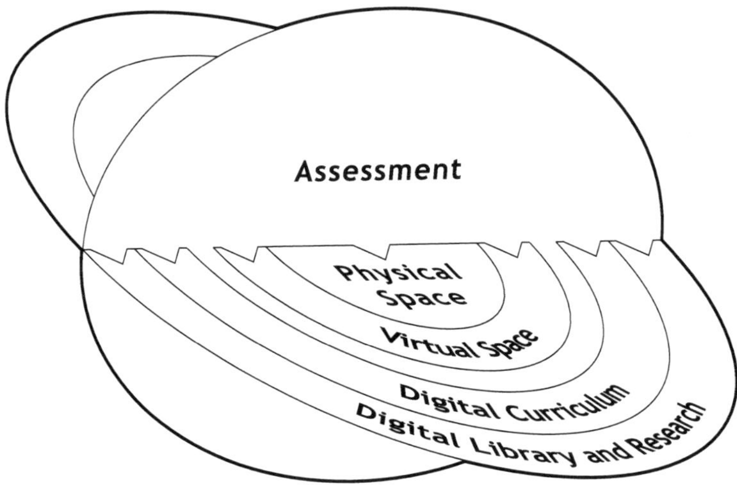

Figure 2. The *mi'raj* of technologies

Muhammad promptly returns to Mecca the same night, which is called *Laylat al-Mi'raj,* or the night of the ladder. Ascending through each circle, he meets and converses with prophets who predate him by centuries. The tradition then introduces *Buraq* (which means lightning) as a technical tool that allows Mohammad to fold space (his rapid travel) and time (his conversation with past prophets). The circles of *mi'raj* are portrayed as spaces that allow communication between different prophetic traditions. *Buraq*'s etymological similarity with electronic media is a convenient metaphor for the role of technology in the reconceptualization of Arab studies.

Answering Michael Thomas and Hayo Reinders's (2010, 1) call to "resist succumbing . . . to uninformed skepticism or uncritical idealism" when exploring the use of technologies in language learning, I propose a five-circle model—"the *mi'raj* of technologies"—that broadly represents their purposeful use in the Arab studies curriculum.

This model represents a blending of in-person and distance technologies to assist a holistic multimodal learning.

First Circle—the Physical Classroom

The physical space of the classroom and how to involve technology therein represents the first circle. Many teachers conceive of the classroom as the proper place for technology, which is a mistake that "wise use" recommendations attempt in part to correct. In the *mi'raj* of technologies, the classroom should be the least technologically enhanced. As the classroom is the primary place for in-person communication and group activities, low and high technologies can disrupt the learning process, so they should be included only when necessary. The least disruptive technology is pen and paper, but depending on the learning goals, the classroom can accept other technologies for presentations, taking notes, and assessment if they are used in their least disruptive manner.

Some questions to address here assess whether the technologies are being used effectively. For example, is PowerPoint used to compare content for translation or media, or does its use consistently keep students from interacting with each other? Are clickers used for counting attendance or are they used for student polling and assessment (Bruff 2009)? Teachers should be deliberate in their use of electronic technology, and any form of technology that disrupts the physical classroom should be abandoned.

Second Circle—Virtual Space around the Physical Classroom

The second circle represents a virtual space around the physical classroom that students visit while away from it. This high-tech circle is usually neglected or underutilized by teachers in Arab studies. In the *mi'raj* of technologies, it is a primary space for educational electronic technologies that take full advantage of the technologies of the mobile, network, and wireless society (Castells 2009). This circle capitalizes on the nature of electronic technology—what I call technology's ability to fold and generate space and time.

The Class Is "Always On"

The strength of the second circle is that digital technologies allow participants to continue engaging with the content of the class after they leave the physical classroom. When digital technologies fold space by connecting two or more individuals who are physically away from each other and generate time before and after the class, they allow students to engage with other students, all of the class's content, and other cultural resources while away from the classroom. Digital technologies also change the speed of the course as announcements, blogs, and so forth can be read immediately after posting. Digital technologies fold time by allowing participants to access information or resources they need in less time; for example, participants do not need to spend time in transit to the library to check out resources but can use them online from home. This allows the class to persist 24/7.

Use of digital technologies in the classroom tends to create a barrier between the participants. Electronic technologies, therefore, should be an integral part of homework when the student is unable to interact with others in person. Effective use of electronic technology in the second circle includes activities that engage students with multimedia content, interactive practices such as with sound- or text-based social networks, creative individual and team projects including research, and engaging with distant Arab culture. Many of these tools reflect the new literacies of digital education (Pegrum 2009), enhance embodied learning, and help learners develop their confidence and personal voice in a more personal and creative way because of an ever-present virtual audience. Web 2.0 tools, some of which can already be accessed through course-management systems as Blackboard, Moodle, or Sakai, already facilitate most of these outcomes. The potential of course-management tools has increased dramatically; using them only to post the syllabus, a few files, announcements, and grades, or to send e-mails is to underuse them. Blackboard, for instance, has evolved into a hub with integrated, simplified social media such as blogs, journals, forums, wikis, peer assessment, Elluminate, a collaborative virtual classroom, and more, as well as tools like ShareStream, which is ideal for engaging with cultural content.

Some questions to address are how to accelerate acclimation (the period between the first time a technological tool is adopted and when it has become effective), how to continue using the tool without feeling lost in it, how to integrate it with sound pedagogy, how not to overload students, and how to guard against the effervescence of online content.

Third Circle—Assessment

The third circle, assessment, intersects and affects all other circles. As Laurillard suggests, learning is a discovery process rooted in a constant dialogue among all stakeholders. The constant dialogue requires regular feedback from all participants and regular redesigning of curricular goals and methods. There has been little research to address how technologies can facilitate and improve assessment. Assessment in the ACTFL era was based on outside experts who decided whether a program was successful and provided recommendations for improvement. It occurred at long intervals and often overlooked the needs of the specific academic environment. ACTFL-era assessment was not integrated into curricular development but was more of "an afterthought" (Watanabe, Norris, and González-Lloret 2009). As a result, by the 1990s educators sought more participatory tools that would help them understand and improve their programs. Assessment should allow for internal and external program performance evaluation, faculty development, and assessment of student-learning outcomes and attitudes.

Assessment is extremely difficult without electronic technologies. They consist of electronic conducting or analysis of interviews, sharing and keeping records of observations and feedback in searchable databases, and providing feedback to all stakeholders. Electronic technologies are also effective in allowing for stakeholder communities to form regardless of the physical distance among their members or their times of availability. Technologies allow for frequent (annual or semiannual) assessment and fast reaction to perceived needs. The rapid follow-up increases the stakeholders' motivation because they feel involved in the improvement of the program.

Among the most effective forms of student-outcomes assessment are quick five-minute assessments called "thin slices" (Bass 2010), self- and peer-assessment done at frequent intervals during the semester, and a blend of self-, peer-, and instructor's evaluation with goals that the student commits to achieving for a particular period following the assessment. Student assessment can double as a progress record in an e-portfolio created throughout the semester and presented at the end in which the students compile samples of their work, assess the class as a whole and the dispositions, knowledge, and skills acquired throughout the semester, compare earlier work with later work, and so forth. Assessment is one of the primary factors affecting student self-motivation, their sense of voice and personal and intellectual significance. For example, in his e-portfolio assessment, Caleb Reed—an elementary student of mine—reflected metacognitively on developing new dispositions: "During this project I learned that I should practice speaking more Arabic. I also learned that my Arab friends think it's great and also funny that we are trying to learn Arabic. I have decided to eat lunch with them more often to practice." Ariana Marnicio—another student of mine—commented on how creating her e-portfolio helped her notice, internalize, and remember her achievements in the class, and as a result her overall satisfaction and motivation increased: "I have learned a lot about myself as a student. I have made so much progress this semester and I don't think I had been able to see it until I completed this e-portfolio."

Tools such as student e-portfolios, interviews, and feedback in the form of questionnaires help the institution and department to understand, improve, and predict future needs. Technologies also allow for developing and conducting placement exams. In Arabic, current digital multiple-choice placement exams still have problems that allow the misplacement of students in a higher level than is appropriate. The open-ended writing alternative is labor-intensive and therefore expensive. This is an area in which any improvements shared with the community of Arab professionals would make an immediate difference.

According to Watanabe, Norris, and González-Lloret (2009) the assessment inspired by the ACTFL culture needs to change from a simple accreditation tool to a pragmatic tool for improvement and raising awareness of the value of language studies. They urge a needs analysis to understand the current learning outcomes and the program's level of performance, indicating that faculty would benefit from "how-to templates" to adapt to their local needs. Technologies can help rapidly develop templates and provide other assessment "how to" materials, through webinars, for example. Technology is also instrumental in facilitating feedback for understanding and building a program's identity, which is, according to Peter Pfeiffer and Heidi Byrnes (2009, 184), the "perceived distinctiveness, attractiveness, value, and overall satisfaction with the major." Post-assessment, technology allows for marketing the successful language-studies program to the entire university.

Some questions to address here are how to develop organized capacity for and a culture of assessment (Davis, Sinicrope, and Watanabe 2009) and how assessment can cyclically improve the curriculum.

Fourth Circle—the Digital Curriculum

This circle is ideal for intensive use of technology, meaning committing to a digital curriculum unique to the institution. The digital curriculum is a joint faculty-owned initiative supported by the department or program. It consists of all lesson content, lesson plans, assignments, exams, research projects, and assessment tools in the entire sequence, saved and organized in secure computer systems. Speed and scale are two profound benefits of the digital curriculum, which allow for an augmented vision of how different aspects and levels of the four-year undergraduate and the two-year graduate course sequence fit together as a whole. The digital curriculum can help identify literary, cultural, and linguistic gaps in the sequence quickly, or easily help spot the lack of a research component throughout the sequence, as well as draw attention to spurious assignments, lack of correspondence between goals and outcomes, and so forth. The digital curriculum of the whole sequence also allows for joint access by all faculty and teaching assistants.

The digital curriculum has at least three immediate benefits. It makes each program unique because the program can become independent of an outside textbook and an outside vision. This raises the program's value for the institution and its students because it allows for a focus on the stakeholders' needs while preventing the outside copying of the program and undermining of its marketing power. If a program develops its own specialization, it becomes unique in the field as well. Second, the digital curriculum can be designed to allow for fast across-the-board changes to any aspect of the curriculum with or without approval from the rest of the team members. Third, it allows faculty to teach different classes easily without the load of developing a new class as changes to the curriculum are constantly being made and communicated. Through social bookmarking and tagging, the digital curriculum allows for adding metadata to help understanding and evaluation of the resources in it, such as voting on a proposed change. This practice involves designing a curriculum not around fitting new technologies into an old framework but around rethinking the foundations of the curriculum periodically.

Questions to be asked include the constant obsolescence of computers and technology standards, effective training of teachers or support through the institution's technology staff, protection from student pranks such as unauthorized alterations, and disaster planning in case of computer failure.

Fifth Circle—Digital Library and Research

Far from the days of Dr. Lorenzo Dow Turner of South Carolina State University, who in the 1930s and 1940s researched the African roots of the Carolina islands' Gullah dialects with a hundred-pound recording machine, today's research is practically unthinkable without high technology. The fifth circle is another high-tech circle designed to make a wealth of information instantly accessible in a digital format to all stakeholders. Digital libraries should be designed as sustainable, digital-born or digitized-information-retrieval systems supported by the department or program. The system may be used by all stakeholders with restricted access as needed, and includes the digital curriculum, assessment databases and templates, archives of e-content (materials for different classes, serious games, e-books, and so forth), movies, music, RSS feeds, and student-generated content (such as wikis, podcasts, calligraphic compositions, research projects, and e-portfolios). Content may be stored locally and thus be accessible through a department/program portal, or users may access it through links to outside networks.

Digital libraries have advantages over the traditional print format as the latter requires ever-increasing overhead: storage space and people. However, digital format does not allow for a range of manipulations such as highlighting, the serendipity of something catching your eye, or the luxury of going through the pages in a moment and getting an overall view of the material. The digital library has no practical limits, is accessible at all times, and allows for multiple and simultaneous users as well as digital enhancement (such as computer-generated speech from text, or vocabulary glossing). E-format requires neither people to move it around nor physical space beyond a computer, making content more mobile, and resolves frequent problems with checked-out, lost, or misshelved books. Subtler advantages of digital content include protection from mutilation, which Arabic and especially Islamic print sources have suffered for decades, and improved user-friendliness, the lack of which drives notorious avoidance of some classic print reference sources, such as Index Islamicus. Furthermore, the option to print the material can fulfill any personal preference for print format.

E-format has changed the nature of the archiving and library business, shifting the emphasis now to access, not ownership. A good library is no longer one that owns a large number of print materials but one that has rapid access to the content of its storage and other libraries' storage. That is why Georgetown University annually spends less than a half million dollars on print materials but 2.5 million dollars on electronic content. Whether in real dollars or in purchasing power, as the share of print format vs. e-format is steadily shrinking, the differences between them become more apparent. Even when electronic content is more expensive, investing in it tends to be best for these reasons.

Even though digital libraries have great advantages, they have a few problems. Copyright infringements need to be resolved on a global level. Digital libraries are in their nascent stage and as a result do not have a lot of content. Lacking content might appear to be a barrier, but at this time digital libraries can still be set up even though they might not have everything the stakeholders desire. Another problem is the short longevity or effervescence of online data. Because the computer revolution is only a few decades old, a permanent digital storage option resembling the millennia-long lifespan of "permanent" paper has not been developed. Having thorough archives and backups is the current solution. A related issue is hardware and software obsolescence because older technologies are frequently incompatible with newer technologies. This problem continues to diminish as businesses and users embrace standards, but eternal standards cannot be guaranteed. No-loss migration is the goal for when standards change (that is, "transfer of digital materials from one hardware/software configuration to another or from one generation of computer technology to a subsequent generation," [Waters and Garrett 1996, 6]). According to Brenda E. Bickett—Georgetown University's Middle Eastern and Islamic librarian—standardization is the biggest issue libraries face today. As the producers and consumers of electronic materials are going to be in different physical places using different equipment (hardware, software, region, rate of updates), libraries and digital archives need to internally standardize what they offer for use. Technologies available through the Internet are presently considered the most stable and user-friendly and so the advice is to invest in them. By contrast, investing in stand-alone supplement hardware is risky. For example, machines like Kindle or Barnes & Noble's Nook are similar to a physical book with an electronic display, but the data on them cannot be transferred to another machine. Arabic dictionaries and complete sets of reference works on DVD do not work very well, for example, Sakar has many of the widespread bugs of 1990s software. Finally, library computers generally have only Roman fonts; they need to add Arabic input and the option to select/change input language to Arabic.

Libraries and digital archives also need to standardize their catalog indexes. In the spring of 2010, the library at Georgetown University's School of Foreign Service in Qatar had its catalog indexed in Arabic, that is, using Arabic script rather than Roman text. The new system is an improvement as the library adds materials in Arabic script from now on, but catalog searches are still inefficient for materials acquired before 2004, which lack Arabic script records. Some libraries have translated their subject headings to Arabic, which is a concern as well because of the lack of standardization. Unless there is a link between the Arabic and the English heading (yet to be set up), the two sets of materials are segregated, so there could be materials in Arabic not found using the Arabic translation of the subject headings. The segregation may inadvertently hide thousands of records.

Gaps in commercial online Arabic collections of e-books like *Kutub Arabiyya* (e.g., no Nagib Mahfuz) or no accompanying set of bibliographic records for each title to be added to the catalog of the library that purchases the collection, as well as typos in the records, are also of concern to digital libraries that support such collections.

Conclusion

In 2009, Pepco Holdings was awarded 168.1 million dollars of federal stimulus funds under President Obama's American Recovery and Reinvestment Act to modernize its electric grid (PHI 2009). Among other improvements, it will be able to notify customers of outages by text message or e-mail. If electric companies become more reliable, then students will expect to be able to connect to faculty and their classmates through stable online applications even in times of dire climate, and university administrations will be better assured of business continuity.

As the power infrastructure evolves, all ranges of technologies and a new generation of technology-savvy faculty will drive a new concept of education in the field of Arab studies rooted in local assessment and high-impact curricular design. The holistic use of technology can succeed only if it is purposeful and supported by the department with its investment of resources and manpower, and very importantly with its technical support, training, and marketing. Classrooms should remain centered on in-person education with nondisruptive low technology, and higher technology should be used sparingly in the classroom. High technology is most effective when used outside the classroom in the virtual space, allowing the class to be always on. Conducting assessment and forming communities of stakeholders essentially requires high technologies, as do designing a digital curriculum and setting up a digital library supported by the department to help learning and research, and to showcase student progress and achievements. Thus, Arab-studies programs can counter the phenomenon of the shrinking humanities by being smart and effective with their use of technology and by becoming unique and valuable to the whole university.

References

Al-Batal, Mahmoud. *The Teaching of Arabic as a Foreign Language: Issues and Directions.* Al-ʿArabiyya Monograph Series 2. Salt Lake City: The American Association of Teachers of Arabic, University of Utah, 1995.

———. "Arabic and National Language Educational Policy." *Modern Language Journal* 91, no. 2 (2007): 268–71.

Al-Batal, Mahmoud, and Kirk Belnap. "The Teaching and Learning of Arabic in the United States: Realities, Needs, and Future Directions." In Wahba, Taha, and England, *Handbook,* 2006, 389–401.

Allen, Elaine, and Jeff Seaman. "Making the Grade." *Online Education in the United States.* Needham, MA: Sloan Consortium, 2006.

———. *Online Nation: Five Years of Growth in Online Learning.* Needham, MA: Sloan Consortium, 2007.

Arnold, Nike, and Lara Ducate. "CALL: Where Are We and Where Do We Go from Here?" In Ducate and Arnold, *Calling on CALL,* 2006, 1–20.

Bäbler, Adriana. "Creating Interactive Web-Based Arabic Teaching Materials with Authoring Systems." In Wahba, Taha, and England, *Handbook,* 2006, 275–94.

Barnwell, David. "Proficiency and the Native Speaker." *ADFL Bulletin* 20, no. 1 (1988): 42–46.

Bass, Randy. "The Problem of Learning in the Post-Course Era." Plenary presentation at the Mid-Atlantic Association for Language Learning Technology Conference. Washington, DC, 2010. http://maallt.org/.

Bickett, Brenda E. Interview by author, November 15, 2010.

Blake, Robert. "Computer-Mediated Communication: A Window on L2 Spanish Interlanguage." *Language Learning and Technology* 4, no. 1 (2000): 120–36.

———. "Two Heads Are Better than One: Computer-Mediated Communication for the L2 Curriculum." In Donaldson and Haggstrom, *Changing,* 2006, 229–48.

———. *Brave New Digital Classroom: Technology and Foreign Language Learning.* Washington, DC: Georgetown University Press, 2008.

Blake, Robert, and Ann Delforge. "Language Learning at a Distance: Spanish without Walls." In *Selected Papers from the 2004 NFLRC Symposium: Distance Education, Distributed Learning, and Language Instruction,* edited by Irene Thompson and David Hiple. Honolulu: University of Hawai'i, National Foreign Language Resource Center, 2005. http://nflrc.hawaii.edu/NetWorks/NW44/Blake.htm.

Brooks, Peter. "A Beginning in the Humanities." *PMLA* 115, no. 7 (2000): 1955–57.

Bruff, Derek. *Teaching with Classroom Response Systems.* San Francisco: Jossey-Bass, 2009.

Burston, Jack. "Working Towards Effective Assessment of CALL." In Donaldson and Haggstrom, *Changing,* 2006, 249–70.

Cahill, Danielle, and Diane Catanzaro. "Teaching First-Year Spanish On-line." *CALICO Journal* 14, no. 2 (1997): 97–114.

Castells, Manuel. *The Rise of the Network Society. The Information Age: Economy, Society, and Culture,* 2nd ed. Oxford: Wiley-Blackwell, 2009.

CBS 6 Staff. "Budget Cuts at SUNY Albany to Hit Academic Programs." *CBS6,* October 1, 2010, www.cbs6albany.com/articles/university-1278894-programs-suny.html.

Chapman, Paige, and Eric Kelderman. "At Rallies across the Country, Students Turn Out in Defense of Public Education." *The Chronicle of Higher Education,* January 11, 2011, http://chronicle.com/article/Students-Turn-Out-in-Defense/124853/.

Chenoweth, Nann A., and Kimmaree Murday. "Measuring Student Learning in an Online French Course." *CALICO Journal* 20, no. 2 (2003): 285–314.

Chun, Dorothy. "CALL Technologies for L2 Reading." In Ducate and Arnold, *Calling on CALL,* 2006, 81–98.

Dandonoli, Patricia, and Grant Henning. "An Investigation of the Construct Validity of the ACTFL Proficiency Guidelines and Oral Proficiency Procedure." *Foreign Language Annals* 23 (1990): 11–22.

Davis, John McE., Castle Sinicrope, and Yukiko Watanabe. "College Foreign Language Program Evaluation: Current Practice, Future Directions." In *Toward Useful Program Evaluation in College Foreign Language Education,* edited by John M. Norris, John McE. Davis, Castle

Sinicrope, and Yukiko Watanabe, 209–26. National Foreign Language Resource Center: University of Hawai'i at Mānoa, 2009.

De Vise, Daniel. "A State University Retreats from Language Study." *The Washington Post*, October 13, 2010, http://voices.washingtonpost.com/college-inc/2010/10/a_state_university_retreats_fr.html.

Donaldson, Randall P., and Margaret A. Haggstrom, eds. *Changing Language Education through CALL*. Abingdon: Routledge, 2006.

Doughty, Catherine. "Acquiring Competence in a Second Language: Form and Function." In *Learning Foreign and Second Languages*, edited by Heidi Byrnes, 128–56. New York: Modern Language Association, 1998.

Ducate, Lara, and Nike Arnold, eds. *Calling on CALL: From Theory and Research to New Directions in Foreign Language Teaching*. CALICO Monograph Series, vol 5. San Marcos, TX: CALICO, 2006.

Eisele, John. "Developing Frames of Reference for Assessment and Curricular Design in a Diglossic L2: From Skills to Tasks (and Back Again)." In Wahba, Taha, and England, *Handbook*, 2006, 197–220.

Feito, Jose. "Allowing Not Knowing in a Dialogic Discussion." *International Journal for the Scholarship of Teaching and Learning* 1, no. 1 (2007). http://hdl.handle.net/10518/4077.

Gass, Susan. *Input, Interaction, and the Second Language Learner*. Mahwah, NJ: Lawrence Erlbaum Associates, 1997.

Gass, Susan, Alison Mackey, and Teresa Pica. "The Role of Input and Interaction in Second Language Acquisition: Introduction to the Special Issue." *Modern Language Journal* 82, no. 3 (1998): 299–307.

Gass, Susan, and Larry Selinker. *Second Language Acquisition: An Introductory Course*, 2nd ed. Hillsdale, NJ: Lawrence Erlbaum Associates, 2001.

Green, Anne, and Bonnie Earnest-Youngs. "Using the Web in Elementary French and German Courses: Quantitative and Qualitative Study Results." *CALICO Journal* 19, no. 1(2001): 89–123.

Henry, Kathryn. "Early L2 Writing Development: A Study of Autobiographical Essays by University-Level Students of Russian." *Modern Language Journal* 80 (1996): 309–26.

Herman, Catherine. "University at Albany Marks 10th Anniversary of Division I Athletics," August 26, 2009, www.albany.edu/news/release_7343.php.

Jaschik, Scott. "Disappearing Languages at Albany." *Inside Higher Ed*, October 10, 2010, www.insidehighered.com/news/2010/10/04/albany.

Kern, Richard. "Restructuring Classroom Interaction with Networked Computers: Effects on Quantity and Quality of Language Production." *Modern Language Journal* 79, no. 4 (1995): 457–76.

Kern, Richard, and M. Warschauer, eds. *Network-Based Language Teaching: Concept and Practice*. Cambridge: Cambridge University Press, 2000.

———. "Theory and Practice of Network-Based Language Teaching." In Kern and Warschauer, *Network-Based*, 2000, 1–19.

Kramsch, Claire. "Proficiency Versus Achievement: Reflections on the Proficiency Movement." *ADFL Bulletin* 18 (1986): 22–24.

———. *Context and Culture in Language Teaching*. Oxford: Oxford University Press, 1993.

Kramsch, Claire, and Roger Anderson. "Teaching Text and Context through Multimedia." *Language Learning and Technology* 2, no. 2 (1999): 31–42.

Krashen, Stephen. *The Input Hypothesis: Issues and Implications*. London: Longman, 1985.

Lantolf, James, and William Frawley. "Oral Proficiency Testing: A Critical Analysis." *Modern Language Journal* 69 (1985): 337–45.

Laurillard, Diana. *Rethinking University Teaching*, 2nd ed. London: Routledge, 2002.

Loewen, Shawn, and Rosemary Erlam. "Corrective Feedback in the Chatroom: An Experimental Study." *Computer Assisted Language Learning* 19, no. 1 (2006): 1–14.

Long, Michael. "Focus on Form: A Design Feature in Language Teaching Methodology." In *Foreign Language Research in Cross-Cultural Perspective*, edited by Claire Kramsch and Ralph Ginsberg, 39–52. Amsterdam: Benjamins, 1991.

Long, Michael, and Peter Robinson. "Focus on Form: Theory, Research, and Practice." In *Focus on Form in Classroom Second Language Acquisition*, edited by Catherine Doughty and Jessica Williams, 15–41. Cambridge: Cambridge University Press, 1998.

Madhany, Al-Husein. "Teaching Arabic with Technology Now: Word-processing, E-mail, and the Internet." In Wahba, Taha, and England, *Handbook*, 2006, 295–304.

McGinnis, Scott. "The Less Common Alternative: A Report from the Task Force for Teacher Training in the Less Commonly Taught Languages." *ADFL Bulletin* 25, no. 2 (1994): 17–22.

Norris, John M., John McE. Davis, Castle Sinicrope, and Yukiko Watanabe, eds. *Toward Useful Program Evaluation in College Foreign Language Education*. National Foreign Language Resource Center: University of Hawai'i at Mānoa, 2009.

Pegrum, Mark. *From Blogs to Bombs: The Future of Digital Technologies in Education*. Perth: University of Western Australia Press, 2009.

Pellettieri, Jill. "Negotiation in Cyberspace: The Role of Chatting in the Development of Grammatical Competence." In Kern and Warschauer, *Network-Based*, 2000, 59–86.

Pfeiffer, Peter, and Heidi Byrnes. "Curriculum, Learning and the Identity of Majors: A Case Study of Program Outcomes Evaluation." In Norris et al., *Toward*, 2009, 183–207.

PHI. "PHI Awarded $168.1 Million for Smart Grid Project," October 27, 2009, www.pepcoholdings.com/about/news/archives/2009/article.aspx?cid=1272.

Pica, Teresa. "Research on Negotiation: What Does It Reveal about Second-language Learning Conditions, Processes, and Outcomes." *Language Learning* 44 (1994): 493–527.

Russell, Thomas. *The No Significant Difference Phenomenon*, 5th ed. The International Distance Education Certification Center, 2001.

Salaberry, Rafael. "Revising and Revised Format of the ACTFL Oral Proficiency Interview." *Language Testing* 17 (2000): 289–310.

Schmidt, Richard. "The Role of Consciousness in Second Language Acquisition." *Applied Linguistics* 11, no. 2 (1990): 219–58.

Smith, Bryan. "The Use of Communication Strategies in Computer-Mediated Communication." *System* 31, no. 1 (2003): 29–53.

———. "The Relationship between Negotiated Interaction, Learner Uptake, and Lexical Acquisition in Task-Based Computer-Mediated Communication." *TESOL Quarterly* 39 (2005): 33–58.

Swain, Merrill. "The Output Hypothesis and Beyond: Mediating Acquisition through Collaborative Dialog." In *Sociocultural Theory and Second Language Learning*, edited by James Lantolf, 97–114. Oxford: Oxford University Press, 2000.

Thomas, Michael, and Hayo Reinders, eds. *Task-Based Language Learning and Teaching with Technology*. London: Continuum International Publishing Group, 2010.

Thompson, Irene. "A Study of Interrater Reliability of the ACTFL Oral Proficiency Interview in Five European Languages: Data from ESL, French, German, Russian, and Spanish." *Foreign Language Annals* 28 (1995): 407–22.

Van Mol, Mark. "Arabic Receptive Language Teaching: A New CALL Approach." In Wahba, Taha, and England, *Handbook,* 2006, 305–16.

Wahba, Kassem, Zeinab Taha, and Elizabeth England, eds. *Handbook for Arabic Language Teaching Professionals in the 21st Century*. Mahwah, NJ: Lawrence Erlbaum Associates, 2006.

Wahba, Kassem, Zeinab Taha, and Liz England. "Preface." In Wahba, Taha, and England, *Handbook,* 2006, xv–xxiv.

Warschauer, Mark. "Comparing Face-to-Face and Electronic Discussion in the Second Language Classroom." *CALICO Journal* 13, no. 2–3 (1997): 7–26.

Watanabe, Yukiko, John M. Norris, and Marta González-Lloret. "Identifying and Responding to Evaluation Needs in College Foreign Language Programs." In Norris et al., *Toward,* 2009, 5–56.

Waters, Donald, and John Garrett. *Preserving Digital Information: Report of the Task Force on Archiving of Digital Information*. Commissioned by the Commission on Preservation and Access and the Research Libraries Group, Inc., Washington, DC: Commission on Preservation and Access, 1996. www.clir.org/pubs/abstract/pub63.html.

Wilmsen, David. "What Is Communicative Arabic?" In Wahba, Taha, and England, *Handbook,* 2006, 125–38.

Winke, Paula, and Rajaa Aquil. "Issues in Developing Standardized Tests of Arabic Language." In Wahba, Taha, and England, *Handbook,* 2006, 221–38.

Agreement and Cliticization in Arabic Varieties from Diachronic and Synchronic Perspectives

■

Elabbas Benmamoun, University of Illinois

Abstract

In this study I discuss some major differences between subject agreement in Arabic and the cliticization of the nonnominative clitics that represent objects and genitive arguments. I present a number of arguments to support the proposal that subject agreement is not due to incorporation but nonnominative clitics are. The arguments come from morphology, syntax, and phonology.

Subject Verb Agreement

In Arabic varieties, including Standard Arabic (SA), the verb and the preverbal subject always agree. This is illustrated below with data from SA, Egyptian Arabic (EA), Jordanian Arabic (JA), and Moroccan Arabic (MA).

(1) l-muʕallim-uun xaraž-uu SA
the-teachers.mp.nom exited-3mp
"The teachers went out"

(2) lə-wlad xərž-u MA
The-children exited-p
"The children went out"

(3) ʔil-wilad ṭəlʕ-u EA
The-children.mp.Npm exited-3mp
"The children went out"

(4) lə-wlad ṭəlʕ-u JA
The-children exited-p
"The children went out"

However, when the subject is in the postverbal position, the modern spoken dialects and SA diverge. In the former, the verb and the subject agree in all features, that is, number, gender and person, but in the latter, agreement is in gender only (and possibly person) as has been extensively discussed (Ayoub 1981; Mohammad 1989, 1999; Benmamoun 1992; Fassi Fehri 1988, 1993; Aoun, Benmamoun, and Sportiche 1994, 1999; Bahloul and Harbert 1992; Benmamoun 2000; Benmamoun and Lorimor 2006; and Soltan 2007, among many others).

(5) a. xaraža l-muʕallim-uun SA
exited-3ms the-teachers-mp.nom
"The teachers went out"

b. xərž-u lə-wlad MA
exited-p the-children
"The children went out"

(6) ṭilʕ-u l-wilad EA
exited-p the-children
"The children went out"

(7) ṭəlʕ-u lə-wlad EA
exited-p the-children
"The children went out"

This agreement asymmetry in SA is not restricted to verbs only but extends to the inflected negative *laysa* and to the participial, which clearly does not agree in person.

(8) a. l-muʕallim-uun lays-uu hunaa
the-teachers-nom neg-3mp here
"The teachers are not here."

b. laysa l-muʕallim-uun hunaa
neg.3ms the-teachers-p.nom here
"The teachers are not here."

Table 1. Agreement Patterns

Variety	Standard Arabic	Colloquial Arabic
SVO	Full Agreement	Full Agreement
VSO	Partial Agreement	Full Agreement

Thus we see a clear difference between SA and the modern colloquial Arabic dialects. This difference as it relates to subject agreement is summarized in table 1.[1]

The controversy that has consumed the Arabic syntax debates, particularly within the principles and parameters framework, concerns the nature of the agreement asymmetry that is found in SA. The main issue at stake concerns the complementary distribution between full agreement, particularly number, and the lexical postverbal subject in (5). The complementary distribution seems to reflect a competition for position between agreement on the verb and the postverbal subject. Interestingly, the same complementary distribution also arises in the context of object and genitive clitics, but in this case in all the Arabic varieties. Thus, an overt lexical object is not compatible with an object clitic on the verb.[2]

(9) a. šakara l-muʕallim-iin SA
thanked.3ms the-teachers-p.acc
"He thanked the teachers."

b. šakara-hum
thanked.3ms.them
"He thanked them."

c. *šakara-hum l-muʕallim-iin
thanked.3ms-them the-teachers-p.acc

(10) a. škər lə-wlad
thanked.3ms the-children
"He thanked the children."

b. škər-həm
thanked.3ms-them
"He thanked them."

b. *škər-həm lə-wlad
thanked.3ms-them the-children

(11) šakar il-mudarəs-iin EA
thanked.3ms the-teachers-p.acc
"He thanked the teachers."

(12) a. šakar lə-mʕalm-iin JA
thanked.3ms the-teachers-p.acc
"He thanked the teachers."

b. šakar-hum
thanked.3ms.them
"He thanked them."

c. *šakar-hum lə-mʕalm-iin
thanked.3ms-them the-teachers-p.acc

This apparent competition for position makes it tempting to aim for a unified analysis and argue that in the context of subject agreement, full agreement in SA competes for position with the postverbal lexical subject. The straightforward way to implement this idea is to say that the agreement on the verbs starts off as a full-fledged pronoun occupying the subject position, which then gets merged with the verb. A version of this analysis has been advanced in various studies, such as Fassi Fehri (1993), and is consistent with other analyses advanced for languages, particularly the Celtic languages, where slightly similar phenomena hold.

However, there is one significant difference between full subject agreement on the verb in SA and the object clitics on verbs. In the context of a lexical noun phrase, no agreement is manifested on the latter. By contrast, in the context of a postverbal subject, gender, possibly together with person, is present on the verb. Thus, for this analysis to be maintained, one has to say that in addition to the incorporated pronoun (full agreement) on the verb in SA there is a paradigm of partial agreement that realizes only gender (and person). Thus, SA would have two paradigms, one paradigm that is essentially the merging of a weak pronoun with the verb and a partial paradigm that is a manifestation of genuine agreement. This is clearly problematic because the relevant cells of the paradigms (third-person singular) are identical in both the perfective and imperfective verb (Benmamoun 2000).

A more serious problem has to do with the fact that in the imperfective verb, subject agreement is realized as a prefix and a suffix on the verb (table 2). The general pattern seems to be that the prefix realizes person and the suffix realizes number. This follows automatically if the two components (prefix and suffix) are independent of each other.

Table 2. Imperfective paradigm in standard Arabic

	Singular	**Dual**	**Plural**
1	ʔu-ħaawil		nu-ħaawil
2m	tu-ħaawil	tu-ħaawil aan	tu-ħaawil-uun
2f	tu-ħaawil-iin	tu-ħaawil-aan	tu-ħaawil-na
3m	yu-ħaawil	yu-ħaawil-aan	yu-ħaawil-uun
3f	tu-ħaawil	tu-ħaawil-aan	yu-ħaawil-na

In fact, there is strong evidence in Arabic that this is the case. Thus, in positive commands (imperatives) the person prefix does not surface (a general feature of Semitic languages), but the number suffix does surface as illustrated in (13).

(13) a. ħaawil-ii
try-fs
"Try."

b. ħaawil-uu
try-mp
"Try."

c. ħaawil-na
try-fp
"Try."

There is strong evidence that in Arabic the imperfective verb and the imperative verbs are related due to the fact that both display identical stem vowels and carry the same gender and number suffixes. The difference has to do with the fact that the imperative does not carry the person prefix.[3] In this context, we see that the imperative verb is the mirror image of the imperfective verb in the VS sentence. The former shows number but no person while the latter shows person but no number. This distribution of the person and number features strongly demonstrates that they have independent morpho-syntactic existence, at least in the imperfective paradigm. No such behavior is displayed by the nonnominative clitics, such as the accusative clitic, which always behaves as a single unit, either present or absent as a single item.

In addition, the masculine number suffix in the imperfective is identical to the masculine number suffix on the participial, which in turn shows that number is independent of person agreement.

(14) a. ya-žlis-uun
3-sit-mp
"They are sitting."

b. hum žaalis-uun
they sitting-mp
"They are sitting."

Based on the above facts, it is safe to conclude that the person and number morphemes are dissociated and do not form a discontinuous agreement morpheme. This in turn casts doubt on any analysis that assumes that full agreement on the verb in SA is a merged pronominal that is composed of phonologically dependent gender, number, and person features. There is no evidence that such a pronominal exists because it never shows up as a single phonological unit.

Table 3. laysa and laazaala paradigms

	darasa	**laysa**	**laazaala**
1s	daras-tu	las-tu	laazil-tu
1p	daras-naa	lasn-naa	laazil-naa
2ms	daras-ta	las-ta	laazil-ta
2fs	daras-ti	last-ti	laazil-ti
2md 2fd	daras-tumaa	lastu-tumaa	laazilt-tumaa
2mp	daras-tum	las-tum	laazil-tum
2fp	daras-tunna	las-tunna	laazil-tunna
3ms	darasa	laysa	laazaala
3fs	daras-at	laysa-at	laazaal-at
3md	daras-aa	lays-aa	laazaal-aa
3fd	daras-ataa	laysa-ataa	laazaal-ataa
3mp	daras-uu	lays-uu	laazaal-uu
3fp	daras-na	las-na	laazil-na

Therefore, the idea that there is a weak subject pronoun that gets merged with the verb does not seem to be tenable. However, this does not mean that there was never a point in the history of Arabic and its Semitic relatives at which the verb incorporated the subject pronoun. It is an accepted assumption within historical Semitic studies that agreement on the verb, particularly person agreement, evolved from a merged pronoun, as is the case for the evolution of agreement in many languages around the world. Benmamoun (2000) adopted this very assumption to explain the otherwise odd agreement pattern we see on the negative *laysa* and the aspectual markers such as *laazaala* (still). These markers occur in present-tense sentences but carry the agreement inflection that is found on verbs, such as *darasa*, that have a past-tense interpretation (that is, the perfective conjugation). Consider the paradigm for the negative *laysa,* which negates present-tense sentences, and the aspectual marker *laazala,* which is tense neutral and can occur in a number of temporal contexts.

(15) a. laysa l-walad-u f-l-bayt-i
neg.3ms the-boy-nom in-the-house
"The boy is not in the house."

b. laysa l-walad-u ya-drusu
neg.3ms the-boy-nom 3m-study
"The boy is not studying."

(16) a. lazaala l-walad-u f-l-bayt-i
still.3ms the-boy-nom in-the-house
"The boy is still in the house."

b. laazaala l-walad-u ya-drusu
still.3ms the-boy-nom 3m-study
"The boy is still studying."

The agreement inflections on *laysa* and *laazaala* are identical to the suffixal agreement inflection on the verb *darasa* though the latter has only a past-tense interpretation. Benmamoun (2000) explains this behavior by arguing that the subject in Arabic and its Semitic relatives occupied a different position in clause structure. In sentences with verbal predicates, it occupied a lower position in the past tense and a higher position in the present tense relative to the verb. A possible representation is shown in (17).

(17)

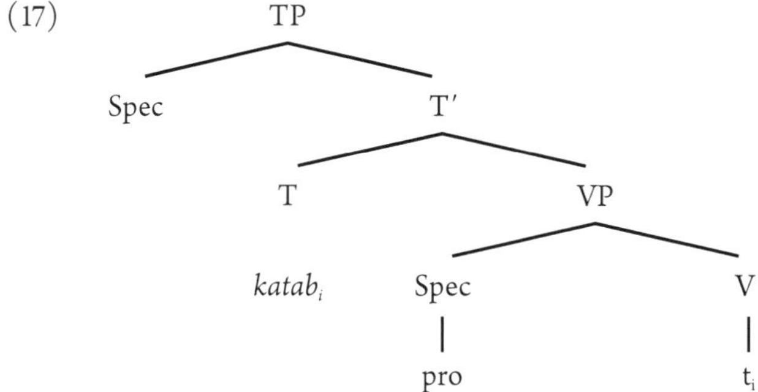

In (17) the verb is moved to T, a position that precedes the pronominal subject, which ends up as an enclitic on the verb. The same analysis applies to the derivation of *laysa* and *laazaala*.

(18)

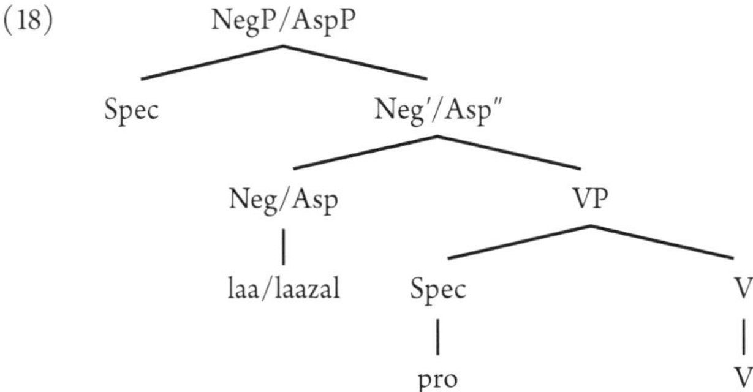

The reason, then, that *laysa* and *laazaala* inflect like the past tense has to do with the nature of the configuration of the past-tense verb and the negative. In both cases, the subject pronoun follows and encliticizes onto the verb and the negative.

Putting aside the details of the analysis, which have to do with the nature of tense and clause structure, the relevant point is that the suffixal pattern arose due to the encliticization of a pronominal subject on the perfective verb, the negative *laa* and the aspectual *laazaala*. Over time, the encliticized pronoun became a full-fledged agreement marker. This is precisely the pattern we should expect when we deal with a path of grammaticalization from strong pronoun to weak pronoun/clitic to inflection. The strong pronoun should have a distribution similar to that of noun phases because it is not restricted phonologically by the need for a host. The weak pronoun always needs a host, but it may have to make do with what is available (to the left or to the right), though it could still impose some restrictions on the host (to be of certain category level, such as a head, and of a certain type, such as a verb). The third path in the grammaticalization process is the inflectional stage, in which the inflection is fully integrated into the structure of the verb. In this stage, the position of the affix is fixed, but it may still impose restrictions on the way it is linearized relative to other morphemes and features.

It seems that subject agreement in SA was already at the inflectional stage at the time when the language was still spoken natively as a first language, though the history is not very clear.[4] At the time when the Arab grammarians embarked on their painstaking and monumental project to document and analyze SA, subject agreement on the verb was firmly at the inflectional stage.

Given the distribution of the subject-agreement inflection in SA, it seems reasonable to say that it is indeed an agreement inflection and not an incorporated pronoun that starts its syntactic history in an argument position. SA does have nominative pronouns, and if indeed the language deployed incorporation of nominative pronouns, we would expect the independent nominative pronoun to incorporate, which is not the case in the context of verbs. That this is what we should expect under an incorporation analysis is confirmed by the fact that nominative pronouns in the modern dialects do incorporate but with sentential negation as the following paradigms from Moroccan Arabic and the Sanʿani dialect of Yemen (Benmamoun and Al-Asbahi 2012).

In table 4, we see that the nominative pronoun either merges with negation as in Moroccan Arabic and becomes flanked by the negative proclitic *ma a*nd the negative enclitic *š*, or it encliticizes onto negation as in Sanʿani. In both dialects the merged and encliticized pronouns are identical to the independent nominative pronouns; though

Table 4. Negative pronouns

Pronoun	Sanʿani	MA
1s	miššana	mana-š
1p	miššiħna	maħna-š
2ms	miššanta	manta-š
2fs	miššanti	manti-š
2mp	miššantum	mantuma-š
2fp	miššantum/miššanten	mantuma-š
3ms	miššu	mahuwa-š
3fs	mišši	mahiya-š
3mp	miššum	mahuma-š
3fp	miššum/miššen	mahuma-š

they may be weakened phonologically, there is no mistaking that the two forms are related. This shows clearly that the agreement inflection we see on the verb in the SV order in SA is not an incorporated pronoun. The pronouns in table 6 are incorporated, and as incorporated pronouns they form a single phonological unit and do not look different from the independent pronouns.

The upshot, then, is that the cliticization or incorporation account is correct as far as diachrony is concerned, but it is not the right mechanism to explain the synchronic agreement asymmetry in SA. The explanation must be found elsewhere, but incorporation of a weak pronoun does not seem to be a viable option.[5]

Nonnominative Clitics

Let us now turn to the nonnominative clitics, which occur on verbs, nouns, prepositions, and other particles such as complementizers. As shown in table 5, the object clitics are exclusively suffixal, that is, on the right of the verb stem, which is exactly the canonical position of the object.

There are a number of differences between subject agreement and nonnominative clitics. First, unlike subject agreement, nonnominative clitics are realized by a single phonological piece that is suffixed to the head. In other words, there are no discontinuous nonnominative markers in any Arabic variety that I am aware of.

Second, there is only one paradigm for the object clitics, which is not the situation with subject agreement. That is, the object clitics are the same for perfective and imperfective verbs.[6]

Table 5. Object clitics in perfective contexts

	Singular	Dual	Plural
1	šakara-nii		šakara-naa
2m	šakara-ka	šakara-kumaa	šakara-kum
2f	šakara-ki	šakara-kumaa	šakara-kunna
3m	šakara-hu	šakara-humaa	šakara-hum
3f	šakara-haa	šakara-humaa	šakara-hunna

Table 6. Object clitics in imperfective contexts

	Singular	Dual	Plural
1	ya-škuru-nii		ya-škurun-naa
2m	ya-škuru-ka	ya-škuru-kumaa	ya-škuru-kum
2f	ya-škuru-ki	ya-škuru-kumaa	ya-škuru-kunna
3m	ya-škuru-hu	ya-škuru-humaa	ya-škuru-hum
3f	ya-škuru-haa	ya-škuru-humaa	ya-škuru-hunna

Table 7. Genetive clitics

	Singular	Dual	Plural
1	kitaab-ii		kitaabu-naa
2m	kitaabu-ka	kitaabu-kumaa	kitaabu-kum
2f	kitaabu-ki	kitaabu-kumaa	kitaabu-kunna
3m	kitaabu-hu	kitaabu-humaa	kitaabu-hum
3f	kitaabu-haa	kitaabu-humaa	kitaabu-hunna

Table 8. Oblique/prepositional clitics

	Singular	Dual	Plural
1	maʕ-ii		maʕa-naa
2m	maʕa-ka	maʕa-kumaa	maʕa-kum
2f	maʕa-ki	maʕa-kumaa	maʕa-kunna
3m	maʕa-hu	maʕa-humaa	maʕa-hum
3f	maʕa-haa	maʕa-humaa	maʕa-hunna

The object clitics are also almost identical to their counterparts on prepositions and nouns. This is significant because it shows that object clitics are not sensitive to the category type and to the aspectual or temporal properties of the head that hosts them.

Third, there is always one nonnominative clitic per clause whereas we can have more than one occurrence of subject agreement in the clause. Thus, while the object clitic is on the verb only, subject agreement occurs on the verb and the auxiliary verb or the verb and the negative marker *laysa.*

(19) a. kaan-uu ya-ktub-uuna-hu
were-3mp 3-write-mp-it
"They were writing it."

b. lays-uu ya-ktub-uuna-hu
neg-3mp 3-write-mp-it
"They are not writing it."

Fourth, it is possible to have more than one nonnominative clitic on the verb in SA, a situation that reflects the double-object nature of classical Arabic.

(20) ʔaʕṭaa-ni-hi
gave.3ms-me-it
"He gave it to me."

While this is not a strong argument against analyzing the clitics as agreement markers, the fact that the two clitics in (20) are from the same paradigm raises questions about the interaction between the paradigms, which would incline one to expect some type of competition leading to bleeding relations.

Fifth, perhaps the most striking difference between subject agreement and non-nominative clitics relates to the fact that the latter, particularly object clitics, are subject to repair strategies which is clearly not the case with the former.

Consider the following sentences from SA.

(21) a. ʔaraa-nii ʔiyaa-hu
showed.3ms-me ʔiyya-it
"He showed it to me."

b. ʔiyaa-hu nu-riidu
ʔiyya-him 1p-want
"We want him."

c. laa nuriidu ʔillaa ʔiyya-hu
neg want only ʔiyya-him
"We only want him."

d. kaana muttahiman ʔiyya-hu bi-l-xiyaanati
was.3ms accusing ʔiyya-him with-the-treason
"He was accusing him of treason."

Here we see that the object is not realized on the verb in (21a–c) or the noun (21d), but on *ʔiyya*. This is evidently a case of repair, which is to say that when the clitic fails to attach to the verb, it is realized on *ʔiyya* because it needs phonological support. Since the issue of repair and the exact status of the *ʔiyya* construction is not the main focus of this paper, suffice it to say that the object clitic occurs on *ʔiyya* when the verb or participle does not host it.[7]

The fact that the object clitic is subject to repair follows straightforwardly if the object clitic occupies its own position in the syntactic representation. As such, it can be fronted by syntactic processes that typically move elements around the clause, usually to the left or right periphery. In such contexts, an element that is phonologically dependent would require the presence of an element to support it. This is the popular analysis of the do-support construction in English sentences such as (22):

(22) a. Mary didn't play.
b. Did Mary play?

The idea is that the past tense in English is generated independently of the verb but the presence of negation or the fronting that takes place in the context of questions prevents it from merging with the verb, which is the preferred option. *Do* comes to the rescue to support the stranded tense marker. This analysis crucially assumes that tense is generated as an independent syntactic element, which may or may not end up affixed to the verb, depending on the syntactic context. This seems to be the same situation that arises in the context of *ʔiyya*. If this is correct, then nonnominative clitics are indeed syntactically independent elements that get cliticized onto their hosts, an operation that may be aborted in some syntactic contexts.

Turning to subject agreement, as far as I know there are no similar repair cases. In other words, to the best of my knowledge, there isn't a single case where subject agreement is on a dummy element. It always occurs on the expected element regardless of syntactic context.

Phonological Evidence for Treating Subject and Object Markers Differently

According to Brame (1974) subject and object markers in Palestinian Arabic have a different impact on their host as far as stress and vowel deletion are concerned. For example, the first-person plural subject marker and the first-person plural object marker are homophonous. However, the former induces high vowel deletion whereas the latter does not. The relevant examples are given in (23):

(23)	fh'imna	we understood	fih'imna	he understood us
	sm'iʕna	we heard	sim'iʕna	he heard us

Assuming that the underlying stem is *fihim*, the suffixation of the subject marker *na* leads to deletion of the high vowel on the first syllable, following syncopy rules of the language, which are sensitive to stress assignment. Interestingly, the suffixation of the object marker does not lead to high vowel deletion, and neither does the suffixation of the negative marker as in (24):

(24)	f'ihim	he understood	ma fih'imiš	he did not understand
	ʔ'ibil	he accepted	ma ʔibiliš	he did not accept
	s'imiʕ	he heard	ma sim'iʕiš	he did not hear
	š'irib	he drank	ma šir'ibiš	he did not drink

Brame (1974) adopts a rule-ordering (cyclic) approach, but the main insight that is relevant to the present study is that the subject marker and the object do not pattern together. Unlike the object and negative markers, the subject marker seems to be well integrated into the prosodic structure of the word and does interact with its syllabic structure. In Brame's (42) words, "all verbs in Palestinian require the presence of a subject pronoun . . . , but not all verbs require the presence of object pronouns or the negative clitic –š. Thus, the subject pronouns are much more intrinsically bound to the stem. On the other hand, the encliticization of object pronouns and the incorporation of negative particles are the kinds of operations we frequently encounter in the syntax of natural language." This is consistent with the claim that the subject marker is an agreement marker that is probably generated on the verb at an earlier point in the derivation than the object marker or, for that matter, the negative marker.

Conclusion

This study presents morphological, syntactic, and phonological argument to support the analysis whereby subject agreement in Arabic realizes genuine agreement morphology rather than incorporated pronouns. In this respect, they behave differently from nonnominative clitics, which are genuine weak pronouns that get merged with verbs, possibly in the postsyntax. Though historically there is strong evidence that subject agreement started off as an incorporated subject pronoun, it gradually becomes purely an expression of an agreement relation with a subject. This implies that the agreement asymmetry manifested in SA must have an alternative explanation along the lines of Benmamoun (2000) or Soltan (2006, 2007).

Notes

Elabbas Benmamoun's research for this paper was supported by NSF grant BCS 0826672. Thanks to Mahmoud Abunasser, Rania Al-Sabbagh, Abdelaadim Bidaoui, and Dana Shalash for their help.

1. Note that the focus is on definite subjects. Indefinite subjects do display agreement asymmetries in some spoken dialects (Aoun, Benmamoun, and Sportiche, 1994), which very likely arise for different reasons.

2. The same restriction applies to genitive clitics on prepositions and nouns.

3. See Brame (1974) and Benmamoun (1998) for a possible derivational relation between the imperfective and the imperative.

4. This is a trivial point, i.e., that standard/classical Arabic was a native language at some point in its history. All recorded languages had that status at some point.

5. See Aoun, Benmamoun, and Sportiche (1994), Benmamoun (2000) and Soltan (2007) for different accounts of the agreement asymmetry in standard Arabic that do not assume incorporation of a weak pronoun.

6. The only difference between verbs and their nonverbal counterparts is the presence of the consonant *n* on the object clitic of the former.

7. The failure to host can be due to morphological saturation or lack of adjacency due to fronting or the presence of an intervening element.

References

Ayoub, Georgine. *Structure de la Phrase en Arabe Standard*. PhD diss., Universite de Paris VII, 1981.

Aoun, Joseph, Elabbas Benmamoun, and Dominique Sportiche. "Agreement, Word Order, and Conjunction in Some Varieties of Arabic." *Linguistic Inquiry* 25 (1994): 195–220.

———. "Further Remarks on First Conjunct Agreement." *Linguistic Inquiry* 30 (1999): 669–81.

Aoun, Joseph, Elabbas Benmamoun, and Lina Choveiri. *Arabic Syntax*. Cambridge: Cambridge University Press, 2010.

Bahloul, Maher, and Wayne Harbert. "Agreement Asymmetries in Arabic." In Mead, *Proceedings,* 1992, 15–31.

Benmamoun, Elabbas. "Arabic Morphology: The Central Role of the Imperfective." *Lingua* 108 (1998): 175–201.

———. *The Feature Structure of Functional Categories: A Comparative Study of Arabic Dialects.* Oxford: Oxford University Press, 2000.

———. *Inflectional and Functional Morphology: Problems of Projection, Representation and Derivation*, PhD diss., University of Southern California, Los Angeles, 1992.

———. "Null Pronominals in the Context of NPs and QPs." In Mead, *Proceedings*, 32–43.

Benmamoun, Elabbas, and Khaled Al-Asbahi. *Negation and the Subject Position in Sana'ani Arabic.* Champaign: University of Illinois Press, in press.

Benmamoun, Elabbas, and Heidi Lorimor. "Featureless Expressions: When Morphological Markers Are Absent." *Linguistic Inquiry* 37 (2006): 1–23.

Brame, Michael. "The Cycle in Phonology: Stress in Palestinian, Maltese, and Spanish." *Linguistic Inquiry* 5 (1974): 39–60.

Fassi Fehri, Abdelkader. "Agreement in Arabic, Binding and Coherence." In *Agreement in Natural Language: Approaches, Theories, Descriptions,* edited by Michael Barlow and Charles A. Ferguson, 107–58. Palo Alto: Center for the Study of Language and Information, 1988.

———. *Issues in the Structure of Arabic Clauses and Words.* Dordrecht: Kluwer, 1993.

Mead, J., ed. *Proceedings of WCCFL 11*. Stanford: The Center for the Study of Language and Information, 1993.

Mohammad, Mohammad. *The Sentence Structure of Arabic.* Ph.D diss., University of Southern California, Los Angeles, 1989.

———. *Word Order, Agreement and Pronominalization in Standard and Palestinean Arabic.* Amsterdam: John Benjamins, 1999.

Soltan, Usama. "Standard Arabic Subject-Verb Agreement Asymmetry Revisited in an Agree-Based Minimalist Syntax." In *Agreement Systems,* edited by C. Boecks, 239–65. Amsterdam: John Benjamins, 2006.

———. *On Formal Feature Licensing in Minimalism: Aspects of Standard Arabic Morphosyntax.* Ph.D diss., University of Maryland, College Park, 2007.

Review of Arabic, Self and Identity

A STUDY IN CONFLICT AND DISPLACEMENT

■

Yasir Suleiman

Yasir Suleiman builds on his previous research on the symbolic use of the Arabic language as a marker of identity, moving from the assumption that language as a proxy may reflect conflicts emerging in the process of identity construction. He shifts the attention from the study of group identity to the analysis of individual identity and argues for the importance of conducting a qualitative study with the use of autobiographical and autoethnographic material. His approach to language and identity as a teaching instructor in Qatar and to the role of language conflict in the life of four Arab intellectuals living in the West provides an original vantage point for the study of linguistic variation in Arabic.

In the second chapter the author outlines seven fault zones in the study of Arabic sociolinguistics. He criticizes the application of the Western "correlationist-variationist approach" to the study of linguistic variation in Arabic. Starting from the assumption that sociolinguistic variables depend highly on the social context, Suleiman asserts that previous sociolinguistic studies have analyzed language variation through variables originally selected and fine-tuned to study Western society and have disregarded the important political force of language in the Arab world. Consequently, these correlationist-variationist studies have marginalized the role of "meta-discourse about language" (11) metalinguistic factors deriving from the ideological use of Arabic in the discourse revolving around ethnic-national identity construction.

A second fault zone consists of the exclusive reliance of correlationist-variationist studies on quantitative data. Suleiman argues, however, that quantitative data does not speak for itself, but requires a qualitative analysis based on interdisciplinary sources. Third, he makes the case for qualitative research, arguing that the risk of bias may be minimized if the researcher clarifies his or her positionality. Fourth, he argues that a correlationist-variationist approach has neglected the study of identity as an important link between language and society, thus privileging the study of the instrumental use of language over its symbolic function. The fifth fault zone lies in the "rejection or marginalization of nativist dualism in discussions of diglossia in the literature in English, whether by Arab or non-Arab scholars" (29). According to Suleiman, duality and diglossia "accord . . . well with how the Arabs generally conceptualize their language situation" (29). The author relates the refusal of the nativist perspective to the tendency of correlationist-variationist approaches to disregard nativist folk-linguistics tradition as an authoritative source of analysis. However, it is worth noting that although Suleiman attributes the concept of continuum to the literature in English, this concept is deeply rooted in the theory of the levels of speech, written in Arabic by Badawi, an Egyptian scholar (1973).

Suleiman rightly argues that both a folk-linguistic and a scientific perspective are needed to approach the complex nature of Arabic. Moreover, he argues that while the nonnativist perspective on diglossia has identified ʿāmmiyya as the mother tongue of the Arabs and speculated on the role of fuṣḥā, he proposes a model in which both fuṣḥā and ʿāmmiyya are strongly related to the identity of the Arabic native speaker. Drawing from Blommaert (2006) and Silverstein (1996, 1998), he argues that while the former "acts as a site of loyalty for Arabic speakers as a linguistic community," the latter consists of "sites of loyalty for speech communities" (31). Suleiman argues that rather than distinguishing ʿāmmiyya from fuṣḥā in terms of natural versus socially constructed forms of language acquisition, a focus on the nativist distinction between standard versus nonstandard varieties allows for the study of "language centred debates about modernization, authenticity, identity and conflict in society from a nonideological position" (31).

The sixth fault zone consists in Suleiman`s criticism towards the Western contemporary taxonomy of Arabic based on ethnic boundaries. The study of Middle Arabic provides an example of how this construct is based on ideological rather than mere linguistic assumptions. He criticizes, for example, Blau's early arguments (made in 1959 and 1968) that defined Judaeo-Arabic as a distinct variety, speculating that these arguments may have been more influenced by the contemporary political climate than by an alleged symbolic use of the variety by the authors of the Middle Arabic texts. In the seventh fault zone, Suleiman stresses the need to use interdisciplinary tools to analyze the political dimension of the Arabic language, which has been neglected by a highly compartmentalized system of academic disciplines.

Beginning with a chapter on "Arabic, Self, and Autoethnography," Suleiman takes up the task of justifying his call for a "symbolic turn" in the study of Arabic sociolinguistics (70). While acknowledging that a correlationist-variationist approach, with its focus on linguistic data, has resulted in important contributions to the study of Arabic in society, his arguments focus on the importance of the "symbolic meaning" of Arabic. In order to demonstrate the value of a shift to qualitative data that addresses this symbolic function of language, Suleiman conducts an autoethnographic study of his experiences conducting a teacher training in Qatar, in which the participants were all native speakers of Arabic from different dialectal backgrounds. This includes an in-depth description of his thought process and consequent language use in the context of this environment, but with no samples or specifics of actual linguistic data. Beginning from the premise that fuṣḥā is a matter of "perception and degree" (47), he describes the reasoning behind his language choices with particular reference to notions of self and identity: He strives to speak a variety that he identifies as Badawi's fuṣḥā al-muthaqafīn while explicitly attempting to disguise linguistic features that would reveal his own Palestinian identity; at the same time, he imposes a ban on English-Arabic code switching during the training for both ideological and personal reasons. Suleiman himself recognizes that while this reflective exploration provides a nuanced perspective concerning the many personal, ideological, and symbolic factors that inform language choices, those factors cannot always be isolated or parsed objectively.

The autoethnographic approach, while ideal for exposing the complex layers informing the role of particular varieties of Arabic in a particular setting, will benefit even more from additional ethnographic data gathered from a similar environment (for example, through surveys of other participants in the training). Suleiman points out that the type of linguistic situation he analyzes (a training in a Gulf environment with speakers of many different Arabic dialects engaging in a common endeavor) is a common one, meaning that additional data should theoretically be easily available. Such additional data would contextualize Suleiman's autoethnographic observations and bolster its robustness at the same time by confirming its claims. In fact, in evaluating the autoethnographic approach, Suleiman himself calls for such data "to authenticate the veracity of the behaviours being reported" by the researcher; although such confirmation is not included in the present book (235). Hence, the exploration of autoethnography illustrates a crucial point about the possibilities for sources of meaningful data about the relationship between Arabic, self, and identity while pointing to the means by which future researchers may further the application of this approach.

Suleiman analyzes a number of other descriptive textual sources to further explore the relationship between Arabic and identity, starting with the autobiographies of Edward Said and Leila Ahmed, who describe this relationship in very different ways. He distinguishes autobiography from autoethnography, noting that the study of autobiography "affords the researcher greater cognitive and emotional distance from the researched" (235). One of the primary objectives of this analysis is to demonstrate that the nature of identity is rhizomatic—a claim that represents Suleiman's attempt to strike a balance between an essentialist view of identity that neglects the role of human agency in identity formation, and what Suleiman calls "poststructuralist and postmodernist views that insist on the fracture, fragmentation, incoherence, amorphousness, decentring or incessant flexibility of identity" (45). An exploration of autobiographical narratives charts not only changing attitudes towards language but also the contexts that produce them—and the widely divergent possibilities of how this process occurs. While Said and Ahmed both discuss language in psychologically and symbolically significant ways, expressing "a multiplicity of feelings, including belonging and alienation" (236), they represent very different accounts of the "language-identity-Self" link (233). Said, for example, describes Arabic as an important index of belonging, while Ahmed considers fuṣḥā in particular to be the language of various state- and gender-based oppressive forces. Suleiman demonstrates that while attitudes toward language shift over the course of both autobiographies, both authors accord language a central role in the formulation of their identities. Thus, Suleiman asserts, "one thing . . . is certain: no matter where subjects locate themselves in the social world, language will continue to act as a linchpin of their identity" (236).

The same chapter also analyzes the writings of Amin Maalouf and Moustapha Safouan to further illustrate the symbolic significance of language in identity formation amidst globalization and national traumas. The chapter illustrates a useful new avenue for mining qualitative data about the symbolic functions of Arabic in society, opening the door to further analysis of a broader range of sources. Future ethnographic or textual research to solicit other perspectives about how Arabic-speaking subjects "locate themselves in the social world" in relation to language will build on these findings, which draw primarily from works by highly educated Arabic speakers who have lived significant portions of their lives outside of the Arab world (236). Both the autoethnographic and autobiographical analyses point to new research possibilities.

In the fifth chapter Suleiman stresses the importance of onomastics and the symbolic function of names, the study of which has been marginalized in both the sociolinguistic and political fields. He argues that names as a marker of identity play an important role, particularly in situations of conflict. The choice of personal and place names is an intentional instrument of assimilation and dissimilation. He questions Borg and Kressel's (2001) thesis on the use of common Arab names among Muslim, Christian, and Jewish Arabs, hypothesizing that such choice is not an attempt to dissimulate their sectarian identity, but rather a deliberate decision to highlight their Arabness. Moreover, the author argues that names are related to issues of modernization. Both the choice of foreign Western names and the use of new names from the Qur'an reflect a drift towards modernization. Conversely, the wide use in the Western world after September 11 of names such as Muhammad may be explained as an intention to challenge the stereotypes about Islam.

Concerning place names, Suleiman shows how these have played an important role in the Palestinian/Israeli conflict. Eventually, the author highlights the sociopolitical valence of ethnonyms, bringing examples from his previous study (Suleiman 2004). Suleiman's study on names in the Arab world outlines the potential that the field of onomastics offers to the analysis of cross-disciplinary issues such as modernization and identity. This chapter suggests areas for future potential research in fields that might enrich our understanding of Arabic sociolinguistics.

Overall, Suleiman makes a compelling argument for the inclusion of language's symbolic function in the field of Arabic sociolinguistics. One of the work's strengths is its focus on the perspective of the native Arabic speaker. Even symbolic "fictions" about the nature of language, Suleiman points out, can become "founding myths" and thence "psychological truths" with real implications, both social and political (234). Suleiman's suggestion to include native dualistic perspective in the study of sociolinguistics and his emphasis on the importance of Arabic's symbolic function lay a foundation for an array of future research possibilities. These include a continued exploration of autoethnographic, autobiographical, and onomastic source material through the lens of Arabic's symbolic functions, as well as the integration of the symbolic dimension into a deeper analysis of the native Arabic diglossic perspective that accounts for it.

—*Anny Gaul and Francesco Sinatora*

References

Badawi, E.S. *Mustawāyāt al-ʿarabiyya al-muʿāṣira fī Miṣr* (Levels of contemporary Arabic in Egypt). Cairo: Dār al-Maʿārif, 1973.

Blau, Joshua. "The Status of Arabic as Used by Jews in the Middle Ages: Do Jewish Middle Arabic Texts Reflect a Distinctive Language?" *Journal of Jewish Studies* 10 (1959): 15–23.

———. "Judaeo-Arabic in Its Linguistic Setting." *Proceedings of the American Academy for Jewish Research* 36 (1968): 1–12.

Blommaert, J. "Language Policy and National Identity." In *An Introduction to Language Policy: Theory and Method*, edited by Thomas Ricento, 238–54. Oxford: Blackwell, 2006.

Borg, Alexander, and Gideon M. Kressel. "Personal Names in the Negev and Sinai." *Zeitschrift fur Arabische Linguistik* 40 (2001): 32–70.

Silverstein, M. "Encountering Language and Languages of Encounter in North American Ethnohistory." *Journal of Linguistic Anthropology* 6 (1996): 126–44.

———. "Contemporary Transformations of Local Linguistic Communities." *Annual Review of Anthropology* (1998): 401–26.

Suleiman, Y. *A War of Words: Language and Conflict in the Middle East*. Cambridge: Cambridge University Press, 2004.

———. *Arabic, Self and Identity: A Study in Conflict and Displacement*. Oxford: Oxford University Press, 2011.

Review of Ordinary Egyptians

CREATING THE MODERN NATION THROUGH POPULAR CULTURE

▪

Ziad Fahmy

Ziad Fahmy's *Ordinary Egyptians* examines the formation of Egyptian national identity via mass culture, arguing that the rise in nationalism was a result of the dissemination of colloquial mass media instead of the top-down propagation of national awareness by intellectuals. The book is comprised of an introduction, six chapters, a conclusion, and two appendices. It chronologically traces the history of Egyptian mass colloquial culture beginning in the 1870s through the 1919 Revolution, focusing on the development and impact of different types of colloquial media.

In the first chapter, Fahmy outlines the use of colloquial and formal speech varieties in Egypt and establishes that only Cairene dialect is viewed as the "true" Egyptian language and is a marker of a "real" Egyptian. The notion of "media capitalism," based on Benedict Anderson's "print capitalism," is also introduced as a concept that is central to the formation of an imagined community and, ultimately, nationalist sentiments. In chapter 2, the author discusses the impact of infrastructure development and increasing centralization on the growth of print media in general and the satirical press in particular in the latter half of the nineteenth century. Satirical periodicals were especially popular due to their use of colloquial Arabic, which was accessible to the masses and easy to read aloud to an illiterate audience. Chapter 3 examines the beginnings of mass culture in the late nineteenth century by analyzing three newspaper editors who also wrote *azjal* (colloquial poems) and plays in colloquial Arabic. During this time, the distribution of colloquial periodicals helped give rise to increased social awareness, which resulted in the beginnings of nationalist sentiments and mass mobilization in national events such as the ʿUrabi Revolt. In chapter 4, Fahmy discusses new forms of mass media from the beginning of the British occupation in 1882 to the Dinshaway incident in 1906 and its aftermath. Through comedy sketches performed by improvisational theater troupes, satirical periodicals, and songs recorded using new gramophone technology, colloquial Arabic was used to express themes of oppression, disenchantment with Western influence, and stronger ideas about what it meant to be a true Egyptian, thus demonstrating an increasing national awareness. Media capitalism, first introduced in chapter 1, receives elaboration in chapter 5 with an analysis of the growing influence of nonprint audiovisual media on mass culture from the beginning of the twentieth century through World War I. As the recording industry grew, consumers of all social classes had access to the same music and recorded comedy sketches, resulting in a consumer-demand-driven recording industry where the most popular material was always performed in colloquial Arabic. Finally, Fahmy examines in chapter 6 the role of street politics and mass mobilization as precursors to the 1919 Revolution, which resulted in some concessions from the ruling authorities, although not complete independence. Weary and frustrated after years of stringent wartime economic policies, glaring class disparities, and general oppression, the Revolution was characterized by mass movements in the streets that included men and women, Copts and Muslims, in nonhierarchical displays of political expression. Fahmy argues that the public, inclusive, nature of these marches and protests was the result of a more coherent sense of Egyptian identity and belonging to a larger, national collective, which had been developed through mass colloquial culture.

Fahmy's arguments throughout the book are thoroughly researched and well supported while presented to the reader in an accessible, engaging manner. As mentioned in the book's introduction, little research has been done on the impact of colloquial sources on the development of Egyptian identity and its modern narrative; this work strives to fill that gap, especially in its frequent use of the era's primary sources to support its claims. The author examines various types of colloquial media as both instruments of veiled political commentary and the means by which the largely illiterate masses came to develop a sense of national Egyptian identity. Through colloquial, not formal, Arabic, nationalism went from being an abstract, intellectual theory to a rallying force among a newly mobilized populace.

Ordinary Egyptians also opens the door for many opportunities for further research. For example, Fahmy mentions that the rise of Cairene dialect and its status as the true Egyptian language led to the decline of provincial dialects but does not elaborate much on this. While the book's focus is largely on urban centers, it would be interesting to delve further into the relationship between Cairene and provincial dialects and the views of the latter's speakers on Egyptian identity. Fahmy's work is an important contribution to the field of Arabic sociolinguistics and one that greatly informs perspectives on the historical narrative of modern Egypt.

—*Clara Shea*

Contributor Information

Mahmoud Abdalla is associate professor of Arabic studies at Monterey Institute of International Studies and director of Middlebury College Arabic School. He earned his master's degree and PhD in applied linguistics at Essex University and the University of Edinburgh. He has taught and lectured extensively on linguistics, Arabic pedagogy, and Arab culture and society in several academic institutions in Egypt, Europe, and the United States. His research interests include second language acquisition, second-language pedagogy, and language, culture, and identity. Abdalla has published on topics on immersion language education, the place of media in the Arabic curriculum, and L2 reading comprehension. He has served on the executive board of the American Association of Teachers of Arabic. He was also a member of the ACTFL leadership team that revised the ACTFL Arabic guidelines. In 1999, he received the outstanding teaching award from the Council of Students of Arts and Sciences at Washington University in St. Louis.

Ghazi Abuhakema is a professor of Arabic language and Arab culture and the coordinator of the Arabic program housed within the Department of International and Interculturtural Studies at the College of Charleston in South Carolina. He is the academic director of the Critical Language Scholarship Program in Amman-Jordan. He is the founding dean of the Arabic Language Village in Minnesota and served in that capacity for three years. He is also an online adjunct professor of Arabic at the National University in California. Abuhakema has taught courses on Arabic language (all proficiency levels), Arab culture, Middle East politics, and Islam. He taught at several institutions such as the University of Texas in Austin, Middlebury College, Montclair State University in New Jersey, and National University. He is the recipient of the College of Charleston Teaching Excellence Award and was a Fulbright scholar. He is an ACTFL-certified OPI tester and an ACTFL/ILR tester. Abuhakema obtained his PhD from the University of Texas at Austin. He is an applied linguist and his main interests include heritage learners, learner corpora, discourse analysis, the teaching of culture in foreign-language classroom settings, and the use of technology in the classroom.

Mahmoud Al-Batal is associate professor of Arabic and director of the Arabic Flagship program in the Department of Middle Eastern Studies at the University of Texas, Austin. He received his PhD in Near Eastern studies with specialization in Arabic linguistics from the University of Michigan, Ann Arbor. He is one of the authors of the *Al-Kitaab* Arabic textbook series (Georgetown University Press). His main area of research is teaching Arabic as a foreign language (TAFL), and he has written numerous articles in this area. He regularly offers teacher-training workshops for college-level teachers of Arabic and is the designer and developer of *Aswaat Arabiyya*, an Arabic listening materials website for learners and teachers of Arabic.

Ali Algryani is a staff member at the Academy of Graduate Studies, Tripoli, Libya. He is currently a PhD candidate in linguistics and English language at Newcastle University, England. His research interests are syntactic theory, comparative syntax, language acquisition, and translation studies. Some of his recent publications include "Text Cohesion in English-Arabic Translation," published in J. Giaber's edited volume *Translation across Cultures: Proceedings of the First Annual Translation Conference*, edited by Academy Publishing House in Tripoli in 2007; "Preposition Stranding in Libyan Arabic Sluicing," published in *Newcastle Working Papers in Linguistics* in 2010; "VP Ellipsis in Libyan Arabic," in *Newcastle Working Papers in Linguistics* in 2011; and "Stripping and Negative Contrast in Libyan Arabic," in *Newcastle Working Papers in Linguistics*, in press.

Elabbas Benmamoun is professor of linguistics and director of the School of Literatures, Cultures, and Linguistics at the University of Illinois. He received his PhD in linguistics from the University of Southern California. His research focuses on comparative syntax and morphology and on the acquisition of Arabic as a first and second language. He is the author of the book *The Feature Structure of Functional Categories* (Oxford University Press, 2000) and is coauthor of *The Syntax of Arabic* with Joseph Aoun and Lina Choueiri (Cambridge University Press, 2010). His current projects include research on comparative studies of Arabic varieties from different regions of the Arab world and Arabic as a heritage language. His research has been supported by the National Science Foundation, the Qatar National Research Fund, and Fulbright.

Anny Gaul is a doctoral student in the Department of Arabic and Islamic Studies at Georgetown University. She received her master's degree in Arab Studies from Georgetown in 2012 and her bachelor's degree from Yale University in 2007. Her research interests include literacy and language policy, rights-based approaches to development, and the politics of food. She has a forthcoming article titled "Charting a Course for Minority Rights: Language and the Amazigh Question," due to be published in a conference volume with Editions l'Harmattan in November 2012.

Hala Ghoneim, a native of Egypt, received her PhD from the Department of African Languages and Literatures at the University of Wisconsin-Madison. She is currently assistant professor of Arabic in the Department of Languages and Literatures at the University of Wisconsin-Whitewater. She earned her master's degree in African languages and literature from the University of Wisconsin-Madison and her bachelor's degree in English literature and translation from the University of Ain Shams, Cairo, Egypt. Her areas of specialization are Arabic and Anglophone African literature, postcolonial theory, modernism, Arabic language, literary theory, and Islam. Her recent publications include "Docile and Dissident Agencies: Female Authorship, Modernism, and the Nationalist Challenge in Post-independence Egyptian Literature," published in the Proceedings of the Hawaii University International Conferences on Arts and Humanities, Honolulu, Hawaii, January 2012, and "Walking in Author's Tracks: Translating Ahmed Fu'ad Nigm," published in *Packingtown Review*, 2009.

Sadam Issa earned his bachelor's degree in English for specific purposes (ESP) from the Jordan University of Science and Technology in 2003. He joined the graduate school at the same university and earned his master's degree in 2006. He came to the United States on a Fulbright scholarship and taught Arabic at Beloit College in Wisconsin from 2006 to 2007. He joined the graduate school at the Department of African Languages, Literature, and Linguistics at the University of Wisconsin-Madison, where he earned his second master's degree in linguistics and is now pursuing his PhD in the same field. He is the recipient of the Honor Instructor Award from the University of Wisconsin-Madison, an award he has won twice. His research interests range from discourse analysis and sociolinguistics to visual rhetoric and political cartoons. Currently, he is a teaching assistant for Arabic in the African Languages, Literature, and Linguistics Department.

Natalie Khazaal is a visiting assistant professor at Georgetown University, where she teaches innovative courses on comparative media, literature, and Arabic culture. She earned her PhD at the University of California, Los Angeles, where she wrote a dissertation about linguistic idealization and parody in Lebanese television, film, and literature under the guidance of the distinguished scholar Michael Cooperson. Khazaal was first interested in Lebanese broadcasting after witnessing the government crackdown on the Lebanese media in the 1990s while living in Beirut. Related to her interest in the battle of the Lebanese media over its exclusion is her concern with ethnic exclusion. Her recent publications include exploring how the Amazigh origins of the renowned Moroccan autobiographer Mohamed Choukri prompted his literary exclusion.

Mouna Mana currently works with the STARTALK Central at the National Foreign Language Center at the University of Maryland. She serves as an Arabic-language education specialist and a member of the STARTALK research team. Mana is an alumna of UCLA's Graduate School of Education and Information Studies, where she earned her PhD in second-language literacy and formative assessment. She also holds a bachelor's degree in linguistics and English, and a master's in education with a focus on cognitive development and second language acquisition. Her areas of research include second/foreign-language education, Arabic-language education, language teachers' professional development, and formative assessment. She has taught Arabic privately and at weekend community schools and has translated contemporary Arabic poetry by writers in the Middle East. She has also trained Arabic-language teachers on various topics and assisted in developing online reading material for Arabic learners. Her most recent publications include a 2011 report to the Abu Dhabi Educational Council on standards-based instruction in teaching Arabic. She has also coauthored a book chapter on formative assessment and literacy instruction.

Gunvor Mejdell is professor of Arabic language and culture at the University of Oslo. Her research interests include mixed styles (between standard and vernacular Arabic) in spoken and written texts and literary translation between Arabic and European languages and cultures. Her publications include *Mixed Styles in Spoken Arabic in Egypt: Somewhere between Order and Chaos* (Brill Academic Publishers, 2006); "Code-Switching," *EALL* I, (Brill Academic Publishers, 2006); "Lugha wusta," *EALL Online* (Brill Academic Publishers, 2010); "A Modern Egyptian Literary Classic Goes West: A Comparative Study of Paratextual Features of Translations of Ṭāhā Ḥusayn´s Novel *al-Ayyām* into English, French, Swedish, and Norwegian" in *Literature, Geography, Translation* (Cambridge Scholars Publishing, 2011); "Playing the Same Game? Notes on Comparing Spoken Contemporary Mixed Arabic and (Pre)modern Written Middle Arabic" in *Middle Arabic and Mixed Arabic: Diachrony and Synchrony* (Brill Academic Publishers, 2012); and "The Elusiveness of Luġha Wusṭā, or, Attempting to Catch Its 'True Nature'" in *Arabic Language and Linguistics* (Georgetown University Press, 2012).

Clara Shea received her master of arts degree in Arabic from Georgetown University in 2012. She is currently the editorial assistant for languages at Georgetown University Press with a focus on Arabic texts. Shea's research interests include TAFL pedagogy and issues in Arabic-English translation.

Francesco L. Sinatora received a master of arts degree in Afro-Asiatic studies from the University of Pavia, Italy. He is currently pursuing a PhD in Arabic and working as a teaching assistant at Georgetown University. His areas of study and research interests include Arabic diglossia, Arabic in the media, cognitive linguistics, discourse analysis, early Arabic poetry, and the teaching of Arabic as a foreign language. He recently published the article "Rethinking Arabic Diglossia: Language Representations and Ideological Intents," with coauthor Manuela E. B. Giolfo in P. Valore's edited volume, *Multilingualism: Language, Power and Knowledge* (Pisa: Edistudio, 2011).